# INTRODUCING

# LATINO/A
# THEOLOGIES

# INTRODUCING

# LATINO/A THEOLOGIES

## Miguel A. De La Torre and Edwin David Aponte

ORBIS BOOKS

Maryknoll, New York 10545

Founded in 1970, Orbis Books endeavors to publish works that enlighten the mind, nourish the spirit, and challenge the conscience. The publishing arm of the Maryknoll Fathers and Brothers, Orbis seeks to explore the global dimensions of the Christian faith and mission, to invite dialogue with diverse cultures and religious traditions, and to serve the cause of reconciliation and peace. The books published reflect the views of their authors and do not represent the official position of the Society. To learn more about Maryknoll and Orbis Books, please visit our website at www.maryknoll.com.

All scripture quotations have been taken from the New Revised Standard Version Bible, copyright © 1989, by the Division of Christian Education of the National Council of the Churches of Christ in the United States of America.

Queries regarding rights and permissions should be addressed to: Orbis Books, P.O. Box 308, Maryknoll, New York 10545-0308.

Published by Orbis Books, Maryknoll, NY 10545-0308

Manufactured in the United States of America

Library of Congress Cataloging-in-Publication Data
Torre, Miguel A. de la.
    Introducing Latino/a theologies / Miguel A. De La Torre and Edwin David Aponte.
        p.  cm.
    Includes bibliographical references and index.
    ISBN 1-57075-400-4
    1. Hispanic American theology.  I. Aponte, Edwin David.  II. Title.
BT83.575 .T67  2001
230'.089'68073 – dc21
                                                            2001036717

*To our children*
*David, Victoria, and Vincent*
*May they always remember their roots*

# Contents

# Preface

A well-meaning scholar suggested that it might be in the best interest of our academic careers if we could identify those parts of this book that we each wrote. Such a separation would be desirable so that it could be determined who would get credit for which part. Yet, such a suggestion flies right in the face of the nature of this work. This book is a collaborative product. It is about collaborative theology that emerges from communities of Latinas/os. In a very true sense it was written together by two persons of different backgrounds, learning to work together, and growing in their relationship with one another as scholars and *hermanos* (brothers), that is, growing in community together. Likewise, Hispanic theology is at its heart a communal endeavor. Therefore, this book is not just about collaborative Latino/a theology, but hopefully it is also an example of it. This is a book about theological cooperation emerging from, in the words of Dietrich Bonhoeffer, our "life together" as Hispanics in the United States.

Yet, this is not solely the product of two people. As we come to the end of this project, we have discovered in a deeper way what we knew before: that we are part of a larger community. We are members of a community of Latina/o scholars of religion, from whom we have learned, who have guided and at times challenged us, sometimes chastised us, but with whom we have always maintained our connection as part of a *comunidad* (community). The influence of others is manifold, as can be seen from the notes and bibliography in the text. Furthermore, the input of these larger communities is present under the text as well. Countless conversations, sermons, lectures, church services, late night talks, and e-mail correspondence influenced our thinking and writing.

We are aware that our perspectives on Hispanic theology and religious history have many sources that cannot be acknowledged adequately. At the same time there are some who gave particular help for this specific project, often giving invaluable comments even when there was disagreement in our approach. These *colegas* (colleagues) who commented on portions of the manuscript or provided other helpful comments include Efraín Agosto, María Pilar Aquino, Orlando Espín, Gastón Espinosa, Luis León, Luis G. Pedraja, Jeanette Rodríguez, and José David Rodríguez. We appreciated all the wise advice we received, even when we felt compelled to go down a different path. We also offer our thanks to all those who responded to the electronic survey on Latina/o theology. All of this input reminded us that we were not alone in this enterprise, and also that there are larger communities with which we need to keep faith. This book is better for it, and any final shortcomings are our responsibility and not that of our colleagues.

We would also like to express our appreciation to others who provided different types of technical help without which we would have been lost. To our editor at Orbis Books, Susan Perry, we owe a debt of gratitude that cannot be repaid. She saw the need for this project, gave us the opportunity to try our approach to the subject, and shepherded us from start to finish. Susan Perry shared with us her wisdom, editorial astuteness, and helped us to overcome any residual fear of the "red pen." Jonathan Schakel also provided editorial assistance for which we are deeply appreciative.

Librarian Anthony Guardado at Hope College helped us immensely in providing countless hours researching and checking census information. Dan Griswold, instructional technologist at Perkins School of Theology, provided help above and beyond the call of duty in setting up the on-line survey and providing technical help throughout the course of this project. Jeremy Latchaw, research assistant to Miguel A. De La Torre, performed outstanding work in helping us pull together material for the book. Frank Leib's work in proofreading sections of the text helped make this a better book. Finally, we would be remiss if we did not thank our collective classes of students who were the first exposed to the unpublished manuscript and gracefully provided feedback to improve its overall quality and readability. The contributions of all these people are another way in which this book is a collaborative effort.

The collaborative help we received for this work includes the wise counsel, support, and occasional nudge of our wives, Deborah L. De La Torre and Laura J. Aponte. Through their steadfast love and encouragement they have made this journey along with us and indeed have made its completion possible. It is no overstatement that we could not have done it without them.

This book does not simply look at the past and present of Hispanic theologies in the United States; it is also deeply concerned with their future. That future will be characterized increasingly by new generations of Latinas/os born and raised in the United States, shaping their own identities in ways different from their parents, grandparents, and great-grandparents. The challenges that younger generations of Hispanics will face cannot be foreseen totally. It is with that future in mind and with the firm hope that it will be better, more peaceful, and filled with greater justice, that we dedicate this book to our children, Vincent and Victoria De La Torre and David S. Aponte.

Miguel A. De La Torre
Holland, Michigan

Edwin David Aponte
Dallas, Texas

*Epifanía (Epiphany)*
*El Día de los Tres Reyes Magos*
*(Day of the Three Magi Kings), 2001*

# Introduction

In March 1981 a conference on urban ministries was held at the famous Riverside Church in New York City. Riverside Church is located on the upper West Side of Manhattan, just south of Harlem and a few blocks from Spanish Harlem, a major center of the Latino/a population of New York City. Unfortunately, the conference organizers failed to include Hispanics on the program, the very people for whom these urban ministries were geared. The oversight was interpreted as another example of Latinas/os being ignored by the dominant religious institutions and social groups. This exclusion prompted a group of Hispanics calling itself the Coalition of Hispanic Christian Leadership to interrupt the conference and protest this gross omission. The protest became known as the "Riverside Manifesto." It specifically charged that Latino/a social issues were not sincerely considered and that the contributions of Hispanics to the church in ministry, theology, and liturgy continued to be ignored. Furthermore, the manifesto charged that Latinas/os experienced discrimination in seminaries and schools of theology and that the religious establishment (defined in the document as "Mainline Protestants, Conservative Fundamentalists, and Establishment Evangelicals") in the United States shared some of the responsibility for this state of affairs.[1]

Almost twenty years later, a widely read weekly newsmagazine, *Time,* published a special section focusing on important trends in the United States for the new millennium. Father Virgilio Elizondo, a Mexican American Latino, appeared in the article as one of the "New Lights of the Spirit." The *Time* article described Elizondo to its vast audience as "a priest-academic [who] has taken the stigma of Hispanic otherness and transformed it into a triumphant Catholic theology of *mestizaje.*"[2] By focusing on Elizondo and his work, *Time* magazine highlighted the importance of Latina/o religion in the United States, especially at a moment in history when tradi-

1

tional religious establishments seem to be losing their influence. How can we explain this twenty-year transformation from Hispanic Christians protesting omission from the theological discourse in New York City to becoming a national focus, heralded as part of the "next wave"?

Increasingly people are becoming aware of the social and cultural importance of Hispanics or Latinas/os in the United States. A key aspect of Hispanic American life and culture is religion in its various articulations, of which Christianity is a major expression. The purpose of this book is to introduce Christian concepts from the perspectives of Latinas/os in the United States and provide a foundation for more specific and advanced study of Hispanic Christian theology, culture, and religion. As an introductory text, the book exposes the reader to the body of works being produced by Latino/a scholars. The intention here is, not to unpack fully all the tenets of Hispanic theology nor to introduce perspectives not present in the current Latino/a theological discourse, but to provide an orientation and direction for more in-depth research, while simultaneously noting the importance of the organic connection of the personal and the communal contexts of Hispanic theology. This project is further complicated by the fact that there exists no such thing as one unified or monolithic Latina/o theology. Indeed, there are many variations, due to a number of diverse factors. But common to many — if not all — is the importance of stories on the varied life journeys of what it means to be a Hispanic in the United States. Accordingly, we have briefly described here our journeys into Latino/a theology as entryways into this rich topic.

## A Personal Journey:
## Edwin David Aponte

When I mentioned to colleagues the possibility of cowriting an introductory textbook to Hispanic theology, some of them expressed surprise. "You're not a theologian!" one said, and in the technical sense that is accurate. For the record I am a cultural historian who focuses on the connection between religion and culture in North America, specifically Latina/o religion and culture. As such, I do occasionally venture into the areas of historical theology, but not technically as a theologian. In a very real sense theology, and especially Hispanic theology, is the province or property, not solely of the theological specialist, but of the whole community.[3] Furthermore, I approach Hispanic theology from two additional social and cultural perspectives. As a Latino, specifically a Puerto Rican Protestant Christian and member of the church, I do theology every day — individually, in my family, and as part of a larger Christian community. As a Hispanic cultural historian, I do theology every day as a member of a theological faculty serving those preparing for and engaging in ministry because my theological perspectives are grounded in the reality, wisdom, and experience of the entire Hispanic community. So what were some of the specific factors that brought me to this project with Miguel De La Torre?

For many years now I have described myself as a Puerto Rican Yankee. By this term I seek to indicate the multifaceted complexity of my being Hispanic in the United States of America. After World War II my parents, as U.S. citizens, moved from the island to the mainland along with tens of thousands of Puerto Ricans. I was born and raised in Connecticut, along with five of my seven brothers and sisters. Because of the local school system's prejudices, my parents decided we would be an English-dominant household to enhance our chances of success in society. One unfortunate result of this decision has been the continuing rejection by some within the Spanish-dominant Hispanic community because we are not "Hispanic enough." My sisters, brothers, and I all experienced some rejection by the local Latino/a community. After primary and secondary education in Connecticut I went to college and seminary in Massachusetts. I had been inculcated with New England cultural values while simultaneously experiencing constant prejudice and rejection by the dominant culture. This led to a growing awareness that I would never be fully accepted by many of my fellow New Englanders. At various points in my life I wanted to say to those who had marginalized me, "Fine, I'll do without you." Yet, I realized I could not sever my roots and survive, for my roots went in several directions.

Gradually, I came into a new awareness of who I am as a Puerto Rican Latino. I might not fit any stereotype, but I am still Puerto Rican, Hispanic, and Latino. My roots are in Puerto Rico, in New England, and in the church. Without a doubt I am a Puerto Rican, but I am neither from the *isla* (island), nor a *Nuyorican* (from El Barrio or El Bronx in New York City). Indeed, many times I knew that a stereotype was at work when, upon learning that I was Puerto Rican, a well-meaning person would say, "Really?! You don't seem Puerto Rican." As a Puerto Rican Yankee, I am a New Englander without a doubt, but not one who traces his ancestry back to the Mayflower, nor one who had access to the dominant social networks of New England life and culture. I knew that a stereotype was at work when I was told by a fellow Latino that I looked "too Presbyterian." My sisters and brothers and I are different kinds of Hispanics, but ours is not a unique story, rather one that is retold across the United States by other Latinas/os of the second and third generations.

While working as a university administrator I attended a conference where the speaker informed us about the growing Hispanic population in the United States, how the corporate and business worlds were taking steps to address this phenomenon, and how colleges and universities should do the same. As I listened, I thought that someone in the church should also focus on Latinos/as. At that moment, I consciously started on the path of Hispanic theology, although with a great deal of anxiety and ignorance. I had only the vaguest idea of where to start, since I was disconnected from and still feeling the pain of prior rejections by the Hispanic community. Eventually the sense of calling led to the decision to study the history of Hispanic Christianity.

Early in my doctoral studies I was introduced into the community of Hispanic scholars of religion and theology. It was refreshing and encouraging to discover that others had blazed the trail through their diverse, comprehensive, and innovative scholarship. It was an additional pleasure to be welcomed into the informal but very real community of Latina/o scholars of Hispanic religion, who are sources of encouragement, inspiration, and motivation as well as dialogue partners and friends. Hispanic theology became a way of coming home.

Through my personal discovery of Hispanic theology I came to a new appreciation of the importance and reality of the Latino/a community of faith in the United States. The study of Hispanic theology is simultaneously personal, communal, historical, contextual, creative, and essential for the common good of all society.

Hispanic theologies nurture people spiritually and culturally, both as individuals and as community. Not simply an academic articulation, Hispanic theology is a means and expression of survival and meaning at the grassroots level.

## A Personal Journey: Miguel Angel De La Torre

With a certain degree of apprehension, I signed up for the required theology course during my first year as a seminarian. I anticipated a rational and systematic approach to understanding the mysteries of the Divine. Theology, the study of God, would elevate my rudimentary comprehension of the Deity learned in my Sunday school classes. Throughout the course, I took meticulous notes as we reviewed the works of the intellectual giants of the faith, the *men* who "pierced into God's truth," men like Luther, Calvin, Troeltsch, Barth, Brunner, and Bultmann. I sat at the feet of my professors, drinking fully from the cup of their wisdom as they contributed to the formation of my theological outlook.

Then, when exploring the "hamartiological question" — a term that refers to the flawed nature of fallen humanity, or sin — I experienced a shift in my theological thinking. Our professor attempted to enlighten us as to the fourfold essence of sin. He walked to the blackboard and wrote the numeral 1, followed by the word *hubris*, "pride." I copied it into my notebook. Then he wrote 2, *hamartia*, "rebellion." Amen, sounded good to me. Then he wrote 3, *concupiscentia*, "greed." Preach on, I thought. Finally, he wrote 4, the foundation of sin, *acedia*, "sloth." Sloth? Isn't that laziness? Grant you, sloth is no virtue, but is sloth the foundation and essence of sin? The fact that we only studied white European or Eurocentric male theologians never bothered me. Instead, what did disturb me was the inclusion of sloth in this list as foundational to Christian understanding of sin. It sounded exaggerated to me. But why was I so perturbed?

The first image that flashed though my mind as I wrote the word "sloth" in my notebook was the U.S. stereotypical image of a Mexican, leaning against a cactus, taking a siesta under his large sombrero. Contributing to this image of Hispanics is the fact that the United States celebrates the so-called Protestant work ethic as a basic element of its ethos. This work ethic causes the dominant culture to see indolence and sloth as the common denominator of all Hispanic culture. Part of the North American myth is that if (any)body can become a (some)body through hard work, then a (no)body cannot blame (any)body but himself or herself for failing to do so. Hispanic "laziness" becomes a fatal flaw defining us as a sinful people, responsible for the economic privation we face in this country. After all, idle hands are the devil's handiwork.

Could it be possible that this fourfold essence of sin was arbitrarily defined by a dominant culture? Would not a culture whose salient characteristic is hyperindividuality produce a list of sins void of any communitarian dimension? As so defined, this fourfold essence of personal sin requires personal repentance to a personal Savior in order to establish a personal relationship with a solitary God. Absent from this construction of sin is its role as a source of social injustice and human oppression. The privatizing of sin led our theology class to consider it a purely private affair. Nevertheless, any exclusively private sin is never actually personal. All sins are communal. While the Eurocentric theologies I was studying in seminary taught me to categorize sin as an essentially private affair, Latin American theologians like Gustavo Gutiérrez and Jon Sobrino showed how sin always negatively affects the whole community.

Why was I so surprised to discover that a society that defines itself first and foremost as "industrious" would use the antonym "sloth" as the foundation of all sins? "Sloth," then, characterizes groups seen as nonindustrious. Additionally, sloth becomes the foundational sin that fatally threatens the dominant ethos of the culture. Thus the dominant culture offers salvation for the Latinas/os only through hard work, the capitalist solution for all socioeconomic ills. For Hispanics to become productive citizens who share in the North American dream, they must first pull themselves up by their "bootstraps," according to dominant social attitudes, most particularly the North American Protestant work ethic. The dominant culture's need to protect itself from the threat of sloth finds its justification by creating a theological perspective that puts any blame on the victims of socioeconomic abuses. I concluded that theology had just as much to do with understanding *who we are* as understanding who God is.

Anyone examining or forging theological texts does so from a particular context, what is termed a "social location." The idea of studying God or reading the biblical text from a position of complete "objectivity" is a myth. In fact, neither theology nor biblical interpretation occurs in a social vacuum. We are all born into an ongoing society that shapes us. When we turn our attention to the biblical text as the source of our theological perspectives, we participate in a dialogue, a dialogue between the written word and the meanings our community taught us to give to this word. We inform the text with the presuppositions we bring to the reading. We become part of the reading as done through our own eyes. And then we are informed by the text. Such a reading inevitably shapes a theology tied to our particular community.

How then does my location as an exilic Cuban theologian influence my theological perspective? I am a former practitioner of an African Cuban religion known as Santería. Does this background in Santería affect my understanding of the Divine? Does the fact that I am male, possess cultural capital, and am seen by fellow Hispanics as white (though I am seen by the dominant culture as a person of color) influence how I define the Divine? As I struggled with questions like these, I sought guidance from the teaching assistant assigned to my class. I shared with him these concerns, asking how a theology from a Latino perspective might differ from that of Euroamericans. He laughed, stating that we do not need any more "chicken-bone theologies," a reference, no doubt, to the rituals of Santería.

I could not understand why he was hostile to my inquiries. Until now, I had assumed that a theologian had to have a Eurocentric worldview. Now I began to question this presupposition. I attempted to perceive the Divine, not as a "wannabe" Euroamerican, but as a Hispanic. My first order of business was to research the works of Hispanic theologians. Knowing little about Latina/o theologies, I went to the library and began to check out the few books in the collection written by individuals with Hispanic surnames. During this time, I was exposed to liberation theologies done in the Two-Thirds World and the United States. While these books resonated within my soul, it was a tedious venture. Most of the books assumed that the reader possessed a fundamental understanding of Latino/a theologies. What I needed was a systematic review of how these theologies developed and of their common denominators. I needed a survey of the formation and the challenges of these theologies. I needed a book like this one.

## Goals for a Common Journey

Why is a book like this important? Few Hispanic religious scholars have written basic introductory texts dealing with Latino/a Christianity in the United States. Individuals wishing to be introduced to Hispanic theological perspectives are limited to books that are challenging and academically rigorous but fall short of providing the newcomer to the field with the fundamental principles of how Latinas/os do theology. Most of these books are designed for advanced students who already have a grasp of the basic concepts of Hispanic Christianity. As previously mentioned, our intention is, not to unpack fully all the tenets of the different Hispanic perspectives, but to orient the reader and provide direction so the reader can conduct more in-depth research.

This is a basic introductory text on the fundamental principles and various perspectives of how Hispanics from different faith traditions do theology. This book is not solely De La Torre's or Aponte's perspective on Hispanic theology. Rather, it explores the numerous perspectives of many Latinas/os, some of which are complementary, some conflicting. We have made a conscious commitment to inclusiveness by soliciting input from our Hispanic colleagues, including a survey e-mailed to the Latino/a theological community. We wrote this book for the individual who has little knowledge of Hispanics and their unique Christian perspectives. This book attempts to inform and challenge. With this in mind, we invite you to read about the perspectives of our diverse peoples, our "chicken-bone" theologies that confound stereotypes even as they fight the struggle for life, confident in the presence of the One who accompanies them on the journey.

## Chapter 1

# U.S. Hispanics:
# Who Are They?

Take a moment to look at Map 1. What do you see? It is not surprising if your response is "a map of the world." In fact, such a response is expected. Most of us grew up seeing this type of map on our classroom walls, our church bulletin boards (with red pins demarcating where the church-sponsored missionaries live), and in our educational textbooks.

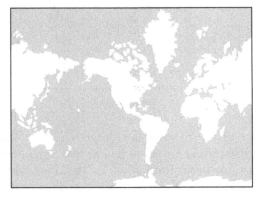

*Map 1*

The orientation of Map 1 is normal only because we have been taught to "see" the world in this fashion. This traditional way of "seeing" masks the power and privilege of those who made the map. We are conditioned to "see" the world in this way, even if it fails to accurately represent the configuration of landmasses. For example, look at Greenland and then look at South America. Which one seems larger? According to Map 1, Greenland has

9

a greater landmass than South America. Yet, Greenland contains 2,175,600 square kilometers while South America has 17,891,100 square kilometers. In other words, South America is almost nine times larger than Greenland, a fact not obvious in Map 1. Also, look at Asia. Notice that this continent is cut in half so that the United States can retain the position of "center."

Now take a moment to look at Map 2. This map represents how the world actually appears. Why, then, the difference between the two maps? Map 1 makes North America the center of the world, forcing other areas to be disproportionately represented. For example, if a picture is taken of an individual with her hand extended forward, the hand would appear larger than normal. Map 2 is drawn with the equator as the center, as it is in fact.

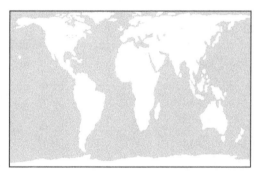

*Map 2*

For most of us, the world as represented in Map 2 appears unnatural, even though it is more accurate. It appears strange because it has not been normalized by the dominant culture. In a way, this is the difference between the dominant culture's theologies and theologies done at the margins. Once the dominant culture is de-centered, an indigenous way of seeing develops, appearing at first to be abnormal since it departs from what we are accustomed to.

Before we get too comfortable with Map 2, we need to realize that this representation is also arbitrary. Why is north chosen as top and south as bottom? Why must the North Atlantic countries be "on top"? If the sixteenth-century explorers and mapmakers had come from the Southern Hemisphere, would south be up?

When one sees the planet from outer space, there is no sign stating, "This side up." Hence, the earth can also be represented by Map 3.

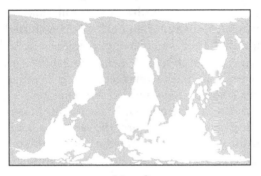

*Map 3*

"Seeing" is not an entirely innocent physiological phenomenon involving the simple transmission of light waves. It encompasses a mode of thought that transforms the object being seen into a concept for intellectual assimilation and possession. This book deals with "seeing" theology. Like the world of Map 1, theology has been legitimized and normalized through the eyes of the dominant, "white," Euroamerican culture. The intention of this book is to explore how the dominant culture "sees" Latinos/as, how Hispanics "see" themselves, and, more importantly, how Latinas/os "see" the Divine, the biblical text, their churches, and their rituals.

## Seeing Hispanics

When members of the dominant culture gaze upon Latinas/os, what do they see? This image is significant because the "seeing" done by many Euroamericans defines the existential selves of Hispanics; it affects the way Latinos/as internalize who they are, and it may compel them to behave and act according to the way in which the dominant culture constructs them. More specifically, when a "true" American gazes upon a Hispanic, the American often perceives a person who is dark, lazy, immoral, and backward. Fernando Segovia compiled a popular conception of Latinas/os as seen through the eyes of the dominant culture. For a large number of Euroamericans, Hispanics are

(a) lazy, unproductive, unenterprising — the sleeping Mexican with the wide *sombrero,* drinking tequila and whiling away the day against a wall, or a bunch of open-shirted Caribbean men drinking beer and playing dominoes at a local, run-down park; (b) carefree, fun-loving, romantic/sensual — latin-lover types with bushy mustachios and beguiling *señoritas* in bright-colored, low-cut dresses; *maracas*-swinging trios and voluptuous vedettes with plenty of flowers or fruits upon their heads; (c) disorderly, undisciplined, violent — uncontrolled progenitors, breeding like rabbits, and knife-wielding gangs, killing one another like animals; (d) vulgar, unintelligent, unteachable — short, swarthy, and primitive people, with funny broken accents and happily occupying the most menial and servile of occupations.[1]

In short, Hispanics are seen as inferior, ignorant, and uncouth, which contributes to the Euroamerican self-definition as superior, intelligent, and civilized. What it means to be a "red-blooded" American is defined by emphasizing the perceived differences with Latinos/as. Defining Hispanics as the antithesis of Euroamericans produces an advantageous space for the latter. The power of seeing becomes internalized, naturalized, and legitimized in order to mask the dominant culture's position of power. Rarely are the self-perceptions of Hispanics solicited.

One of the first modern and still most influential Euroamerican presentations of a Latino was the television character Ricky Ricardo, played by Desi Arnaz, in the popular 1950s sitcom *I Love Lucy,* which continues to be shown in reruns, allowing new viewers to become acquainted with this character. Throughout living rooms in this country since the 1950s, the Euroamerican public has gazed upon this fictitious figure. Although the character of Ricky Ricardo was Cuban, the dominant culture watching the show saw him as part of an overall homogeneous group, labeled in the popular imagination as "Hispanic."

The second episode of the show, "Be a Pal," which was broadcast on October 22, 1951, demonstrates how the dominant culture abuses and confuses Hispanics by seeing them as one monolithic cultural group. In this episode, Lucy, fearing Ricky is losing interest in her, transforms the living room of their apartment to resemble Ricky's Cuban homeland. The viewers gaze upon icons that help define a Latino. They see a chicken coop, a donkey, bananas, palm trees, and a woman (Lucy's friend and neighbor Ethel) dressed as a Latino man wearing a serape under a sombrero. Five children run out of the bedroom, emphasizing the Latino's fecundity. Lucy, with fruit in her hair, performs as the Brazilian Carmen Miranda, singing "Mamâe eu quero" ("Mama, I Want"). In this Portuguese song, the singer asks her mama for a *chupeta,* literally a "sucker." Without any apparent distinction between very different cultural types, Brazilian and Mexican symbols in the popular imagination are merged indiscriminately to create a "sucker's" reflection, not only of Ricky's Cuban homeland, but also of all Hispanic homelands.

This episode illustrates that under the Euroamerican gaze all Hispanics are the same. Latinas/os are seen as one monolithic group with few differences existing between a Puerto Rican, a Brazilian, an Argentine, and a Chicano. However, contrary to this illusion, Hispanics are a *mestizaje* (racial mixture or combination of ethnicities), a *mestizaje* of races, a *mestizaje* of cultures, a *mestizaje* of kitchens, a dense stew of distinct flavors. Unlike the still common Euroamerican "melting pot" paradigm, which pictures immigrants placed into one pot where they all "melt down" into a new "American" culture that nevertheless remains essentially Eurocentric, our Latina/o stew always retains the differing flavors of its diverse roots while enriching all other elements. Some "ingredients" may dissolve completely in the mixture, while other ingredients remain more distinct, yet all provide flavor to the simmering stew, which by its very nature is always in a state of flux. For this reason, the Hispanic stew, whether it is called an *ajiaco* or a *sancocho,* is and should be unapologetically the Latinas'/os' own authentic reality, their *locus theologicus* (theological milieu), from which Hispanics approach the wider world.

Latinos/as are heirs of several different Amerindian or indigenous cultures (such as Taino, Mayan, Aztec, and Zapotec), of medieval Catholic Spain (influenced by Muslims and Jews), of Africa (primarily in the Caribbean and Brazil), of Asia, and due to a continuing presence in the United States, of various European backgrounds. Latinos/as are truly a multicultural people, the heirs of many cultural traditions, yet fully accepted by none of them. Within their veins, the blood of conquerors and conquered converge. Although their presence *aquí* (here) in the United States binds them together as Hispanics, they remain unwelcome. Also, because they have been absent from the cultural land of their births, or the birth of their progenitors, they cease to belong *allá* (there).[2] For some, like Chicanos/as, there is no *allá*. Although seen as foreigners by the dominant culture, they are actually occupying their ancestral lands. The Europeans are the foreigners. From these existential in-between spaces, Latinos/as construct the theological bases upon which Hispanics reconcile their several selves to their theological beliefs.

Consequently, there is no such thing as a "typical" Hispanic. They are white with blond hair and blue eyes, they are black with curly hair, and they are everything in between. Some have Native American features, others Asian features. They are Catholics, Protestants, worshipers of the *orishas* (African deities), Jews, atheists, spiritualists, and followers of Amerindian religious traditions. Some speak "pure" Spanish; others speak Spanglish (a mixture of English words with Spanish phonological and morphological rules), while others speak only English. Still others converse in Cholo, Mayan, Náhuatl, or Pocho. Some have recently arrived in this country, while the ancestors of others were here centuries before the formation of the United States. They live in the blank despair of the barrio and in the comfortable illusions of the suburbs. Some pick apples and grapes; others pick stocks and bonds.

The common Euroamerican vision of Hispanics, as portrayed in the *I Love Lucy* television series, can easily delude us into assuming that there can be only one Hispanic theology. But because Hispanic cultures and contexts are so varied, we cannot speak of one Latino/a theological perspective. Instead we must speak of perspectives. While some commonalties exist, divergences flourish, depending on the group's gender, race, economic class, ethnic identity, national background, years in this country, and location. Hispanic theologies are neither imported nor created by theological professionals for the uniform consumption of Latinas/os. Hispanic theologies, at their best, reflect believing communities seeking to understand their own locations, while remaining strangers and exiles in a foreign land that may also be home.

## Hispanic or Latino/a?

Should the term "Latino/a" or "Hispanic" be used? The etymology of the word "Latino/a" is rooted in ancient Rome, while "Hispanic" is derived from the word *España* (Spain). For some, using the "wrong" terminology can be insulting or a sign of betrayal; thus, considerable debate has taken place over ethnic self-identification. Broadly speaking, those who prefer the term "Latino/a" tend to be older and liberal (if not radical). Those who insist on the term "Hispanic" are usually younger, conservative, college educated, and more assimilated into the dominant culture.

The term "Hispanic" is accused of overemphasizing the Euro-Spanish element of the heritage, ignoring the contributions made by non-Spanish Europeans, Africans, Asians, and Native Americans. Additionally, "Hispanic" is the official term imposed by United States governmental agencies (specifically the Census Bureau) in the 1970s to officially identify people of Latin American and Spanish descent living in the United States. Before the 1970s "Hispanic" as a census category did not exist. As a governmental construction designed to lump everyone who comes from a Spanish-speaking culture together in one group, the term "Hispanic" can be found only in the United States. Nowhere else in the world do people use this pan-ethnic term.[3]

While popular among many who reject the term "Hispanic," the gender-sensitive label "Latino/a" is also a neologism. Some argue that "Latino/a" emphasizes the importance of the Latin American context. Linguistically, however, this latter term emphasizes a Latin (European) culture while overlooking other groups. Like the expression "Hispanic," "Latina/o" is a nebulous term used as a catch-all label to homogenize diverse groups.

In a recent presidential tracking poll conducted by Hispanic Trends, Inc., the majority of those surveyed prefer the term "Hispanic." Of the twelve hundred Latina/o registered voters polled, 65 percent preferred to identify themselves as Hispanics, while 30 percent chose the term "Latino/a." These demographics held true regionally. However, it must be noted that those who are registered to vote tend to be second- and third-generation Hispanics who have undergone some assimilation, hence possibly skewing the results.[4]

Although an ethnic label is an abstraction from reality, the necessity of using a term for Hispanics or Latinos/as leads the authors of this book to use both terms interchangeably. Any prolonged debate over which term should be used is self-defeating. Both labels fail to deal with the complexity of the Hispanic existence. In any case, few Latinas/os ordinarily use the terms "Hispanic" and/or "Latina/o" in common parlance, for both are artificial constructions created for the dominant culture's convenience in naming those who are "Other" to Euroamericans. Even ethnic labels like "Mexican American" or "Cuban American" are artificial designations amalgamating "who Hispanics are" with "where Latinos/as live." These are names given by the dominant culture, not names chosen by the groups being named. Hence, it should not be surprising that when Hispanics talk among themselves, they seldom use labels like "Hispanic" and "Latina/o," nor do they use compounded identities that attempt to reconcile two distinct and separate cultures into one being. Instead, they commonly use the country of their origin to identify themselves. They call themselves Salvadoran, Dominican, Puerto Rican, and so forth (Fig. 1).

## Demographics and Diversity

Chances are you know a Latina/o or have heard people speaking Spanish in an elevator, in a grocery line, or on campus. It is common to hear Spanish spoken throughout the United States; in fact, Spanish is the second most spoken language in the United States, surpassed only by English. At the start of the 1990s, about 7 percent of the 230 million inhabitants within the United States spoke only Spanish in their homes.[5] Among the nations in this hemisphere, the United States has the fourth largest Spanish-speaking population. Only Mexico, Argentina, and Colombia claim more Spanish-speaking people.

According to the latest Census Bureau information, Hispanics are the fastest-growing group in the United States. Among

## Figure 1. How Hispanics/Latinos Describe Themselves

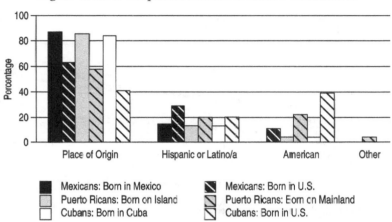

Mexicans: Born in Mexico          Mexicans: Born in U.S.
Puerto Ricans: Born on Island     Puerto Ricans: Born on Mainland
Cubans: Born in Cuba              Cubans: Born in U.S.

*Source:* Graph was created from information provided by Rodolfo O. de la Garza, one of the authors of the Latino National Survey involving 2,817 interviews in 1989 and 1990, as reported in Davis Gonzalez, "What's the Problem with 'Hispanic'? Just ask a 'Latino.' " *New York Times* (November 15, 1992), E6.

the top ten ancestry groups, Latinos/as rank number four, tied with African Americans. They are surpassed (in order) by those with German, Irish, and English backgrounds. The 2000 census information estimates a Hispanic population of 36.4 million individuals. However, these figures exclude 3.5 million Puerto Ricans who live on the island of Puerto Rico and about 5.5 million undocumented "immigrants," treating them as nonentities.[6] This flaw is further complicated by the Census Bureau's own admission of underrepresenting Hispanics (and other minority groups) by as much as 3 percent. If these figures were adjusted, there would appear to be more than 46.5 million Hispanics under the domain of the United States. Hispanics would then outnumber those of purely English or Irish descent. Only Germans would have a larger ancestry group.[7]

Regardless of the bureau's concession of undercounting minority groups during the 1990 census, the U.S. Supreme Court refused to allow the figures to be calibrated correctly, thus denying Latinas/os (and other minority groups) hundreds of millions of dollars per year in federal money for health, highways, social services, community development, and other governmental programs, as well

Figure 2. U.S. Ethnic Growth Rate Projection (in thousands)

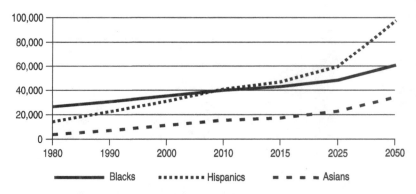

Source: United States Census Bureau

as greater legislative representation. Misrepresented in the national consciousness, Hispanics become misrepresented also in demographic statistics, which, in turn, leads to unjust social policies. This lack of proper representation is part of the continuing history of refusing to recognize or treat Latinos/as in the United States as visible citizens. As the 2000 census information is being tallied, it is conservatively estimated that people of color again were uncounted by as much as 3 percent. Regardless of this fact, Congress is refusing to adjust the figures.

The Hispanic population at the start of the twenty-first century is roughly 11.3 percent of the U.S. population. In 1950, there were only 4,000,000 Latinas/os residing in this country, or about 2.6 percent of the population. These figures indicate an increase of more than 900 percent during the last fifty years. The majority of Latinos/as are chiefly of Mexican origins (64 percent), followed by Puerto Ricans (11 percent), and exilic Cubans (5 percent).[8] Latinas/os are younger than the overall population. In 1998, the median age of Hispanics was 26.4 years, with a large percentage below the age of 16 (31 percent). Compare this to the U.S. population's median age of 36.3 years, with only 23 percent below the age of 16.[9] As the Hispanic population grows and remains younger than the overall U.S. population, this country's future workforce will be disproportionately composed of Latinos/as. This under-

### Figure 3. Middle Series Resident Population
### Percent Distribution Projection (in thousands)

| Year | Total Population | Whites | Blacks | Asians | Latinos/as |
|------|------------------|--------|--------|--------|------------|
| 2000 | 274,634 | 71.8% | 12.2% | 3.9% | 11.4% |
| 2010 | 297,716 | 68.0% | 12.6% | 4.8% | 13.8% |
| 2020 | 322,742 | 64.3% | 12.9% | 5.7% | 16.3% |
| 2030 | 346,899 | 60.5% | 13.1% | 6.6% | 18.9% |
| 2040 | 369,980 | 56.7% | 13.3% | 7.5% | 21.7% |
| 2050 | 393,931 | 52.8% | 13.6% | 8.2% | 24.5% |

Source: United States Census Bureau

explored reality has profound implications for the future economic structures in the United States.

The Latino/a population is growing at a faster rate than any other ethnic or racial group in this county. In the year 2000, Hispanics contributed to 37 percent of the nation's growth. It is estimated that between the years 2000 and 2014, Hispanics' contribution to growth will be 43 percent. The growth rate is expected to increase to 57 percent between the years 2030 to 2050. These growth trends project that Hispanics will soon become the largest ethnic group in the United States. The U.S. Census Bureau estimates that Latinos/as will compose 13.8 percent of the U.S. population by the year 2010, 16.3 percent of the population by the year 2020, and 24.5 percent of the population by the year 2050.[10] This means that one out of every four residents of the United States will be Hispanic (Figs. 2, 3)!

Besides internal growth, immigration contributes to the rapid increase of the Latino/a population. During the 1980s, 33 percent of all "legal" immigration came from Latin America. By 1993, of the 900,000 "legal" immigrants admitted into this country for that year, 238,000 were of Latin American origin. Hispanics represent the second largest documented immigrant group (Asians being the largest), with Mexicans accounting for 14 percent of it.[11] No one knows how many undocumented immigrants are presently in the United States. The Immigration and Naturalization Service conservatively estimates there are 3.2 million undocumented immigrants, with an additional 200,000 to 300,000 arriving each year. The majority of undocumented immigrants are from Mexico, followed by sizable minorities from El Salvador and Guatemala. The favorite port of entry is the penetrable border of Baja California. About 90 percent of all expelled undocumented aliens from 131 countries are from Latin American countries, with Mexico representing 66.6 percent of all expulsions.[12]

Demographically, by 1997 approximately 80 percent of the Hispanic population resided in five states. They are California, Texas, New York, Florida, and Illinois. All other states report less than one million Hispanic inhabitants. Those states with the highest concentration of Latinas/os are New Mexico (40.1 percent), California (30.8 percent), Texas (29.4 percent), and Arizona (21.9 percent).[13] (See Fig. 4.) The majority of Hispanics live within an urban area, with 76.9 percent of all Latinos/as living in twenty cities. As of 1997, about half of this number populate the following five metropolitan areas: Los Angeles (37.8 percent Latina/o of the total metro area population), New York City (16.8 percent), Miami (36.6 percent), San Francisco/San Jose (18.6 percent), and Chicago (13.1 percent).[14] Several major urban centers consist mostly of Latinos/as. The six top cities are Hialeah, Florida (70 percent of the city's inhabitants are Hispanic), El Paso, Texas (69 percent), Santa Ana, California (65.2 percent), Miami, Florida (62.5 percent), San Antonio, Texas (55.6 percent), and Corpus Christi, Texas (50.4 percent).[15] Among Central Americans, many have immigrated to the United States as political and economic refugees, often as a result of the economic and political policies and actions of the United States. The majority of Central Americans reside in Los Angeles, with other major population areas in Houston, Washington, D.C., New York, Chicago, New Orleans, and Miami.[16]

Of the 6.6 million Hispanic households in 1993, 80 percent were classified as families, a higher figure than the nation as a whole at 71 percent. These families tended to be larger than the general population, with 3.8 persons per family instead of the U.S. figure of 3.2 persons per family.[17] Also, their 1998 median income appears to be substantially lower at $28,330 ($40,912 for Euroamericans). Their 1998 mean income of $38,280 ($54,207 for Euroamericans) also reveals the financial plight of Latinas/os. This income gap is widening, causing Hispanics to experience pauperization at a faster

# Figure 4. 1997 Hispanic State Population (in thousands)

| State | Total Population | Latina/o Population | Percentage |
|-------|------------------|---------------------|------------|
| Ala. | 4,319 | 39 | 0.9% |
| Alaska | 609 | 23 | 3.8% |
| Ariz. | 4,555 | 999 | 21.9% |
| Ark. | 2,523 | 45 | 1.8% |
| Calif. | 32,268 | 9,941 | 30.8% |
| Colo. | 3,893 | 556 | 14.3% |
| Conn. | 3,270 | 259 | 7.9% |
| Del. | 732 | 24 | 3.3% |
| D.C. | 529 | 38 | 7.2% |
| Fla. | 14,654 | 2,106 | 14.4% |
| Ga. | 7,486 | 207 | 2.8% |
| Hawaii | 1,187 | 95 | 8.0% |
| Idaho | 1,210 | 86 | 7.1% |
| Ill. | 11,896 | 1,183 | 9.9% |
| Ind. | 5,864 | 137 | 2.3% |
| Iowa | 2,852 | 53 | 1.9% |
| Kans. | 2,595 | 133 | 5.1% |
| Ky. | 3,908 | 30 | 0.8% |
| La. | 4,352 | 113 | 2.6% |
| Maine | 1,242 | 9 | 0.7% |
| Md. | 5,094 | 179 | 3.5% |
| Mass. | 6,113 | 359 | 5.9% |
| Mich. | 9,774 | 254 | 2.6% |
| Minn. | 4,686 | 81 | 1.7% |
| Miss. | 2,731 | 22 | 0.8% |
| Mo. | 5,402 | 82 | 1.5% |
| Mont. | 879 | 15 | 1.7% |
| Nebr. | 1,657 | 68 | 4.1% |
| Nev. | 1,677 | 253 | 15.1% |
| N.H. | 1,173 | 17 | 1.4% |
| N.J. | 8,053 | 959 | 11.9% |
| N.Mex. | 1,730 | 693 | 40.1% |
| N.Y. | 18,137 | 2,570 | 14.2% |
| N.C. | 7,425 | 149 | 2.0% |
| N.Dak. | 641 | 7 | 1.1% |
| Ohio | 11,186 | 173 | 1.5% |
| Okla. | 3,317 | 122 | 3.7% |
| Ore. | 3,243 | 190 | 5.9% |
| Pa. | 12,020 | 302 | 2.5% |
| R.I. | 987 | 61 | 6.2% |
| S.C. | 3,760 | 46 | 1.2% |
| S.Dak. | 738 | 8 | 1.1% |
| Tenn. | 5,368 | 57 | 1.1% |
| Tex. | 19,439 | 5,723 | 29.4% |
| Utah | 2,059 | 133 | 6.5% |
| Vt. | 589 | 5 | 0.8% |
| Va. | 6,734 | 239 | 3.5% |
| Wash. | 5,610 | 340 | 6.1% |
| W.Va. | 1,816 | 10 | 0.6% |
| Wisc. | 5,170 | 128 | 2.5% |
| Wyo. | 480 | 28 | 5.8% |

Source: United States Census Bureau

rate than any other ethnic/racial group. By 1998, 25.9 percent of
Latino/a families lived on a total household income of $14,999 or
less, an increase from 23 percent in 1993 (Fig. 5). Of these families,
57.8 percent lived on less than $10,000.[18] This figure is shocking
when we consider the 1998 poverty line to be $16,530.

**Figure 5. Hispanic/Euroamerican Household Comparisons**

| 1998 | Hispanics | Percentage | Euroamerican | Percentage |
|---|---|---|---|---|
| Number of Households | 9,060 | – | 87,212 | – |
| Current Dollar Incomes of: | | | | |
| Under $5,000 | 441 | 4.9% | 2,263 | 2.6% |
| $5,000–$9,999 | 912 | 10.1% | 5,352 | 6.1% |
| $10,000–$14,999 | 989 | 10.9% | 6,468 | 7.4% |
| $15,000–$24,999 | 1,620 | 17.9% | 11,937 | 13.7% |
| $25,000–$34,999 | 1,477 | 16.3% | 11,480 | 13.2% |
| $35,000–$49,999 | 1,432 | 15.8% | 14,230 | 16.3% |
| $50,000–$74,999 | 1,271 | 14.0% | 16,862 | 19.3% |
| $75,000–$99,999 | 503 | 5.6% | 8,730 | 10.0% |
| $100,000 and over | 416 | 4.6% | 9,889 | 11.3% |
| Median Income | $28,330 | – | $40,912 | – |
| Mean Income | $38,280 | – | $54,207 | – |

*Source:* United States Census Bureau

    Among Hispanics, those of Cuban origin appear to do better fi-
nancially. Exilic Cubans' 1997 median family income of $35,616
is closer than any other Hispanic group to the overall U.S. population's median of $49,692. Contrast this with Mexicans at $25,347
or Puerto Ricans at $23,646. Sixty-three percent of exilic Cubans
own businesses (the highest rate among Latin Americans), contrasted with 19 percent of Mexicans and 11 percent of Puerto
Ricans. Unemployment rates of 6.1 percent for Cubans are lower
than for Mexicans at 9.5 percent and for Puerto Ricans at 11.4
percent. Only 17.2 percent of exilic Cubans find themselves below
the poverty line, as opposed to 30.9 percent of Mexicans and 35.4
percent of Puerto Ricans. Finally, 22 percent of exilic Cubans hold
managerial or professional employment, much higher than the 9
percent of Mexicans and 12 percent of Puerto Ricans (Fig. 6).[19] If
the statistical information of exilic Cubans were excluded from the
overall Hispanic category, the reality of poverty among Latinos/as
would be greater than official records indicate.[20]
    Latinas/os are more likely to be victims of crime (39.6 per

## Figure 6. Ethnic Economic Comparison

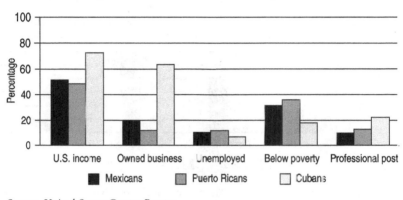

*Source:* United States Census Bureau

1,000) than non-Hispanics (35.3 per 1,000).[21] If convicted of a crime, they are more likely to serve longer sentences. According to statistics of the U.S. Bureau of Justice, Hispanics are likely to be released in only 26 percent of their cases. Non-Latinos/as are usually released before trial in 66 percent of their cases.[22] Furthermore, Hispanics (as well as other minority groups) face substantial abuse by law enforcement agencies. For example, a study conducted by Amnesty International concerning police conduct in Los Angeles found that the two largest enforcement agencies (the Los Angeles Police Department and the Los Angeles Sheriff's Department) committed abuses too numerous to count, including police shootings, cruel use of dogs, and police brutality.[23]

Additionally, Latinas/os are more likely to live with pollution (19 percent) than Euroamericans (6 percent) or African Americans (9 percent) combined. Approximately 34 percent of Latinos/as live among dust and soot, 57 percent with high concentrations of carbon monoxide,[24] while 19 percent of Hispanic children (ages six months to five years in cities with more than one million persons) reported high blood levels of lead (Fig. 7).[25] Additional health concerns are many: Latinos/as are less likely to receive preventive medical examinations (15 percent for Hispanics vs. 9.7 percent for non-Hispanics); Latinas tend to receive prenatal care later than the general population, with only 61 percent receiving such care in the

## Figure 7. People Living with Pollution

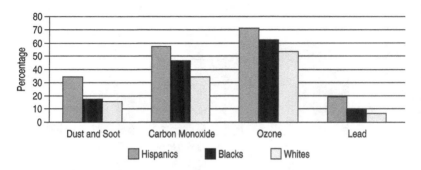

Source: Robert Suro, "Pollution-Weary Minorities Try Civil Rights Tack," *New York Times* (January 11, 1993): A-1; and the Environmental Protection Agency.

first trimester; Hispanics are also less likely than African Americans and Euroamericans to carry health insurance.[26]

When it comes to education, Hispanic children find themselves within a social environment that contributes to their failure in obtaining adequate schooling. According to the 2000 census, Latina girls are dropping out of school at a far greater rate than any other group of U.S. girls. Hispanic girls represent 26 percent of dropouts among female high school students age sixteen to twenty-four (African American girls represent 13 percent, and white girls represent 6.9 percent). These girls are more likely to drop out of school earlier than any other group, male or female, and least likely to return and complete their high school education. The only group that has a higher dropout rate than Latina girls is Latino boys at 31 percent (compared to African American boys at 12.1 percent and white boys at 7.7 percent) (Fig. 8). The most often cited reasons for such excessive dropout rates among Hispanics are the high rates of poverty among Latinos/as and language barriers. Latina girls are additionally burdened by machismo paradigms that expect them to marry young, cook meals, and raise children.[27]

A poll of Hispanic religiosity was conducted by the Barna Research Group in the year 2000. Based on the responses of more than four thousand adults, this survey revealed that Latinas/os are shifting from traditional Catholic-oriented spirituality to a more

## Figure 8. 1999 High School Dropout Rates according to Race/Ethnicity

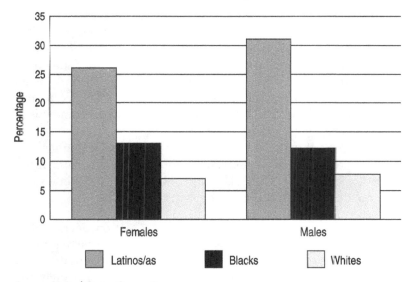

*Source:* United States Census Bureau

diverse spiritual hybrid, which is not necessarily mainline Protestant. In 1990, 68 percent of all Hispanic adults claimed affiliation with Roman Catholicism. A decade later, 53 percent of the population said they mostly attended the Roman Catholic Church. Yet, no single Protestant denomination can claim exclusivity in incorporating these Hispanics into their congregations. This group of Latinos/as who left the Catholic Church during the 1990s spread themselves among dozens of evangelical and charismatic churches, with an above average tendency to fellowship at Pentecostal and charismatic churches.

Although the Barna Group survey revealed that Hispanic spiritual practices tend to be similar to the spiritual practices of non-Latinas/os (40 percent attend church, 24 percent volunteer at their church, 81 percent pray, and 15 percent participate in small groups that gather for spiritual reasons), a significant distinction exists. Hispanics are less likely to read the Bible (outside of a church service) than non-Latinos/as (33 percent vs. 40 percent). Also, Latinas/os are less likely to use the term "born-again" when referring to themselves (25 percent vs. non-Hispanics at 44 percent).[28]

The Latinas/os who left Roman Catholic churches for Protestant denominations face serious challenges. These Protestant churches will be forced to face the spiritual perspectives of their new parishioners who are not necessarily evangelical nor fundamentalist.[29] Either these Hispanics will have to change their theological views, or the congregations they are joining will have to transform some of their theological tenets in order to welcome this new contingency.

Based on these broad statistical data concerning Latinos/as, we can make some initial observations about how Hispanics construct theological perspectives. These brief observations will be explored in greater detail in subsequent chapters.

- Hispanics are seen as "exiles, aliens, and outsiders." Hence, they have become accustomed to seeing themselves through the eyes of Euroamericans as the marginalized "Other" of the dominant culture. This way of seeing acutely influences the Latino/a approach to theology by incorporating a profound sense of "Otherness." Because they exist beyond the center of U.S. culture, they construct their theological perspectives from within this disenfranchised space, making a conscious effort to avoid "importing" their perspectives from Latin America or transplanting them from Eurocentric theologies. Instead, Latinos/as attempt to forge theologies from the faith and life experience of Latinas/os themselves. Until recently, a Euroamerican male hand has written their history, defined their theology, and shaped their identity. Yet as Hispanics grow in number, they have begun to write their own stories, a process that consequently makes their perspectives subversive to the dominant theological discourse.

- Theology does not exist in a social vacuum; rather, it reflects sociopolitical location. The majority of Latinas/os live in this nation's densely populated urban centers, which makes *el barrio* a key context in which to analyze the Latino/a social reality and to construct their theological perspectives.[30] Hispanics occupy the bottom stratum of the economy, receiving the lowest weekly wages of any major group in the labor market. During the 1990s Hispanics suffered substantially greater increases in unemployment than other ethnic/racial groups. Hence, any Latino/a theology tends to represent the struggle of its people. Hispanics forge their perspectives from the underside of U.S. economic structures. From the bottom, their voices provide a needed critique of the status quo.

- Hispanics are a people with conservative cultural roots. Many Latinos/as come from conservative religious backgrounds that are less receptive to birth control measures or abortion. Their internal cultural mythology celebrates early marriage and large families, which contribute to a younger and more fertile ethnic group when compared to the rest of the nation. As present growth trends continue, the U.S. labor force in the new millennium will have a disproportionately greater numbers of Latinas/os. As global capitalism continues to expand, the future workforce of the United States, which will be predominately Hispanic, will find itself occupying the lower paying service industries, will face greater economic struggles than previous generations, and will also find the so-called American Dream far more elusive. The hope of transcending the dismal economic space Hispanics occupy will continue to be more and more illusory.

- Latinos/as have disproportionately low levels of educational attainment and thus represent an undereducated class. Hispanics account for the largest dropout rates of all major racial/ethnic groups, with few continuing on to higher education, where the most deplorable Latino/a absence exists. Not surprisingly, this underrepresentation is also evident in theological education, where Latinos/as account for less than 3 percent of the total enrollment in seminaries and schools of theology. The disproportionately low number of Hispanic theologians makes it difficult for institutions to offer curriculum with a genuine Hispanic component, thus contributing to a monolithic and Eurocentric education that ignores the variety of religious life within the United States. This in turn continues a vicious cycle of discouraging some Latina/o stu-

dents from pursuing theological education because of the
lack of Hispanic faculty serving as mentors and advisors.
The continued underrepresentation of Latino/a scholarship
is measured proportionately to the number of Hispanic faculty.[31] Hence Euroamericans will continue to dwarf Hispanics
in contributions to the overall formal theological discourse of
our time.

In short, current demographic information indicates Hispanics
are a diverse and growing minority group that constructs its religious perspectives from locations of imposed marginality and
disenfranchisement. To see and understand Hispanic theological
perspectives, one must understand both their present locations and
their social, cultural, and religious roots.

## Seeing the Background
## of Latino/a Religion in the U.S.

Understanding the social locations and religious life and practices
of Latinos/as in the United States involves considering a wide range
of rich and diverse multicultural backgrounds and roots. An important primary consideration is that religion in both Latin America
and among U.S. Hispanics is not exclusively Christian, while those
U.S. Latinos/as who are Christian are not exclusively Catholic or
Protestant. Various Hispanic groups often practice religious faith
in ways that are at a variance with dominant mainstream cultures.
Generally speaking, the diversity of cultural and religious roots
of Hispanics falls into three main categories, namely, (1) the European, (2) the numerous and diverse Amerindian or indigenous
cultures of the Americas, and (3) the complex and innovative beliefs and practices of Africa, primarily West Africa. These three
streams are brought together historically and culturally into a
Latin American synthesis with profound regional differences. They
then undergo further development and innovation in the context
of North America, with the ultimate result that while there are
discernible links between Latin American religions and Latino/a
religions in the United States, each is a distinct phenomenon.

## European Religions

The European dimension in Latin American religion is primarily Spanish, but not exclusively so. Even the term "Spain" needs to be considered carefully, for Spain has been and is a multicultural entity with a complex cultural and religious history. Often when people in the United States think of Christianity in Spain, they have a vague notion of mysterious and exotic Roman Catholicism, a hint of an oppressive, unenlightened Inquisition, and a sense of some sort of connection with Latin America. They may also assume that the common people hold belief in widespread superstitions. Occasionally, people in the States may be aware of some sort of link between Spain and peoples in the United States who are called Hispanics; however, the overall impression is one of fuzziness about something that is deemed of little importance to mainstream life in the United States.

Religious cultural systems are complex, and that of Spain is no exception. In historical terms, that is in part, because not all the religions in Spain were Christian, nor was Christianity in Spain ever monolithically conceived and practiced. Throughout its long history, the Iberian Peninsula has witnessed waves of settlements of many peoples including the Phoenicians, Celts, Greeks, Carthaginians, Romans, Goths, Arabs, Berbers, Jews, Franks, and the original native peoples. Moreover, although Iberia is mistakenly perceived as being on the fringe of Europe, throughout its history it has been a crossroads of peoples, civilizations, and cultures. In considering the history of Christianity in Spain, one must deal with the substantial presence and influence of Judaism and Islam, both of which settled for a time at this crossroads.

When a Muslim presence on the peninsula first emerged, Christians reacted with efforts that would later come under the common rubric of the *reconquista* (reconquest). This idea of holy war had a significant impact on the development of the Spanish kingdoms and the subsequent colonization of Latin America. The seven-hundred-year-old struggle to reclaim the land and vanquish Muslims by way of Christianity merged nationalism with Catholicism. A Christian was one who was obligated to fight the enemies of the faith. Holy war became an expression of faith. As the last crusade against the Muslims came to an end in Old

Spain, a new, vaster campaign became available in New Spain. This reconquest spirit, where Roman Catholic orthodoxy and Hispanicity became synonymous, defined the entire Spanish colonialization process.

Although periodically the object of persecution under both Christian and Muslim regimes, the Jewish community in Spain sustained itself. The mystical aspects of Judaism were explored in Jewish Spain. Many Iberian Jews served as advisors, linguists, and financiers in the courts of both Muslim and Christian rulers. Jewish practices, often through *conversos* (converted Jews), entered the larger culture as the *conversos* sought to maintain a dual heritage. Even when Islam was no longer in ascendancy and the Jews were expelled from the peninsula, the influence of both communities continued to be felt in the Old World *mestizaje* religious-cultural systems of Iberia and in the new *mestizaje* cultures of the Spanish colonies (for more on the concept of *mestizaje*, see p. 37).

Spain's religious and cultural adaptability was always practiced as times and circumstances dictated. Alternative expressions of Christianity were continually present throughout the long history of Spain. The geography of Iberia contributed to the development of regional identities and distinct cultural perceptions that were transported across the Atlantic. There were popular practices that sometimes differed from official observances. All of this Iberian diversity made the journey across the Atlantic and encountered the native populations there.

## Indigenous Native American Religions

Just as the assumption of the monolithic nature of the Spanish colonizers needs to be reexamined, so does the perception that Columbus encountered a single people he erroneously called *indios*. The second major stream in the development of Latin American religious cultural systems and an important factor in understanding Hispanic religiosity are the beliefs and practices of the native peoples of the Americas. When the Spaniards encountered indigenous populations in the Caribbean in 1492, they did not find a single entity; rather, the Europeans stumbled upon numerous groups with ethnic, linguistic, and historical variety. Furthermore, the Spaniards came upon, not a religious and cultural vacuum, but creative and ancient cultures with various developed social-political systems and worldviews.

In many of the islands of the Antilles were peoples eventually called collectively Taino, and on some islands closer to the continent were other peoples now called the Island-Caribs, although interestingly the indigenous peoples seemed to refer to themselves by their locality rather than by a larger collective name. The word "Taino" itself means "good" or "noble" and seems to have been used as a descriptor to distinguish them from the Island-Caribs. In Puerto Rico, eastern Cuba, and Hispaniola, the advanced cultures took the form of large permanent villages governed by a *cacique* (chief). Villages of at least two distinct social classes were organized into district chiefdoms. The Taino religious cosmology included belief in deities known as *zemis*, ancestral spirits, and spirits of nature. Although Spanish colonization in the Caribbean led to virtual cultural and racial genocide, the seminomadic Island-Caribs and Tainos left a cultural legacy through amalgamation into a new religious cultural synthesis of their actual and cultural descendants.

Likewise the Spanish encounter with the indigenous Mesoamerican populations of the Aztec and the Mayan was with highly developed societies with their own historic classical civilizations. The urban civilizations of Mesoamerica, which had developed advanced math and astronomy and sophisticated methods of construction, were among the major sites of advanced civilization in the history of the entire world, albeit unknown to the Europeans. As they expanded from their Caribbean bases in search of new wealth, the Spanish came in contact with many peoples on the continent, including the Zapotec in Oaxaca and Maya and the Chichimeca peoples, including the Aztec or Culhua-Mexica. The region was dominated by a complex urban-based culture. The religious world of the various Mesoamerican peoples was characterized by the important role of the calendar cycle ordering space and time. A dualistic dimension expressed itself in the opposition of day and night, but this was a dualism in which both sides were necessary for life. Twins figure prominently in various Mesoamerican cosmologies, and the sacred accounts tell of the creation of the world and social behavior. The Mesoamerican people also kept genealogies as well as the histories of various migrations.

In the Spanish conquest of Mexico, Hernán Cortés and his

colleagues viewed the long-established Mesoamerican religions as false and believed it was their duty to vanquish the religion of the "heathens" with the truth of their own Spaniard faith, the cross, and the sword. With the final surrender of the Aztecs in 1521, a new civilization began that combined indigenous and European cultures. Central to this creation of a new people and their evangelization was devotion to the Virgin of Guadalupe.

In what came to be known as South America, the largest existing political entity at the time of the Spanish conquest was the Inca Empire, an advanced civilization with a long history. The empire included major parts of modern Ecuador, Peru, and Chile. Indeed, throughout these modern states are found the direct descendants of the Quechua people of the Inca Empire, called Quichua in contemporary Ecuador and Quechua in contemporary Peru. The Inca Empire was crushed during the years 1532–72.

The culture of the Inca Empire was characterized by reciprocity in everyday relations, closeness to nature, and reverence for the sun, in particular. Quechua religion included belief in a supreme creator deity who was mirrored on earth by the Inca emperor, although the creator was perceived to be somewhat removed from humanity. Also present in the supernatural council were other deities of sun, stars, moon, earth, and the elements, who had more everyday connections with humanity. Major Inca public rites were associated with agricultural events, indicating the ceremonial importance of an Incan calendar. Although initially the Spaniards perceived similarities with Catholicism, ultimately Andean religious beliefs and practice were viewed by the Spanish as false and of the devil.

As in Mexico and the Caribbean, the Spanish continued the dual effort of (re)conquista and the spread of Christianity. The conflicting natures of these impulses were never reconciled effectively during the Spanish colonial period and have left a conflicted cultural legacy to the present day. Though the Spanish evangelized the various indigenous peoples, a great deal of variety in the appropriation and practice of Christianity appears to have developed. In the Andes, Mesoamerica, the Caribbean, and the rest of what became Spanish America, indigenous beliefs and practices were combined with elements of the imported Spanish Christianity, both in its official and popular/folk expressions. In some locations alternate and sometimes "underground" religious-cultural systems sustained people in their everyday life.

## African Traditional Religions

A third major component important for understanding Latino/a religiosity is the African religious-cultural cosmos of those persons forcibly brought to the Western Hemisphere as slaves. As with the European and indigenous Amerindian sources, the extent of this influence varies from region to region; the religious-cultural heritage of the African Diaspora is "a family of traditions" with a shared social history of subjugation and racism.[32] African religious-cultural traditions shared an emphasis on maintaining good or balanced relationships between human beings and "spirits," which was accomplished through various ceremonies in which beliefs were combined with symbolic objects and actions. African beliefs and practices persisted through adversity to empower the new community and were reformulated particularly as they came in contact with European Christianity (official and popular) and indigenous beliefs and practices. Examples of this re-creation and continuity are widespread throughout much of Latin America. A prominent example is the religious expression practiced among Cubans known as Santería. During the period of slavery, the Africans' attitudes, music, dance, and religion exerted a major influence on the developing Cuban culture. In Cuba a distinct slave religion developed, one characterized by a fusion of African beliefs and practices with Spanish Catholic folk culture.

Throughout Latin America wherever there was an African presence, including the islands of the Caribbean, portions of Mexico, Central America, and South America, such synthesis was a religious way of life that saw all aspects of life infused with the spiritual and connected to the supernatural.[33] The ultimate concern was to maintain balance in life and good relationships between the different realms of existence and to obtain the resources needed to negotiate daily life. Those adopting the synthesis honored and recognized their ancestors as exerting a continuing influence in life and believed in a supreme being, known as Olodumare, who contributed all of life, as well as the presence of intermediary quasi-deities known as *orisha*.

Santería and similar religious-cultural systems emerged as a means of maintaining continuity with the African past. At the same time they appropriated elements of Spanish Christianity (especially folk or popular religion) along with aspects of the indigenous cosmology. Typical of many African-based religious traditions in Latin America are divination rituals to address spiritual problems, to seek knowledge, and to align human action with the spiritual realm. These often involve a type of sacrifice intended to establish deeper relationships with the spirits (*orisha*). Drums and dances figure prominently as divination and sacrifice combine into one event/experience.

Today, there are indications of the ongoing influence and presence of African religious traditions among U.S. Hispanic groups that have no direct connection with Africa. An example is found in the many *botanicas* and spiritualists' establishments found throughout U.S. urban centers that contain a large Hispanic population. Among these urban populations one finds specialty shops with the names of *orishas* like Changó and Obatala and other evidence of the belief in *orishas*.

## Hispanic Christianity and Christianity in Latin America

Given the varied streams and influences that converge to create Christianity in Latin America, the latter cannot be viewed as a monolithic entity. There was and is a great deal of regional variety, even within a given modern nation. Generally speaking, Latin American Catholicism was numerically and culturally dominant, although often expressed in two distinct ways. It was manifested first in the hierarchy-focused type of devotion that has been termed "official religion," drawing heavily upon the upper classes. Second, it was and continues to be expressed through the spirituality of the common people of the lower classes, who are far greater in number. In some parts of Latin America this latter group contains indigenous Amerindian peoples who survived the colonization period. In recent years their understandings and practices of Christianity have been termed "popular religion" or "popular religiosity." Such forms of popular religion have always been an important part of Roman Catholicism in Latin America. Historically, Latin Americans drew upon their popular religiosity as a resource for their daily struggle to survive socially, politically, economically, and religiously. In the 1960s a Latin American Catholic reformation movement known as liberation theology began to emerge. Increasingly, liberation theology showed an appreciation for the important role popular religion plays in the faith of the people.

Latin American liberation theology has exerted a profound influence in the development and character of U.S. Latino/a theologies. Emerging from Roman Catholic contexts, liberation theology is a type of systematic theology whose starting point is the experience and realities of the poor in society. As an interpretation of the Christian message from the perspective of the poor, liberation theology understands poverty as a result, not solely of individual failings, but of societal and systemic forces. Liberation theologians in Latin America associated themselves with local grassroots communities known as *comunidades eclesiales de base* (Christian base communities). These base communities, composed mostly of poor people, provided opportunities for new appropriation and practice of the Christian faith *a la luz de la fé* (in the light of faith) and directly reflected the social, ecclesiastical, and economic marginalization of the majority of Catholics in Latin America. The practice and theological reflection upon reality emanating from liberation theology has influenced the development of Hispanic theology in the United States. Even given this significant influence, one must not confuse U.S. Hispanic theologies with Latin American liberation theologies, nor vice versa.

Protestantism gradually appeared in Latin America during the early days of the new republics, first as the religion of small communities of European expatriates whose faith was eventually adopted by a few Latin Americans. No significant growth in Latin American Protestantism occurred until the appearance of Pentecostal Christianity around the turn of the twentieth century. During the 1970s and 1980s, as liberation theology made some inroads in revitalizing portions of the Catholic Church, a greater Protestant presence in Latin America developed, but it was misinterpreted, unnoticed, or underestimated by some. By the 1990s it was clear to all observers that Protestantism in the region had a significant presence. While quantifying the number of Latin American Protestants (*evangélicos*) has always been problematic, some estimate that by the year 2010 Protestants will grow from 2 to over 50 percent of the population of specific countries.[34]

More recently, observers of religion and culture in Latin America have begun to explore why Protestantism, particularly in its Pentecostal manifestations, is growing at comparatively phenomenal rates. While Catholic liberation theology has its adherents, it has not grown at the pace earlier observers anticipated. Adding to the complexity are the numbers of Protestants, including some Pentecostals, who display characteristics in their ministry and theology similar to those of liberation theology. It is important to note that the multiplicity of religious and political options in Latin America indicates that Latin American Protestantism is not a carbon (colonial) copy of North American Protestantism. Nor for that matter is Latino/a Catholicism in the United States a carbon copy of the situation in Latin America. Christianity among Hispanics in the United States must be seen in its own context. All the factors mentioned above and many others come together to form U.S. Hispanic Christianity. Furthermore, the roots of Hispanic Christianity in the United States are not limited to events in the Caribbean and Central and South America but are also found in North America, including the United States and Mexico.

The social and political histories of Mexico and the United States have been intertwined at least since the 1820s. In addition, one must also consider the influence of Spanish colonial missions and settlements in what is now part of the United States. These include the expeditions to Florida by Juan Ponce de León in 1513 and the establishment of St. Augustine in 1565 as the first permanent European settlement and mission in what would become the United States. An early Spanish presence also affected those areas that became New Mexico, Texas, Arizona, and California. Unfortunately, the early Spaniards believed that the "Indians" had no religion or were devil worshipers. The basic mission structure imposed the *encomienda* system, a type of colonial feudalism. The word *encomienda* connotes the entrusting of a person or thing into the care of someone or something else. As subjects of the Spanish Crown, Native Americans were entrusted to the conquistadores for the purpose of religious and cultural evangelization. Through this arrangement, the Spanish settler acquired both free laborers and fertile soil. This arrangement became more insidious than slavery because the settler invested nothing in the worker, having no obligation for his or her well-being.

Many historians view this period as the decimation of an indigenous people, masked by the overblown claims of forced evangelization. Nevertheless, through intercultural mixing, new religious cultural systems were created. Today's Hispanic Christian popular religiosity and devotion find a wellspring of resources from this nexus: the U.S. Southwest is highly influenced by the indigenous cultures of that region; peoples of Caribbean origin experience the influence of both indigenous cultures and the African Diaspora; and the growing number of Latinos/as from places like Peru and Chile exhibit an Andean influence.

## Seeing Latino/a *Mestizaje* and Spirituality

The term *mestizaje* has been used throughout this chapter. Important to understanding Hispanic spirituality and theology, *mestizaje* is an existential awareness of cultural complexity. Recall the obvious, but usually overlooked, fact that the United States is not Latin America. While people of Latin American descent and heritage live in the United States, the respective cultural, social, political, and religious contexts are very different. The rich religious-cultural systems of Latin America cannot be forgotten, but both continuity and discontinuity exist. In the different context of North America, a new cultural identity emerges as Latinos/as hold on to other identities of importance.

One way Hispanic theologians have described their religious identity is based on the concept of *mestizaje*. A leader in this effort has been the Catholic *Tejano* (Texan) theologian Virgilio Elizondo, who states that "the borderlands between the U.S. and Mexico form the cradle of a new humanity."[35] For Latinos/as in the United States, the borderlands are not solely a geographic location but also a social location. The profundity of this reality is sometimes better felt than explained. The poet Aurora Levins Morales provides a good illustration of this new cultural identity in her poem "Child of the Americas":

I am a child of the Americas,
a light-skinned *mestiza* of the Caribbean,
a child of many diaspora, born into this continent at a
    crossroads.

I am a U.S. Puerto Rican Jew,
a product of the ghettos of New York I have never known.
An immigrant and the daughter and granddaughter of
    immigrants.
I speak English with a passion: It's the tool of my
    consciousness,
a flashing knife blade of crystal, my tool, my craft.

I am *Caribeña*, island grown, Spanish is in my flesh,
ripples from my tongue, lodges in my hips:
the language of garlic and mangoes,
the singing in my poetry, the flying gestures of my hands.
I am of *Latinoamerica*, rooted in the history of my continent:
I speak from that body.

I am not african. Africa is in me, but I cannot return.
I am not taína. Taíno is in me, but there is no way back.
I am not european. Europe lives in me, but I have no
    home there.

I am new. History made me. My first language was spanglish.
I was born at the crossroads
and I am whole.[36]

Each Latina/o in the United States is a "child of the Americas."
Hispanic communities are profoundly aware of their roots and
their present realities, including the daily struggle to be whole. Hispanic Christian faith communities draw on their many resources
*aquí* (here) in the United States and *allá* (there) even as they
struggle with defining their identity in a sometimes hostile social
environment. Hispanic Christians of different denominations work
within their communities to construct a theology to help them
clearly see themselves and the present reality of their struggle.

In attempting to define the Latina/o identity, it is important
to consider the significance of a minority perspective, meaning
the perspective of both a religious minority and a racial/ethnic

minority in the United States. Part of the backdrop is the U.S. nature of race. Both Hispanic Catholics and Protestants experience abuse and neglect from within their own denominations. The creation of *comunidad* (community) serves as resource, becoming an important unifying factor in the new *mestizaje* of the United States.

Another significant issue for Latinos/as is their marginalization from two directions, the legacies of providentialism and Manifest Destiny. The concept of Manifest Destiny significantly shaped the ethos of the dominant culture in the United States, particularly in the early 1800s. Manifest Destiny held that the lands that became the United States were divinely given to those Europeans who settled the eastern seaboard of North America; their destiny as well as their mission was to claim and settle the land between the two seas as a new promised land for a new chosen people. "Providentialism" refers to the fact that Spain conceived itself as the "providential guardian of Catholic devotion" and was chosen by God for a special mission in the world. This resulted in the problematic "discovery-conquest-conversion" of the indigenous peoples.[37] Both Manifest Destiny and the providentialism of the Spanish colonies objectified the indigenous peoples as a lesser "Other." The legacies of these injustices form part of the deep background of Hispanic cultures in the United States.

## One Way of Seeing and Mapping

The preceding historical and sociological information demonstrates that no one simple way of looking at Hispanic religious life in the United States exists. Just as it is possible to look at a map of the world from different viewpoints, so too it is possible to look at Latina/o Christianity from different perspectives. Whatever map is used, as one gazes at Hispanic Christianity in the United States, it becomes abundantly clear that the "terrain" is richly varied with many important features to consider. Despite deeply ingrained social habits of perception, it is clear that not all Latinas/os are the same. In fact, many factors need to be pondered in getting a clear picture of Hispanic religious and theological thought. An awareness of the nature of these communities and their histories helps avoid serious distortions.

The subsequent chapters present a particular way of "mapping" Latina/o theology in which the full complexity of Hispanic cultural life is considered along with its religious expressions. This map recognizes other equally legitimate ways of seeing Latino/a religion. Of particular concern is how Hispanics in the United States "see" the Divine, the biblical text, their church, their own stories, and their rituals, particularly as these perspectives appear in some of the shared common features of Latino/a theology.

# Chapter 1 Study Questions

## Definition Questions

1. What is the difference between "the center" and "the margins"?

2. What does it mean to be an "Other," or to have a profound sense of "Otherness"?

3. What is *la reconquista,* and how did it influence the Spanish conquest of the Americas?

4. What are the differences between Manifest Destiny and providentialism?

5. Define the following terms: *mestizaje, encomienda,* Christian base communities.

## Essay Questions

1. How are Hispanics depicted in the media? When you think of a Latino/a, what images come to mind? Within your community, what positions (economically, socially, politically, etc.) do Hispanics normally occupy?

2. By 2050, Hispanics will compose 25 percent of the United States population. How does this make you feel? What impact, if any, do you perceive it will have upon your lifestyle? Do you envision this as positive or negative for the United States? Why? What strategies should be employed now to prepare for these rapidly changing demographics?

3. In what ways does the social location of Hispanics influence their theological views? Should theology occur from a group's social location? Why or why not? If all theologies represent the social location of a group, can there be such a thing as an "objective" theological perspective? Are your theological views (or lack thereof) a reflection of your own social location?

4. How does a Hispanic theology confront, critique, subvert, and challenge how Euroamericans do theology? What does Latina/o theology share with Euroamerican theology?

5. What are the distinct traditions contributing to the creation of the Latino/a present-day religious expression? How is this *mestizaje* evident in the expression of Hispanic spirituality?

## Chapter 2

# Common Cultural Themes within a Community-Based Theology

Theology is usually defined as "the study of God." Traditionally theologians have emphasized God as the object of their discipline rather than concentrate on themselves as its practitioners. Yet, to understand the function of theology, we first need to focus upon the unmentioned subject of this definition: Who is doing the studying? Theology may aspire toward eternal and universal truths about the nature and essence of God, but all theology is done by human beings, limited by their finite identities and their place in society, culture, and history. Consequently, to do theology is to participate in an ongoing communal process. Traditional theology, as done primarily by Eurocentric men, necessarily differs from the theology done by African Americans, Asian/Pacific Americans, Native Americans, or Hispanics. Yet, Eurocentric theologies have positioned themselves historically and socially as the "center" in worldwide theological thought, as though they were somehow more objective and more legitimate. Any theology constructed by others, perhaps by those on the "margins," automatically becomes a response to, or a dialogue with, the "center." Any attempt by a people to study God apart from the self-appointed center risks ridicule as "nonscholarly." Unless established "authorities" like Rahner, Bultmann, Von Balthasar, Barth, Lonergan, Niebuhr, Tillich, or Brunner are mentioned, theologies from the margins often are considered lightweight and irrelevant. Yet, theology done at the self-appointed center can continue to be relevant to all without ever having to mention, discuss, or understand

Aquino, Elizondo, Espín, González, Isasi-Díaz, Pineda, Segovia, or Villafañe.

The family of Latino/a theologies is the study of God from the margins of North American society and culture. It is a relatively new phenomenon shaped by many different sources and accomplishing many different tasks. While scholars continue to investigate, enumerate, and identify all of these sources, there is agreement that the Hispanic experience is paramount for the development of theological perspectives. If there were no Latinos/as, then there would be no Hispanic theology. Thus, Latina/o theology becomes a distinct type of God-talk whose function is (1) to understand the Divine from within the Hispanic cultural location; (2) to seek God's liberative will in the face of both cultural and economic oppression; (3) to search for a common voice that proclaims salvation, liberation, and reconciliation to the most diverse segments of the Latino/a culture; (4) to create theological harmony between the U.S. Hispanic condition and the scriptural narratives; (5) to struggle against the way Latinos/as are perceived and conceived by the dominant culture; and (6) to provide a prophetic voice that unmasks the racism, classism, and sexism implicit in the theology of the dominant white culture.

If Hispanic theologies are the theological reflections of people labeled Latinos/as, we must begin with an effort to understand how the community sees, defines, and understands itself. We must discern the Hispanic social location to comprehend these conceptions of and dialogue with God. This is accomplished when the study of Hispanic theologies begins by elucidating their own *comunidad,* their community. *Comunidad* must be the touchstone by which we comprehend the Hispanics' perception of God and themselves, the starting point in developing Latina/o theological perspectives.

Latinos/as are not a monolithic group. Any attempt to define their *comunidad* by listing superficial, stereotypical denominators, whether they are positive or negative characteristics, does violence to Latinas'/os' dignity. They are as different as the colors of the rainbow. Yet, some common themes do recur in the shared attempt to understand God. While these recurring themes are neither universal nor applicable to every Hispanic group found in the United States, they do serve as important clues, exposing the basic foundations that underlie and support the multiple perspectives existing in Latino/a theologies. Without a doubt, Latina/o cultural roots shape the community-based theologies of Hispanics, including how Latinos/as regard God and the personhood of Jesus Christ, how they read and interpret the Bible, how they worship and praise God, and how they understand and practice the justice-based teachings of the gospel. This chapter will lay the groundwork for grasping how Hispanics do theology by first exploring the cultural roots that influence the construction of Latina/o theology and then by reviewing some of the significant aspects of the resulting theology.

## Cultural Roots Influencing Hispanic Theologies

Even though Spanish was the first European language spoken in the Western Hemisphere during the time of exploration and colonization, those who speak Spanish in the United States today are viewed as newcomers. Yet, a glance at a map of the United States demonstrates long-term Hispanic influences. States named Nevada, Florida, and Colorado (instead of Snow, Flowered, and Red-Colored) and cities named Los Angeles, Santa Fe, San Antonio, and El Paso (instead of The Angels, Holy Faith, St. Anthony, and The Pass) bear witness to the Latina/o heritage and presence. Regardless of the fact that the first European settlers in what was to become the United States came from Spain, Hispanics, after some five hundred years, are still seen by the dominant culture as exiles, aliens, and outsiders.

Hispanics are viewed in the United States as a people who do not belong. Some are here due to conquest (Mexicans and Puerto Ricans); others, as a result of gunboat diplomacy (Central Americans and Caribbeans). Still others are the victims of geopolitical struggles played out in their homelands (Chileans and Argentines). Mexicans and Puerto Ricans, whose presence is a direct consequence of United States territorial expansion, are foreigners in their own lands. Chicanas/os have occupied the land that would eventually be known as the United States for centuries prior to the European invasion. Virgilio Elizondo states that Mexicans did not cross the border; rather, it was the border that crossed them; the

same can be said about Puerto Ricans.[1] Both were and are the
consequences of Manifest Destiny. Cubans, on the other hand, had
their independence from Spain abrogated due to the United States'
multiple invasions of the island during the period of imperialism
in the late nineteenth century. Likewise, Central Americans from
various nations find themselves in this country because of the civil
wars sponsored by the United States in their homelands, as was the
case with the U.S. Contra war in Nicaragua during the Reagan ad-
ministration. Territorial invasions and the exploitation of natural
resources by U.S. corporations like the United Fruit Company contributed to Latin America's underdevelopment and internal unrest.
Many now find themselves refugees in the same country responsible for their flight from home. In all of these cases, Latinos/as
are a people separated from the land that previously defined them.
How then do Hispanics construct and understand their ethnicity
while separated from the land of their roots?

People usually define their ethnicity by the land that witnessed
their birth. Puerto Ricans or Cubans refer to themselves as such,
in part because they or their parents were born on those particular
Caribbean islands. But what happens when the land that defines
them is no longer available to them in the way it was for their parents and grandparents? How do they understand themselves in a
foreign and, at times, hostile land? How do those born in the States
forge an identity when they are treated as foreigners? What if their
love for their homeland remains stronger than their allegiance to
the land where they presently reside? How do they remain faithful to the land they love and the land they adopted? How does an
outsider status affect their theological understandings? These questions go to the heart of their sense of Otherness. James Clifford,
a cultural anthropologist, said it best when he wrote, "Perhaps
there's no return for anyone to a native land — only field notes
for its reinvention."[2]

Reinventing the past allows older adults who arrive on these
shores to live within their dismembered memories. This reinventing enables them to ignore the pain of displacement, even when
surrounded by constant reminders that they now reside on foreign soil. Young adults and adolescents are forced to live in at
least two worlds, trapped by the tension of trying to reconcile the
constructed ideal of the (former) homeland with the present real-

ity of their adopted land or new homeland. Children and infants who hold no memories of their (former) homeland are condemned to live within the memories constructed for them by their parents. Exiles, aliens, and outsiders feel unable to escape an inner struggle that defines their ethnicity, an ethnicity that frustrates their ability to reconcile their identity with their presence in the United States.

## Exiles, Aliens, and Outsiders

Exiles, aliens, and outsiders are three separate categories of persons, even though many if not all Hispanic national groups experience all three types of otherness. For example, many Salvadorans entered the United States as exiles during the U.S.-sponsored civil wars of the 1970s and 1980s, having left El Salvador in order to preserve their lives. Once hostilities ceased, later refugees were not fleeing tyranny as much as seeking economic stability. As aliens, they closely resembled "classical immigrants," such as the Irish, who were "pulled" by the allure of economic opportunities found in the United States, as opposed to being "pushed" by warfare. The economic pull of the United States complicates the reductionist argument that the sole reason for immigration is political. It ignores the natural flow of people from so-called underdeveloped to developed countries. While the basic reason for an individual to leave any country may be dissatisfaction with the current situation, it is impossible to discern any clear dividing lines between political, economic, and psychological reasons.

As these Salvadoran families settled in the United States, their children, born in this country, grew to adulthood experiencing the pain of being treated like outsiders. Being born here, speaking the dominant language, and eating hamburgers do not make them belong. Within most Latino/a communities, individuals have multiple existential experiences as exiles, aliens, and outsiders. All three of these groups experience the pain and difficulties of being treated as strangers in one's land of residence. The myth of a melting pot has proven to be an empty and selective promise. For purposes of exploring these three categories in greater detail, we will look at the Cuban community when discussing exiles, the Mexican community when discussing aliens, and the Puerto Rican community when discussing outsiders.

## Exiles

Many Cuban Americans best identify with the ethnic construction of *el exilio* (the exile). Deeply embedded in the Cuban psyche exists the realization that they have lost the land of their birth and that when their bodies are finally laid to rest, they will be interred as foreigners in an alien soil. *El exilio* is a term mainly used by exilic Cubans to name' their collective identity. The term connotes the involuntary nature of their displacement and constructs them as sojourners in a foreign land. *El exilio* is an in-between place, a place to wait and hope for a return to the homeland. More than a geographic separation, it encompasses disconnection, displacement, and disembodiment. In Miami, longing for Cuba, or the "rhetoric of return," becomes the unifying characteristic of the Cuban who constructs *el exilio* as a sacred space in which religion and morality become synonymous with nationality.

For Cubans in Miami, *el exilio,* although literally a geographic reality, is a culturally constructed artifact imagined as a landless nation complete with its own history and values. From this imaginary land(lessness), those in *el exilio* have evolved theological perspectives within which ethnic identity assumes religious significance. For example, in 1973, in order to rectify exilic existence, Cubans built on Biscayne Bay a tentlike shrine for La Virgen de Caridad to serve as both a political and sacred space. Upon this sacred ground, exilic Cubans re-created the image of their homeland on foreign shores. In this shrine, religious zeal marries Cuban patriotism, illustrated by the mural behind the altar and the sacred icon before it, a weak substitute for the original shrine on the island. Standing in the shrine, which faces Cuba, one can simultaneously occupy space in both *"la Cuba de ayer"* (yesteryear's Cuba) and the Miami of today. The religious illusion created by this reproduction of an authentic Cuban shrine on U.S. soil only masks the reality and pain of exilic status.

For the older Cuban, the shrine constructs and glorifies a Cuba that never was and never could be, yet somehow by simply worshiping in this space, one can be transported to that other place and time. For those who arrived in Miami as infants or children and are now busy paying mortgages and climbing the corporate ladder, the shrine is a physical representation of the dreams of their parents—

dreams about which they feel a strong, yet fading, sense of loyalty. The shrine provides a space where exiles can safely display their patriotism without having to commit to any action to make those dreams a reality. For children born and raised in this country, the shrine only confirms that their parents' dreams of Cuba amount to little more than an artificially constructed fantasy island.

Every exilic Cuban has heard Celia Cruz sing the popular tear-jerker "Cuando salí de Cuba" ("When I Left Cuba"). The song summarizes the pain of existential location: "Never can I die, my heart is not *here*. Over *there* it is waiting for me, it is waiting for me to return *there*. When I left Cuba, I left my life, I left my love. When I left Cuba, I left my heart buried." This popular Cuban ballad, written by a Chilean and sung as a hymn of faith, illustrates a denial of reality by exiled Cubans: the reality is that they are living and probably will die on foreign soil.

Like the Jews captive in Babylon, Cubans must deal with this incomprehensible pain of being torn from the "promised land." In Babylon, out of their pain, the Jews questioned the sovereignty of a God who would tear God's people from their homes and plant them in an alien land. A major concern for those in exile is their status as deportees. Does removal from the "promised land," by which their identity is constructed, indicate a divine rejection, voiding any future participation in God's plan? Does resettlement in a foreign land mean assimilation to a culture perceived as inferior? Surely names given to children like Jordan Perez or Jennifer Gomez reveal the changing Cuban ethnic identity and the pain caused in assimilating. These children will grow old as new "Americans." They are no more Cuban than their grandparents are "American." They exist in two different worlds, connected only by an in-between generation. Cuban sociologist Ruben Rumbaut has labeled this in-between space the "one-and-a-half" generation. While the first generation, consisting of the parents from the "old" world, faced the task of acculturation, managing the transition from one sociocultural environment to another, the second generation, consisting of the children from the "new" world, faces the task of managing the transition from childhood to adulthood. Those who are caught between these two spaces are forced to cope with both crisis-producing and identity-defining transitions.

## Aliens

Terms like "exile" and "alien" are often used interchangeably. Yet, the term "exile" has political connotations and suggests an inability on the part of the exile to return to the homeland. "Alien," on the other hand, reflects a different type of Otherness, regardless of the cause of expatriation. Aliens may reside in a new land for political or economic reasons. In theory, however, the alien can always return "home," if only for a visit.

Many Mexicans live the life of resident aliens in this country. Of the roughly nine hundred thousand "legal" immigrants annually admitted into the United States, Mexicans account for 14 percent of the group. Moreover, the Immigration and Naturalization Service conservatively estimates that an additional two hundred thousand to three hundred thousand undocumented Mexicans arrive each year. These migration patterns explain the way in which the dominant culture views all who have Mexican roots. To them, all Mexicans are aliens, which is hardly the full reality of the Mexican American experience. Not all Mexicans in the United States are recent arrivals. Many Mexican Americans can trace their connection to what was to become the United States through their Spanish ancestors by more than five centuries. If we consider their indigenous roots, their connection to the land could be traced further back.

Twelve years before the 1620 landing of the Mayflower at Plymouth Rock, Santa Fe, New Mexico, was founded as a Spanish city, having been explored years earlier by Francisco Vásquez de Coronado. In fact, the first European flag to be raised in what later was to be named the United States was the flag of Spain. The Spanish settlement of St. Augustine, Florida, in 1567 actually predates the first English settlement of Jamestown, Virginia, which was established in 1607. These historical facts are problematic and often ignored by the dominant culture, for how can Latinos/as be viewed solely as recent aliens when their presence here precedes the arrival of Anglos? From the Hispanic perspective, Anglos in the southwestern portion of the United States are the aliens, for they are the ones who arrived last. Yet, by constructing all Mexicans as aliens, the power and privilege of the dominant culture are preserved and legitimized while masking the historical reality that Mexican territory once included Texas, New Mexico, Arizona, California, Nevada, and Colorado.

The justification of this massive land acquisition was based on a theology that conceived the dominant Euroamerican culture as especially chosen by God, God's new Israel. The previously mentioned romantic form of jingoism known as "Manifest Destiny" taught that God had manifestly intended Euroamericans to spread their eagle wings over the entire northern continent. To deny this concept was not only treasonous but also blasphemous. The popular theological doctrine of the early 1800s concerning how the world would end, a type of millennialism, suggested that God's kingdom would be realized through the history of the United States. Christ's second coming would commence once the United States executed its apocalyptic mission of manifesting its territorial destiny. This divine mandate extended not only "from sea to shining sea" but also from the snowy wastes of the Arctic to the tropical charms of the Isthmus.[3]

The expansionist war against Mexico is a prime example of Manifest Destiny at work. In July 1845 General Zachary Taylor encroached on Mexican territory by deploying his troops to bait the Mexicans. Once Mexico mobilized to meet its adversary, President Polk (who was elected for his support of the annexation of Texas and the war with Mexico) had the opportunity to request a declaration of war from Congress. A military onslaught by the puissant United States led to Mexico's capitulation and to the 1848 Treaty of Guadalupe-Hidalgo, which ceded half of Mexico's territory to the United States. This land included gold deposits that would be discovered in California in 1849, silver deposits in Nevada, oil in Texas, and all of the natural harbors (except Veracruz) necessary for commerce. John Quincy Adams denounced the government's naked act of aggression against Mexico in his well-known caustic remark to Congress: "The banners of freedom will be the banners of Mexico; and your banners, I blush to speak the word, will be the banners of slavery."[4] Even Ulysses S. Grant, who served in this conflict, viewed the war, so obviously forced upon Mexico for the sake of acquiring land, as unjust.[5]

With the acquisition of land, the "Mexican question" in the United States developed. What would be done with the "alien" inhabitants? First, the U.S. government ignored treaty agreements and historic land titles. Second, Mexican Americans were further marginalized due to their economic value. They represented a "reserve army" of laborers, allowing the overall southwestern economy to develop and function. The new Euroamerican settlements profited by the labor surplus extracted from the barrios. Cities throughout former north Mexico developed by utilizing these "illegal immigrants." Third, segregation insured the privileged space of the newly installed Euroamerican center. Because Mexican Americans, out of necessity, were willing to work at the lowest wage level in the mining and agriculture industry, they were able to consolidate the power and wealth of the Euroamericans. The luxury houses of Los Angeles, San Antonio, and Santa Fe were built at considerable cost so as to distance their privileged space from the menace of *el barrio*, while simultaneously capitalizing on the poverty of this marginalized space.

With the turn of the twentieth century, the United States had created a need for cheap labor throughout the Midwest. The "reserve army" of Mexican laborers moved to manufacturing centers where they and their children faced assimilation, while a Hispanic middle class began to emerge. Yet, with the coming of the Great Depression of the 1930s, the Euroamerican majority increasingly viewed these "aliens" as taking away jobs from "real" Americans; this resulted in the deportation of many Latinas/os to Mexico. Because they no longer served an economic need, more than four hundred thousand Hispanics were returned to Mexico, including those born in the United States.

To be seen as an alien means one is always a foreigner even though the person is born within the artificial boundaries of the United States. Yet being an "alien" has little to do with where one is born and where one migrates. Instead, it has everything to do with how one looks or sounds. Any Hispanic whose appearance demonstrates the physical *mestizaje* of her or his roots or speaks with a "funny accent" is automatically seen as an alien.

## Outsiders

Not all Latinas/os living in the United States are exiles from Latin America (whether political, economic, religious, or a combination thereof), and neither are all Hispanics in the United States aliens in the way the term is usually understood. Nevertheless, a third group of Latinos/as shares the experiences of marginalization with Hispanic exiles and aliens. There is a significant and growing percentage of Hispanics whose only concept of "home" has been the United States, yet within this home they live in ambiguity. Outsiders are Latinas/os born within the United States yet rejected as Americans because of their Hispanic roots. While outsiders can be found in the experiences shared by the children of refugees and immigrants from all Latino/a ethnic groups, Puerto Ricans typify this group.

Puerto Rico was acquired by the United States through the Spanish-American War in 1898. The initial years of North American hegemony were characterized by attempts to "Americanize" and "civilize" this population. In the popular imagination in the United States, "Porto Rico" was seen as a backward place. By 1917 all Puerto Ricans were granted U.S. citizenship, allowing travel from the island to the mainland. Technically not considered immigration, this mobility was rather the movement of U.S. citizens within the United States.

Three major migrations of Puerto Ricans have occurred since 1900: the first wave (1900–1945) is referred to as "pioneers"; the second wave after World War II (1946–64) is known as the "Great Puerto Rican Migration"; and the third wave (1965–onward) is characterized by a pattern of ongoing migration and return, or "revolving door migration." Originally, the Puerto Rican population was centered in the northeastern United States, with New York City the major place of residence, but currently it is more dispersed, with increasing numbers of Puerto Ricans found in Illinois, New Jersey, and Pennsylvania. The majority of Puerto Ricans live outside New York City and exhibit significantly different characteristics from those of New York City Puerto Ricans (sometimes referred to as *Nuyoricans*).

Theologian Samuel Solivan has used the term "citizen-exiles" to describe the existential situation of Puerto Ricans as outsiders. Although Puerto Ricans have been citizens of the United States since 1917, in practice their reality has been of second-class citizens. Continuing his analysis, Solivan identifies aspects of Puerto Rican displacement and ambiguous social location in the popular Puerto Rican folksong from the 1940s "En Mi Viejo San Juan" ("In My

Old San Juan"): "One afternoon I departed toward a strange nation because destiny wanted it so. But my heart stayed close to the sea, in my old San Juan. Farewell, beloved Borinquen. Goodbye, goddess of the sea, I go, but one day I'll return, to look for my love, to dream once again, in my old San Juan."[26]

Another aspect of the outsider experience is the constant threat and reality of rejection by other Latinos/as. Often, later generation Hispanic Americans are treated poorly by others within Hispanic communities as other issues come into play, particularly the level of facility with the Spanish language. Although there is the desire for connection, a realization of disconnection exists. The late *Tejana* singer Selena was extremely popular in Spanish-language settings and on the verge of a breakthrough into mainstream fame at the time of her death. She had built her career with *Tejano* audiences singing in Spanish. Yet, few people knew at the time that she was not bilingual herself.

In conclusion, most Hispanics continue to be seen by the dominant culture as exiles, aliens, and outsiders, regardless of their historical connection to U.S. lands. To be a Latino/a within the United States is never to belong, unless the person can "pass" for a Euroamerican. This deep sense of Otherness informs how Hispanic theological perspectives are developed. In fact, these social locations serve as the starting point for most Hispanics in their quest for understanding the Deity. To ignore these spaces runs the risk of never fully comprehending Latina/o theologies.

## Theologies of Place

The physical space where many Hispanics reside, known as *el barrio*, has an influence on how Latinos/as develop their theological perspectives. As mentioned in the previous chapter, the 2000 U.S. census listed the total number of Hispanics at 36,400,000 nationwide. This growing Hispanic population is concentrated primarily in the urban centers of the United States, where the vast majority of Latinas/os reside. They are often simultaneously young, poor, and highly segregated. The reasons underlying these basic features reflect national trends affecting the several component groups of the Hispanic community and the bleak economic path it faces.

Yet, saying that the Latina/o *comunidad* is mostly urban communicates another obvious, but usually unstated, aspect of that reality — namely, not all Latinos/as live in urban barrios. Latinos/as are found in cities, rural settings, suburban bedroom communities, and the new exurban settings. Many others are seasonal farm workers in places that do not realize there is a rural Latino/a presence, such as Wisconsin, Ohio, and Michigan. Others work in meatpacking plants in Kansas, in service industries in Boston, or in poultry processing in Georgia; some are professionals in Los Angeles. This far-flung community faces difficult day-to-day economic realities, with little, save their own resilience, to draw on to change the position of that community in the overall structure of society.

Living in suburbs, rural areas, small towns, and cities, Hispanics have developed various expressions of theologies of place. Harold Recinos's barrio theology, for example, affirms "that Jesus can be found at the center of social reality."[7] A theology of place such as barrio theology affirms the worth of the *comunidad* to God and God's abiding presence in Christ in the day-to-day economic realities — realities defined by Hispanics who are marginalized, poor, and undereducated.

The barrio creates an environment in which the vast majority of the Hispanic community experiences residential segregation, employment discrimination, and political isolation. Nonetheless, the Hispanic community is beginning to realize the power of the vote. Even though the income gap continues to widen between Hispanics and Euroamericans, and while the Latina/o community represents only 6 percent of those voting in the 1998 midterm election, opportunity does exist to become powerbrokers. Urban Latinos/as are clustered in eleven key states, ones comprising 217 out of the 270 electoral votes needed for the presidency. Hispanics are learning that the best weapon of defense against xenophobic laws is U.S. citizenship and the right to vote. Hispanic leaders attempted to register an additional three million voters by the 2000 election. Is it any wonder that presidential contenders repeatedly made campaign stops in California, Texas, and Florida, greeting their audiences in Spanish? Yet, in spite of the potential opportunity to succeed, Hispanics are constantly threatened by institutionalized racism. Even though Hispanics pump $300 billion a year into the U.S. economy, 40 percent of their children still live in poverty, the highest rate ever recorded in the United States.

Because their children live in poverty, Hispanics now constitute an undereducated class that will soon mature into an underskilled workforce. Hispanics have the lowest levels of educational achievement of any ethnic group. Their children are more likely to drop out of school. According to the Census Bureau, the majority of Hispanics (more than 51 percent) drop out of high school, while 78 percent of non-Hispanics graduate. Dilapidated school buildings and insufficient budgets for books contribute to this rate of attrition. In fact, even before the Latina/o child attends her or his first day of school, she or he is often culturally predestined to fail. For most, college is unattainable; fewer than 10 percent expect to graduate, and only half of the 4 percent of all Hispanics who enter graduate school finish.[8] These conditions of the barrio are further aggravated by the overall racism of the dominant culture.

## Multiracialism

The Hispanic *comunidad* is *mestizo* (multiracial). The commonly used terms "Hispanic" and "Latino" are heuristic devices referring to the diverse groups of people of Iberian European, Native American, and African American descent and heritage living in the United States. At least three major streams feeding into the Latin American experience affect the development of the Hispanic identity in the United States. One source is European, consisting mainly of people from the Iberian Peninsula. The second font is the African heritage brought to the Western Hemisphere through the injustice of slavery. The third stream is the indigenous Native Americans, who suffered exploitation and genocide as a result of European conquest. In the current national groups of Latin America, a different "mix" of these three streams occurs depending on the historic presence of each stream in a given location. Given the diverse origins and complex histories involved, it is not even possible to speak of Latin Americans as a homogenous group. Subsequently, the Hispanic population of the United States is an extremely diverse group with a number of distinct subgroups of identifiable demographic and economic traits that distinguish the various subpopulations.

Latinos/as in the United States live in a two-tiered racist culture that classifies individuals as either white or nonwhite. Because Latinas/os are a multiracial *comunidad,* the dominant culture "sees" all Hispanics as nonwhite, even though Latinos/as see a segment of their own community as white. Regardless of how Hispanics construct racial categories, the dominant culture's racism relegates all Latinos/as to the category of "people of color." Their color is not determined solely by skin pigmentation; rather, they are also considered to be "of color" due to sound. Language becomes a bond that unifies Latinos/as. Their accents and Spanish-sounding surnames determine their race, their "color," and hence their marginality. Yet, "honorary whiteness" awaits those who have a lighter skin, acquire economic or cultural capital, and speak English without a Spanish accent.

Sociologists Frank Bean and Marta Tienda catalog four factors that identify and shape the ethnicity of Hispanics in the United States, particularly when compared with the European immigrations that occurred from 1880 to 1920. First, the period of mass entrance was shorter for Europeans. A long period of restricted migration followed, allowing for the assimilation of two to three generations. In contrast, Hispanic immigration is ongoing. Second, European immigrants were more concentrated in residence and employment, while Hispanics were more geographically dispersed. Third, the earlier Europeans were initially or eventually considered "white"; Hispanics, regardless of their skin pigmentation, are seen as a mixed breed and, therefore, "nonwhite." Fourth, in the context of the United States, the ideology held by the dominant society creates ethnic groups; in other words, the Irish, Germans, and Italians became "white," but Hispanics remained "nonwhite."[9]

Some have suggested that racial designations in the United States — such as Hispanic and Latino/a — are more descriptive of the social construction of the dominant society than a set of characteristics. For example, Michael Omi and Howard Winant describe a type of "racial etiquette" of interpretative codes and meanings that are at work in the everyday experiences of people in the United States. These are unquestioned assumptions that determine "the 'presentation of self,' distinctions of status, and appropriate modes of conduct."[10] Speaking from a theological context, Elizondo arrives at a similar position:

White Western supremacy permeates our way of life to such a degree that even good persons act in racist ways without even realizing that they are being racist. That is the tragedy of the social blindness of North American society. Racism and ethnocentrism are interwoven in literature, entertainment, institutions, marriage relations, finances, and even religious symbolism. This racist culture continues to bombard the non-Western and nonwhite with the message that they are nonhuman. This is not said in so many words, but the message is loud and clear through all the media of communication.[11]

The naming process itself displays the power of cultural codes. Part of the power of naming is that it disguises the nature of social classes that are present in U.S. society. A name can foster false consciousness. If a concerted effort is launched to tell people that they are something other than what they perceive themselves to be, a group's commonsense understanding of reality can become supplanted by someone else's understandings through coercion, deceit, or a combination of the two. When individuals and groups subscribe to a definition of "self" constructed by someone else, they fall into the trap of domination. But unless the cultural codes are known, the trap remains unseen, although clearly felt.[12] Hispanics feel the pressure to ignore known cultural pasts and to accept a new interpretive designation (i.e., dominant cultural myth) in the United States.

Prior to coming to the United States (or the United States coming to them in the case of Mexican Americans and Puerto Ricans), Latin Americans often identified themselves in terms of the nation or distinct subgroups found within their particular nations of origin. They further carried with them their concepts of class divisions as experienced in their nations of origin. Upon arrival in the United States, they perceived another class arrangement at work, one couched in racial or ethnic terms, categories that were alien to them. Jack Forbes says it best:

The concept of Hispanic (which means "Spanish" or "Spanish-derived") is especially absurd as applied to Maya, Mixtec, Zapotec, or other American peoples who often do not even speak Spanish (except perhaps as a second, foreign language), whose surnames are often not of Spanish origin, and whose racial and cultural backgrounds are First American or African or mixed.[13]

Although "for many Latin Americans the division between 'whites' and 'nonwhites' is insufficient to capture the racial, ethnic and cultural gradations to which they are accustomed in their countries of origin," there is a recognition of "the way things work," which compels them to deal with the power of the U.S. color-line.[14]

## Machismo

Another cultural root that influences Latina/o theology is the phenomena of gender relationships, specifically *machismo*. Although the term is used synonymously with "sexism," it originally referred to a celebration of conventional masculinities. Neither solely associated with the oppression of women nor solely used in a pejorative sense, the term "machismo" described the values associated with being a man, a *macho*. Similarly, the celebration of female attributes is known as *hembrismo*. A popular Hispanic saying is "Soy tan hembra como tú macho" (I am as much woman as you are man). Although sexism exists in both the Hispanic and Euroamerican cultures, when Euroamericans use the term "machismo," even though a comparable English term exists, it implies that Latinos are somehow more sexist than Euroamericans, hence absolving the Euroamerican culture of its own chauvinistic structures and attitudes. Although manifested differently, both Euroamericans and Hispanics are equally oppressive toward women.

Hispanic men, like Euroamerican men, are sexist, both products of two distinct patriarchal societies. For Latinos, to be a man, a *macho,* implies both domination and protection for those under them, specifically the females in the family. The *macho* worldview creates a dichotomy in which men operate within the public sphere — that is, the overall community — while women are relegated to the private sphere, specifically the home. The family's honor is augmented by the ability of the *macho* to provide for the family. The wife who works becomes a public testament then to the *macho*'s inability to be a good provider. While family honor is achieved by the *macho*, shame can come to the family via the women. In the mind of the *macho*, the possible sexual infidelity of the women in his household makes his honor susceptible, thus their banishment to the home. By confining women to the private sphere, the *macho* protects "his" women from their supposed sexual urges. Yet, the *macho*'s own sexual urges require no protection. In fact, his actions of infidelity only enhance his machismo.

Latinos' responsibility, their burden, is to educate those below their "superior" standards. Because of the privilege that comes with the male gender, Latinos are complicit with the sexist social structures of both the dominant Euroamerican culture as well as their own Hispanic cultures, a complicity motivated by personal advantage. The sexist attitudes toward women are not simply a belief in the superiority of men; rather, Hispanic men are able to exploit the power that comes with maleness to profit from customs, traditions, and laws designed to limit certain activities of Latinas while not limiting them for Latinos. All things being equal, Latinos prevail over Latinas in the marketplace, in the church, in the *comunidad*, and within the family structure.

Latinas contend that their struggle against sexism is a response to the machismo existing within the Hispanic community and the racial, ethnic, and class prejudice existing within the Euroamerican feminist community, which ignores the fundamental ways white women benefit from the oppression of women of color. Latinas attempt to find liberation as members of the Hispanic community that struggles to obliterate all institutions and communal structures contributing to the poverty and suffering of the entire *comunidad*, a poverty and suffering that lead to systematic death within the Latina/o community. The goal of most Latinas is, not to equate liberation with Euroamerican middle-class males, but to create new social structures in which all — women, men, and children — can find the fullness of life and liberation within a justice-based community. In chapter 4, we will explore the various feminist perspectives among Latinas within the Hispanic community. The current task is to recognize machismo as an active ingredient of the Latina/o ethos. As such, it requires our full attention so that we can include and comprehend the different voices and perspectives of Latinas.

## Cultural Influences on Theology

Latino/a theology is a reflection of the cultural milieu of Hispanics. Understanding the Latina/o ethos allows us to comprehend how social location shapes the community-based theology of Hispanics, specifically in regards to their relationship with the Deity. While it is obvious that these broad generalizations do not apply to every single U.S. Hispanic, they do, however, provide an accurate view into the lives and struggles of many Latinas/os. The present task is to examine how the overall Hispanic culture contributes to the expression of Latina/o theological perspectives.

As we have seen, the Hispanic *comunidad* shares multiple heritages. Not only is the U.S. Latino/a community multicultural; it is an intercultural reality. Common among Hispanics' diverse heritages is their religiosity. Latinos/as, as a group, consider religion to be an important component of their daily lives. The central role Western Christendom (via Iberia) played in Latin America influenced Hispanic customs, idioms, and traditions of Catholic religiosity, even when the Latino/a happens to be Protestant. Catholic theologian Virgilio Elizondo best expresses this thought in his foreword to Protestant theologian Justo González's book *Mañana:*

> Let me be very clear — I do not want to say that every Hispanic has to remain a member of the Roman Catholic Church in order to be Hispanic, but I am saying that when a Hispanic ceases to be catholic (to participate in the religious-cultural expressions of our people), he or she ceases to be a Hispanic. But it should be equally clear that the most cherished religious-cultural expressions of the people are certainly practiced in some Roman Catholic Churches while despised in others, yet they are not the sole property of the Roman Catholic Church.... We can go to any church we choose to go to, but we should not be asked to change our name and destroy our identity in order to be accepted. Being reborn in Christ certainly transforms us from within, but it does not destroy us. We do not cease being Black, Chicano, Cuban-exile, or Puerto Rican, nor do we cease liking *tamales* or *pastelitos,* *cumbias* or *polkitas,* nor do we forget our history or the road we traveled, or give up the treasures of our heritage.[15]

Consequently, *la comunidad* can be understood partly as a religious community due to the cultural influence of Catholicism within specific Latin American contexts. This development was constantly in conversation with indigenous Amerindian and African cultures. The shared cultural roots produced distinctive theological concerns. One focus is the need to convince Latina/o aliens, exiles, or outsiders that they have personal dignity because they are created in the divine image.

While it is true that the majority of Hispanics either actively identify with or are affiliated with Catholicism, it would be erroneous to "see" all Latinas/os in the United States as Catholics. In fact, a Protestant presence, although not large, existed in sixteenth-century Spain. Many *conversos* embraced the new teachings, but the efforts of the Spanish Inquisition either eradicated them or forced them into exile. Some of these exiles made their way to the New World in the regions of European colonization. In the border regions of the English colonies, later the United States, there was contact with the border regions of New Spain, later Mexico. It is possible to trace a Latino/a Protestant community in the United States to at least the mid-nineteenth century. The nineteenth century also witnessed the growth of Protestantism in Latin America, with an exponential increase occurring in the twentieth century. A number of these Latin American Protestants, especially members of Pentecostal churches, made their way to the United States. Recent decades have seen an increasing number of Latino/a Catholics join Protestant denominations, either as a form of spiritual awakening or cultural assimilation. As many as sixty thousand make the switch to Protestantism annually; it is estimated that from 25 to almost 40 percent of the Hispanic population in the United States is affiliated with some Protestant denomination.[16] However, whether a Latina/o might be a first-generation or fourth-generation Protestant, there are still shared cultural roots of the *comunidad* with Catholicism.

## Popular Religiosity

A rich complexity of shared cultural roots exists beyond the recognized boundaries of Christianity. Many Native American and African traditions continue to influence community life. Among these are Vodou, Santería, different types of spiritism, Umbanda, and Candomble. Some of these traditions lived underground due to centuries of racism and oppression, making it necessary to maintain an outward mask of Catholicism. This influence can be viewed as a mask or as an expression of popular religiosity or, as some argue, a direct continuity with pre-Columbian beliefs and practices. What is part of these diverse shared roots is that a cultural *mestizaje* is drawn upon, one in which the supernatural influences everyday life. The Latino's/a's spiritual worldview is an everyday reality that emphasizes the importance of home devotional practices, like home altars, prayers to saints, or *promesas* (vows). A detailed analysis of popular religiosity will appear in chapter 5; for now, we will briefly survey Hispanic spirituality and worship.

## Spirituality

The shared cultural roots of different traditions point to an important aspect of Latino/a culture, namely, popular religion (also known as devotional piety or spirituality). This spiritual expression is situated in a dynamic grassroots religion that is believed and practiced every day. Popular religiosity is a focus point for individual and communal feelings: its religious symbols and actions make sense of the world and provide a concrete point of contact with the Divine.

Latino/a Catholic theologians recognize popular Catholicism as a source for theologizing. Recently, Latino/a Protestant theologians have begun to explore this impulse within their own traditions. Hispanic popular religiosity has widespread appeal, appearing in formal and informal settings and exhibiting the affective dimensions of devotion and spirituality. Examples of popular religion in Hispanic contexts include the *via crucis* (way of the cross), *quinceañeras* (fifteenth-birthday celebration, which is comparable to a "sweet sixteen" or a debutante party), home altars, daily devotions, *coritos* (choruses) and *estribillos* (literally "refrain," another term used for choruses), prayer meetings, *testimonios* (testimonies), *vigilias* (vigils), and *posadas* (processions). Popular religion includes cultural elements of faith but is much more than a mere recovery of cultural roots; it is a source of theology, a creative way of being, a means of cultural self-identification for survival, and a uniting force for the *comunidad*.

Among Protestant and Catholic Hispanics popular religion is widespread and adaptable, crossing denominational lines. This has led to informal and formal ecumenical dialogue on possible common sources of spirituality, including European religiosity, Amerindian spiritualities, and African worldviews, as well as how Hispanics negotiate their multiracial heritage. Among Hispanic Christians, these spiritual practices have become pivotal to their faith and have been incorporated as part of the informal and formal liturgical experiences.

Elements of Christian worship present in Hispanic worship include an emphasis on the importance of a believing community coming together to praise God, who calls them into community. Allan Figueroa Deck states that Hispanic Roman Catholic religiosity "is permeated with a symbolic, sacramental imagination that continues its influence even as these people migrate and experience 'the acids of modernity.' "[17] Likewise, Latino Protestant worship is also richly imaginative.

## Worship

In the fiesta of worship Latino/a Christian communities express their individual and corporate relationship with God. While a great deal of variety exists in the theological approaches employed by different Hispanic congregations, much is held in common in beliefs about worship and actual worship practices, even across Catholic/Protestant boundaries. A good example is the sacred fiesta, which includes an informal time of greeting and assembly, enthusiastic singing, freely expressed praise, a confession of sin, and the confession of faith in the One who forgives sin. Sacred fiesta occurs in community where baptism and the Santa Cena (Holy Communion), the two common ordinances/sacraments, are celebrated.

According to common belief, Hispanic Catholics deem three features of worship to be most important: *misa* (mass), *mesa* (table), and *musa* (muse, i.e., the arts). Also present in Hispanic Protestant contexts, these features are part of the *culto*, or worship service. In the Protestant *culto*, as in the Catholic *misa*, a reaffirmation of community and identity occurs. Elizabeth Conde-Frazier observes this among Hispanic Protestants:

> The *culto,* or worship, is the celebration of the victory of the cross. It is the "fiesta" expression of our spirituality, and music and testimonies reflect this. The *culto* has been described by Hispanic theologians as the place of dialogue between persons and God. This dialogue takes place through verbal and symbolic expressions. It has also been called the *locus theologicus* of the Hispanic community. The preaching, hymns, testimonies, and prayers all express parts of our theology. Worship is our place for using the spiritual tools for struggle and survival as a community.[18]

Conde-Frazier's observation emphasizes the critical reflective aspect of Hispanic worship as expressed in the communal celebration of sacred fiesta, which to the uninformed outsider may seem like unsophisticated frenzy. Indeed, *fiesta* can be translated as "party." This concept of celebration in both Hispanic Protestant and Catholic contexts is, not a remote formalized drama that is watched, but rather a neighborhood party in which all are invited to participate. Justo González, like Conde-Frazier, observes that

> Latino worship is a fiesta. It is a celebration of the mighty deeds of God. It is a get-together of the family of God. It is important to remember this in order to understand some of the features of our worship that sometime disconcert or even upset those of the dominant culture. First of all, because worship is a fiesta rather than a performance, it may be planned, but not rehearsed. Oftentimes, Hispanic worship may seem chaotic. ... But in most cases the difference between our worship and that of the dominant culture is that we think in terms of planning a party more than rehearsing a performance.[19]

Although the specific liturgical manifestations are different, the impulse of celebration is a common feature. For Hispanic Christians (Protestant and Roman Catholic), the language of fiesta, or "party," is a natural and expressive way to speak of the joyful understanding the community has of its present and eschatological (or future) connection with God and its celebration of that connection. The phrases "sacred fiesta" and "sacred party" are suggested by the historian Daniel Ramírez: "The more problematic thing is the English rendering of *fiesta* as 'party.' It is that, but much more. Celebration also fails to do justice to the term. It is communal, and can have both sacred and profane elements to it."[20] This view of the term *fiesta* shows the usefulness of the concept of contextual ritualization. For some members of the dominant culture, both inside and outside the church, viewing worship as fiesta, as party, is inappropriate and even offensive. The contrast in perspectives is another illustration of the nature of Hispanic Christian communities to create their own alternative public spaces for God-talk.

## Religious Beliefs in Practice

How does the ethos of the Latino/a community shape what is theologically important to Hispanics? We have seen how the Latina/o cultural context contributes to the popular religiosity of Hispanics, specifically in the manifestation of their spirituality and worship. Likewise, the social location of Latinos/as also informs what the *comunidad* deems to be important. Before concentrating on the contributions made by Hispanics to specific theological concepts (the task of the next chapter), we turn our attention toward two areas where the Latina/o ethos shapes what becomes important to Hispanics, specifically the concepts of family and justice.

### The Importance of Familia

A central aspect of Latino/a Christianity is the important role of *comunidad*. This sense of community has corporate expressions in the lives of its members, particularly in popular religiosity. In a North American context where individualism is on the increase, a countervailing impulse in *comunidad* among U.S. Hispanics exists. Even within the diversity of national origins, race, language facilities, denominations, and class, the omnipresent prominence of the notion and experience of community is a unifying factor and a resource for ministry, engagement with the dominant Euroamerican culture, and theology.

One common feature found within Hispanic communities is the importance of *familia* (family), which is closely tied to the concept of *comunidad*. Some consider the family to be the basic and perhaps most important social institution in Latino/a cultures. A shared aspect of the concept of *familia* is that it encompasses a broadly extended network of relatives and fictive kinships. Even when Hispanics are not literal blood relations, they often re-create family through the *compadrazgo* system. Among Latino/a Catholics and some Hispanic Protestants that practice infant baptism, the sponsoring godparents (*padrino, madrina*) become "coparents" (*compadres, comadres*) and enter into lifelong relationships not only with the child but also with the family. Indeed, the hope is that the *compadres* and *comadres* (literally "cofather" and "comother") would become part of an extended family (if they were not already part of it), nurturing the child and being reliable companions to the parents, as well as assuming parental responsibility should the parents die.

Within Latino/a Protestant circles that adhere to other understandings of baptism, members of the congregation refer to each other as *hermano* (brother) and *hermana* (sister). Congregations as communities of re-created families provide support, stability, and hope in settings where people are confronted by a host of challenges and difficulties. Whether in Catholic or Protestant settings, many Latinas/os in the United States participate in some re-creation of family as a means to maintain community. For example, among Puerto Ricans in the mainland United States, the phrase "second family" (*segunda familia*) is a common expression.[21]

In U.S. Latino/a communities the sense of family and kinship can cross racial, ethnic, and national categories that might have been impenetrable barriers in Latin America. In that sense Hispanic family relational networks become additional indicators of the distinctiveness of Latino/a communities in the United States, as well as showing continuities with Latin America. Through family and the re-creation of family, larger Latino/a communities are built and maintained.

## The Importance of Justice

"To know God is to do justice."[22] The central tenet of any Latino/a theology is *praxis,* that is, doing the deed of justice. Yet, the word "justice" is itself in need of liberation. Justice has become a worn-out expression constructed to absolve the actions of the dominant culture over against the actions of disenfranchised communities. One person's justice has become the other person's tyranny. We are then left asking, Whose "justice" do we seek?

Along with *agape* (unconditional love), justice is an important component of Christianity. For Hispanic Christians, it is perhaps among the most important components. Justice based on love toward one's neighbor is a reflection of one's love for and by God. Yet, the concept of justice can be lost in the ambiguous term "righteousness" when a biblical text is read in English. Latinas/os who read the biblical text in Spanish use the word *justicia,* which is translated as "justice" rather than "righteousness."

When Euroamericans read "righteous," Hispanics read "just." The dictionary defines "righteous" as "morally right or justifiable, acting in an upright, moral way."[23] The definition implies an action that can be performed privately. However, "justice" can only be exercised in community, never in isolation, for the concrete reality of sin is always manifested in relation to others. Likewise, justice can only manifest itself in relation to others. Stranded on a deserted island, an individual can be righteous by remaining conscientious and God-fearing in thought. Justice, on the other hand, can never be practiced on a deserted island. By its very nature, justice needs others to whom justice can be administered. If there is no community, there can be no justice. Rather than being a private expression of faith, justice is, by definition, a public action, a public manifestation of God's acting grace in the lives of Hispanics. Here is a major difference between the ways in which Euroamericans and Latinas/os do theology.

By using the words *justo* and *justicia,* the Spanish translation reinforces communalism as opposed to individualism. For example, James tells us that "the prayer of the righteous is powerful and effective" (5:16); that is, one who is pious, whose relationship with God is based on an individual conversion, has his or her prayers answered. The Spanish version tells us, "La oración eficaz del justo tiene mucha fuerza" (Reina-Valera). It is the prayer of the just one (the one doing justice within the community in obedience to God) that has much power. Matthew quotes Jesus as saying, "Blessed are those who hunger and thirst for righteousness, for they will be filled" (5:6). In other words, those who hunger for moral purity and thirst for chastity will be rewarded. The Spanish rendering is, "Bienaventurados los que tienen hambre y sed de justicia, porque ellos serán saciados." Those who hunger for justice to be done to all members of the community, especially to the disenfranchised, and who thirst for justice against all oppressors, these are the ones whom God will fully satisfy.

Luke tells us that the centurion who witnessed Christ's crucifixion said, "Certainly this man was righteous" (23:47). Christ was the unsoiled innocent lamb who died for our sins. In Spanish, this same centurion says, "Realmente, este hombre era justo." Christ was a just man who died an unjust death. The advice given to Timothy reads, "The law is laid down not for the righteous but for the lawless and disobedient, for the ungodly and sinful, for unholy and profane" (1 Tim. 1:9). In Spanish, this advice reads, "La ley no fue puesta para el justo, sino para los transgresores e insumisos, para los impíos e pecadores." While Euroamerican readers are assured that the law does not apply to them because by faith in Christ they have been justified and are not ungodly, sinful, unholy, or profane, Spanish readers understand that individuals practicing justice do not need the law, for the law is already internal, and their actions are only an outward expression of their inward conversion. Based on these translations, theology as practiced in the English-speaking world becomes foreign to those who read the text in Spanish.

Through justice, we are able to dismantle the social structures erected and normalized by the dominant culture. When we espouse justice as a universal ideal, we can demand dignity. An "option for the poor" characterizes Hispanic theology, not because the marginalized are inherently more holy than the dominant classes, but simply because they lack the elite's power and privilege. Justice demands the oppressors' repentance for benefiting from social structures that provide them with privilege at the expense of the marginalized. If there is no repentance, then there is no salvation, no liberation, no reconciliation, and accordingly no justice.

## A Concluding Thought

A connection exists between Hispanics' social location and how those cultural roots significantly affect their resulting theology. To explore Latina/o theology without considering these cultural roots runs the risk of creating a theology disconnected from the daily human struggle of a disenfranchised group that looks toward the Deity for solutions to its oppression. This chapter demonstrates that Latina/o theological perspectives do not exist within a vacuum but rather come forth as the consequences of the social space Hispanics are usually relegated to occupy. In fact, the practice and articulation of all theologies, not just Latino/a, are mainly influenced by the social and cultural location from which they arise.

Hispanic theologies are community-based. Usually Eurocentric theologies reject this proposition and claim some sort of objectivity, which divorces their theological perspectives from their social location. Hispanic theologies, on the other hand, openly admit their connections to the communities from which they arose. Since Latino/a theologies emerge from their community contexts, it is possible to identify some of their distinctive theological perspectives, the way these perspectives differ from dominant Euroamerican theologies, and the contribution Hispanic theologies make to the overall discourse. The task that is now before us is to examine how the resulting theological concepts, shaped by Hispanics, differ from the predominant Euroamerican theologies. The purpose of chapter 3 is to systematically review some basic theological concepts from the social perspectives of Latinas/os.

## Chapter 2 Study Questions

### Definition Question

Define the following terms: *comunidad,* barrio, popular religion, sacred fiesta, machismo, *compadrazgo.*

## Essay Questions

1. Explain the differences between exiles, aliens, and outsiders. Can one specific group encompass all three categories? If so, how? How do these categories help explain the differences between the three largest Hispanic groups in the United States (Mexicans, Puerto Ricans, Cubans)?

2. List several cultural roots that inform and influence Latina/o theological perspectives. Are there cultural roots that inform U.S. theological perspectives? If so, what are they? Compare the cultural roots of Hispanics and Euroamericans and attempt to explain how they influence their distinctive theological perspectives.

3. What consequences do Hispanics who live in the barrio face? What responsibility, if any, does society have toward them? Do you think that if barrio conditions change, so will the theological perspectives of Latinas/os? Why or why not?

4. Interview at least two Latinos/as. Ask them how they see themselves, how they view the dominant culture, and if they have ever felt discrimination. Do they consider themselves Americans? Do they believe they are accepted by the dominant culture as being a participating member of that culture? Ask how their views on religion are influenced and shaped by their social location.

5. What are some manifestations of a Euroamerican popular religious expression? Compare this with some examples that occur within the Hispanic context. How do these examples substantiate the proposition that spirituality and worship styles reflect the Latina/o ethos?

6. Why and how is the concept of *familia* important in the practice of Hispanics' religious beliefs?

7. How does the English word "righteous" lead toward different biblical interpretations than the Spanish word *justicia* does?

# Chapter 3

# Theological Perspectives

Latino/a spirituality has always been an integral part of the U.S. Hispanic ethos; however, the formal articulation of what we have been calling Latino/a theologies is a more recent phenomenon. Although its various roots stretch back beyond the European conquest of the Western Hemisphere to include indigenous and African peoples, in the last quarter of the twentieth century Latino/a scholars began to unapologetically and assertively enter the overall theological discourse from the perspective of their own sociocultural location. Their contribution to theology is not reducible to an "interesting" perspective; rather it is central to understanding God's movement within North American culture, a culture that is being redefined by the Latina/o presence. It would be erroneous to assume that the theologies being constructed and practiced by Hispanics are solely for Latinos/as. Instead, these theologies are a practical discourse that seeks engagement with other expressions of Christian theologies.

In chapter 2 we defined theology as the study of God, emphasizing the social location of those who are doing the studying. Such a definition proved useful in our entry into a discussion of Latina/o theology, but it remains limited in its ability to articulate how Hispanics understand the presence of God within their daily struggles. Hence, before turning toward some of the basic theological perspectives existing among most Hispanic scholars, clergy, and congregations, it is crucial that we first define what the term "theology" means to most Latinos/as.

For the Latino/a Christian faith community, theology becomes the verbal expression of faith as practiced, believed, articulated, and celebrated by Hispanics. It moves beyond the Eurocentric Enlightenment project that attempts to rationally understand God

71

and communicate this rationality to unbelievers so that they too can believe. For Latinos/as, theology is more than dogmas or faith formulas; it is the daily articulation of life in community, where it is known that God and the divine activity move and participate within history to save, liberate, and reconcile. In effect, theology becomes the reflection of God's praxis, God's action in bringing about liberation from both corporate and individual sins. To do theology is to participate in the action of God, actions motivated by God's love and best illustrated in the figure of Jesus the Christ. From the U.S. social location of Hispanics, struggling to overcome race and class oppression, theology becomes a religious construction of and for the faith community, which responds to these overt and subtle forms of repression. In short, theology is the Latino/a voice of faith.

What then is the theological voice of Hispanics existing in the margins of the United States? What contributions do Latinos/as make to the overall theological discourse? This chapter will present a brief systematic approach to theological concepts developed by Hispanics during the last twenty-five years. The goal is neither to provide the reader with an exhaustive and complete list of theological concepts nor to unpack fully each concept. Rather, this chapter's modest goal is to highlight some of the more significant theological perspectives developed by Hispanics.

## Methodology

How do we "know" what is "truth"? *Epistemology* is a term that describes the process of discovering how knowing occurs, taking into consideration its validity, limitations, and relationship to truth. For many theologians, epistemology is the relationship between the believer's knowledge of God and the revelation of the Deity. Even if we take the position that all knowledge about God is derived from the Scriptures, the church, tradition, and/or the spiritual experience of an individual, the process of interpreting these authorities becomes the function of epistemology. Simply stated, epistemology attempts to understand the process by which the self-revelatory knowledge about God is derived. For the theologian, the function of theology is the unveiling of an understanding of God through established sources of authority.

Traditionally Eurocentric Christian epistemology has been based on (1) divine revelation as found in the Scriptures; (2) the authority of the institutional church (at least for Roman Catholics) operating under the guidance of the Holy Spirit; (3) the life, death, and resurrection of Jesus Christ; (4) a "scientific" methodology that uses human reason as the basis for any truth; and (5) the unique inner feeling of a spiritual conversion experience (at least for evangelicals). Eurocentric Christians attempt to arrive at truth — orthodoxy (literally "correct doctrine") — through one or a combination of the above listed sources of authority.

U.S. Hispanics have made significant contributions to the field of epistemology. Influenced by Latin America liberation theologians like Gustavo Gutiérrez, Clodovis Boff, and Enrique Dussel, Latinas/os maintain that "knowing" truth is insufficient and that so-called objective concepts of knowledge are problematic. The purpose of Latino/a theology is praxis, the *doing* of theology, known as orthopraxis (literally "correct action"), which is more important than developing abstract philosophical concepts about God. Hispanics strive to ascertain meaning for their existence by being faithful to God's calling in God's overall objective of redeeming creation. The starting point for praxis is found in the location, time, and experience of particular people, especially those living under oppression. The purpose of doing theology, or orthopraxis, is to change the structures causing such oppression in order to liberate those who exist under these injustices.

Latino/a theologies did not develop within a social vacuum; rather, these theological perspectives are directly connected to the social context of Hispanics. To do theology from those particular contexts is to participate in a process that gives voice to the voiceless, a process in which those on the margins articulate as a *comunidad* God's salvific plan. In contrast to the authors of more abstract theologies, Latino/a theologians immerse themselves in the human experience of Hispanic communities, most of which are oppressed. These Hispanic theologians are keenly aware that their theological perspectives — their knowing — are influenced by the community of believers. This methodology that seeks theological truth is an ongoing process called *teología de conjunto* (collaborative theology, connoting unity and communion), the coming together of the community of believers to work collectively in seeking theological precepts.

Central to this methodology is the relationship between praxis (action) and theory. Latinos/as do not reduce praxis to reflections that flow from actions; for them, praxis occurs when reflection is brought to bear upon action. Unlike many Eurocentric theologians, Latinas/os do not reduce praxis to a rational instrument of theory in which only verifiable praxis is relevant. Such reduction discredits alternatives like popular religion as relevant in the search for truth. Contrary to those with this understanding of praxis, Latino/a theologians articulate a praxis-based theology that reflects the struggles of U.S. Hispanics.

## Reading the Bible

If epistemology describes the process of discovering truth, then what are the sources upon which truth is based? For many Latinos/as, the Bible is paramount in the formation of truth for the Hispanic faith community. The process of reading and understanding a historically distant text is known as *hermeneutics*. Biblical hermeneutical studies include the analysis, interpretation, explanation, textuality, language, and historicity of the Bible. One goal of biblical hermeneutics is to provide a theologically sound response that guides humanity toward understanding the biblical text. Traditionally for most Protestants, the object of interpretation is the biblical text, not the church or any of its representatives. The final authority for interpreting the Bible is the gospel message found in the Scriptures. Hence, the text is its own interpreter. For most Catholics, the Bible is the privileged foundation for theological studies informed by church tradition. The church, which established the canon, interprets the text.

Every reader's interpretation of a text is based on what he or she brings to the reading, specifically the reader's gender, social-economic location, and race. In order to understand how Latinas/os approach the text, we need to be cognizant of their social location. Justo González, in his book *Santa Biblia*, attempts to illuminate the text by methodically reading the Bible through Hispanic eyes. By consciously claiming a Latina/o identity, he looks to the text from within the Hispanic context of struggle in order to learn what God wants Latinas/os and the world to be. Yet, which Hispanic eyes should be used? Are Puerto Rican, Peruvian, Dominican, and Mexican eyes identical? For González, the experiences of Hispanics are different; all Latina/o eyes are not the same. Hence, he refuses to provide "the" Hispanic perspective. Instead, he provides "a" Latino/a perspective, while hoping such a perspective resonates among most Latinos/as.[1] However, evaluating the significance of the Hispanic location does not necessarily diminish the importance of the biblical text. For biblical scholar Jean-Pierre Ruiz, if the Bible is the authoritative lens through which the religious experience is focused, the optics of that lens requires scrutiny.[2]

According to González, Hispanics read the Bible from positions of marginality, poverty, *mestizaje/mulatez,* exile, and solidarity. Generally speaking, he is correct. The vast majority of Latinas/os in this country live under such conditions. However, we need to be aware that the vast majority do not read the Bible at all. And many who do look to the text read it through a methodology of popularization, meaning that they recount the biblical stories, at times merging them with stories from other religious traditions, for the purpose of providing a lesson that teaches Latinos/as how to live and survive. Eurocentric theologians usually regard this type of reading as being distorted, but such reading represents how the text is understood in people's daily lives. Because many Hispanics seldom read the biblical text, they often express their deeply held religiosity through customs and traditions, an approach that leads to popularizing versions of the biblical stories, combining at times Amerindian and/or African traditions for the purpose of emphasizing a spiritual point.

Yet, reading the text through Latino/a eyes raises concerns about masking intra-Hispanic repression. The danger of reading the Bible to justify a political position over against others is a real threat. Ada María Isasi-Díaz raises the valid concern of how Jesus has been used by Hispanics in positions of power to marginalize Latina women. For example, those who speak from the pulpit demand obedience (particularly from women toward men) in the application of the Scripture, when in fact they are presenting only their *interpretation* of the Scripture as biblically authoritative.[3]

Although Latinos/as look toward the Bible as a source of salvation and liberation, they also recognize that it has been used as a source of damnation and subjugation. Salvation is made possible and effective by the justice-based praxis rooted in the reading of the Bible, a reading made Hispanic when done from a Latino/a perspective. Such a reading requires a turning away from Eurocentric theological triumphalism toward a search within the Latina/o community for an understanding of the text, which can be accomplished through what Gustavo Gutiérrez calls "a militant reading," one from the perspective of those dwelling in "the underside of history."[4]

To read the biblical text as a Latino/a is (1) to read it identifying with a profound sense of "Otherness"; (2) to read it as a legitimization of alternative perspectives, perspectives that cross traditionally dominant boundaries and social categories; and (3) to read it as a subversive text that radically challenges what the dominant culture has labeled normative truths. If reading the text implies application, then Latinos/as are in a unique position to hear God's Word in the context of their own suffering, which makes their oppressed existence part of the text's interpretation. This subversive way of reading the text makes use of what is known as the "hermeneutical privilege of the oppressed." Because Latinas/os have learned how to function without power in a realm constructed by those with privilege, they know more about the overall U.S. culture than those with power, who only know their own protected space. This circumstance does not confer truth exclusively on those oppressed; it only states that they are in a better position to understand the biblical call for justice than those who deceive themselves into thinking that justice already exists.

### Reading in Spanish

Whenever the dominant culture "sees" a Hispanic, it usually presumes, erroneously, that the Latino/a is able to communicate in Spanish. Some Hispanics speak only English; others speak only Spanish; some are bilingual, while still others speak Spanglish, switching between the two languages depending on which word or phrase best nuances the intended meaning. Moreover, Latinas/os who are able to converse in Spanish are not necessarily literate. Yet, those who do read the Bible in Spanish discover a text that provides theological interpretations different from those issuing from reading the same passages in English. To read the Bible in Spanish affects how Latinos/as discern the Divine, which influences their theological perspectives. We saw an example of this in the preceding chapter when the Spanish word *justicia* was contrasted with the English word "righteousness."

For theologian Luis Pedraja, differences in theological interpretations can arise on the basis of language. The English word "love" is used to characterize how one feels toward diverse objects, persons, and experiences. If the same word is used to describe feeling toward both family and pizza, the word "love" loses some of its intimacy and significance. Spanish makes a distinction. *Te amo* (I love you) is reserved for spouses or lovers. *Te quiero* (literally "I want you") is used to connote love toward family and friends. *Me gusta* (I like it) usually refers to pizza, hiking, and other things or experiences we like. Nevertheless, to refer in Spanish to the love of God, the more intimate phrase *te amo* is used.

Another example is the English word "you," which can be translated into Spanish as either *tú* or *usted*. *Tú* is an informal pronoun used when addressing one's equals those who are friends or coworkers. *Usted,* on the other hand, is a formal pronoun used when addressing those who occupy a higher station in life, for example, one's boss, teachers, political leaders, or elders. When referring in Spanish to God, the informal *tú* is used, not the formal *usted.* Since Hispanics recognize God as one who is in solidarity with them as a fellow journeyer, the informal familiar pronoun is employed.

The final example comes from the Gospel of John. Pedraja contrasts the English and Spanish translations of the first verse: "In the beginning was the Word, and the Word was with God, and the Word was God" and "En el principio era el Verbo, y el Verbo estaba con Dios, y el Verbo era Dios." (In the beginning was the Verb...). In Spanish, Jesus is, not the Word, but the Verb, God's living and active Verb. As a noun, the Divine is static. As a verb, an action word, God's incarnation in flesh continues as a praxis, an action, within the human experience. The difference between the Word and the Verb is significant. Rather than reflecting on a noun as the basis for theology, Hispanics write and talk about "doing" theology.[5]

## Understanding Being Human

*Anthropology* refers to the study of humans. When Christian theologians engage anthropology, they basically study beliefs about the nature of human beings. Such beliefs usually include the Creation story, specifically the origin of humanity in God, and the Fall. A recurring motif within Christian anthropology is the healing of humanity, known as *salvation,* from the consequences of the Fall. Briefly, Christian theological anthropologists emphasize the origins of humans as products of God's creativity. Regardless of whether the scholar accepts or rejects the Creation story of Genesis as historically accurate, the essence of the story is that creation's source is God. As such, humans bear the image of God (the *imago Dei*). Due to humanity's transgression, however, sin entered humanity, alienating humans from God. Yet even while humans remain in need of redemption, the promise of a new humanity exists. The focus of this new humanity is Christ, as the second Adam (Rom. 5:12–21), who is the completion of all humanity.

Latino/a theologians have stressed aspects of the Creation story not necessarily emphasized in the dominant discourse, specifically the means by which God brings forth a new humanity. The Good News, according to Latina/o theologians, is that the biblical narrative proclaims a God who reveals Godself from within disenfranchised communities. Historically God has chosen the disenfranchised as agents of God's new creation. It is the stone rejected by the builders that becomes the keystone of God's new creation (Matt. 21:42). God made God's will known, not to the court of Pharaoh, but to their slaves, the Hebrews. Where did God choose to perform the miracle of the Incarnation? It was not Rome, the most powerful city of the known world, nor was it Jerusalem, the center of Yahweh worship. Impoverished Galilee was where God chose to first proclaim the message of the Gospels. Nazareth was so insignificant to the religious life of Judaism that the Hebrew Bible never mentions it. Had Jesus not been a Nazarene, Galilee may have been just another unknown and unimportant region of the world.

Jesus' contemporaries had a low opinion of the region. According to John (7:52–53), when the multitudes discovered Jesus' origins they exclaimed, "Surely you are not also from Galilee, are you? Search and you will see that no prophet is to arise from Galilee." John also gives us the example of Jesus' future disciple Nathanael, who upon learning Jesus was from Nazareth showed his bias by saying, "Can anything good come out of Nazareth?" (1:46). It would be as if Jesus were born today in the barrios of the Bronx, East Los Angeles, or Miami's *sagüesera,* rather than from the "good" neighborhoods with their ornate sanctuaries. God chooses a stone from the margins that has been rejected by the dominant culture to carry out God's salvific plan.

Latino/a theologians are quick to point out that those marginalized in Jesus' time occupied the privileged position of being the first to hear the Good News. They occupied this position, not because they were holier, but because God chooses sides. God makes an option for those who exist under the weight of oppression. Jesus willingly assumes the role of the ultradisenfranchised. The radical nature of the Incarnation for Hispanics is, not that God became human, but that God assumed the condition of a slave. In his letter to the Philippians, Paul says of Christ, "Who, though he was in the form of God, did not regard equality with God as something to be exploited, but emptied himself, taking the form of a slave?" (2:6). Why is it important to see Jesus and construct theology through the lens of the disenfranchised? By making the disenfranchised recipients of the Good News, Jesus emphasized the political edge of his message (Luke 4:18–19).

Latinos/as expect the Divine to work God's ways through today's marginalized communities. Because of the disenfranchised space of Hispanics, they hold the sacred responsibility to proclaim the Good News to all, specifically to the centers of power and privilege. This is not an attempt to romanticize their marginalization, for there is no glorification in being poor. Instead, it is an attempt to formulate a theological response to their social location. Hispanic theologies do not call people to resign themselves to their economic conditions while hopefully awaiting their reward in the hereafter; rather, they seek the elimination of the sin of injustice in the present. Latino/a theology is a call to participate in a consciousness-raising experience so they can transcend their objectification by the dominant culture and establish their humanity.

# Theological Topics

One final point about the methodology employed in the development of Latino/a theological perspectives: recognizing the differences existing between Euroamerican and Hispanic theological views does not mean that Euroamerican theological views and the theological traditions of the church are identical. It would be erroneous to conclude that any reaction against Euroamerican theological perspectives is automatically a reaction against the historical tradition of the church (either Catholic or any of the several Protestant denominations). The Hispanic perspective does not necessarily oppose the historical tradition of the church; rather, it opposes those perspectives that have dominated the theological discourse while marginalizing important teachings of the faith tradition. The Christian theological traditions that have historically dominated the discourse due to the dominant group's ability to impose its views upon other groups are not necessarily the most important teachings of the faith community. Listening to the theological voices of historically marginalized groups revitalizes the discourse. These voices bring to the forefront valuable concepts of the faith tradition that have been systematically ignored because they challenge the power and privilege of those setting the theological agenda.

## *Sin*

Sin opposes God's benevolent purposes for creation and is responsible for the enslavement of the human race and the corruption of God's created order. An individual's transgressions as well as the sins of those with power and privilege displace the liberation found in Christ. The essence of sin is idolatry, that is, striving to supplant the Creator with something or someone else. This displacement can be voluntary, as when individuals exchange the glory of God for money. However, God can also be deposed involuntarily, as in the case of structural mechanisms that foster the subjugation of many to the privileged few. The consequences of sin are alienation from God, God's community, God's creation, and God's will for each person.

Many Euroamerican Christians often look to the cross as the remedy for sin. Salvation is found in Christ's death, a substitute for the sinner to appease an angry God. Hispanics, while understanding the cosmic importance of Jesus' death, also focus on his life. By paying closer attention to his life, Hispanics are able to overcome their own alienation. For many Euroamerican Christians, Jesus' death saves; for Hispanics, Jesus' life sufferings and resurrection are also the center of his salvific plan. This does not mean that Hispanics minimize or ignore the Passion of Christ. In fact, Jesus' suffering on the cross is graphically depicted in the sacred art found throughout Hispanic houses of worship. The devotions of the Penitentes of northern New Mexico during Holy Week directly connect with Jesus' suffering on the cross.[6] Dramatic re-creations of the Passion during the Holy Week celebrations, such as that at San Fernando Cathedral in San Antonio, Texas, also depict the suffering of Christ. Lest we think these communities are too focused on Jesus' death on the cross, however, remember that many Hispanic Christian communities, such as the San Fernando Cathedral, end Holy Week with a grand celebration of the resurrection of Jesus. Latinos/as look not only toward the cross for the remedy for sin but also to the life and resurrection of Jesus.

Within the North American environment, which is influenced by hyperindividualism, Christians often regard sin as a private matter. Jesus, many Protestant evangelists tell us, has a plan for our *individual* lives only if we repent from *our own* sins and accept him as our *personal* Savior. While Hispanics understand the importance of confessing and repenting sins committed by the individual, we also recognize that sin may be individually committed, but it is never personal. Regardless as to how private we may wish to keep sin, it always affects others because we are communal creatures. Hence, Hispanics maintain that sin has both an individual and a communal dimension.

Unlike the dominant culture, Hispanics emphasize the importance of communal or corporate sin. Rather than simply linking the causes of sin to the inheritance of Adam, Hispanics understand sin, as a result of powers and principalities (Eph. 6:12), to be inherent within social structures. Hence, Jesus' purpose was not solely to save individuals from their sins but also, and just as importantly, to save the community from the sins of its social structures. Race, class, and gender oppression transcend the individual's personal bias by becoming the collective bias of society. These biases, in turn, are institutionalized by the society in the government, the marketplace, and the church. Latinos/as facing discriminatory practices often realize that the source of this form of violence is not necessarily found in an individual within an organization; rather, the organization is constructed to protect the privileged space of the dominant culture at the expense of the disenfranchised. Hence, individual repentance is insufficient to change or challenge the status quo. Institutions also must repent by unmasking their normative procedures.

For many Hispanics, life exists under institutionalized violence, that is, under the consequences of oppression operative within social structures. Those structures, the antithesis of Jesus' life-giving mission, bring death (figuratively and literally) to Latinas/os. The dominant culture usually views those who are victimized by institutionalized violence as responsible for their own suffering. One reason Hispanics are poor, according to many in the dominant culture, is because they are lazy (refusing to implement the Protestant work ethic), ignorant (preferring to live in the mire of the barrio), or violent (responsible for many of our cities' crimes). Absent from the discourse is any examination of the structures of society that have intentionally created an army of low-skilled laborers for the benefit of commerce. Confessing Christians, while sometimes sympathetic to the Hispanic plight, benefit from it and usually fail to realize their complicity with that plight.

Yet, it would be erroneous to assume that Hispanics are the only victims of the dominant culture's corporate sins. Euroamericans are also trapped and negatively affected by the existing relationship between those with privilege and those who are disenfranchised. Members of the dominant culture must live up to a false role of superiority, always in danger of losing their status. Those whom social structures privilege are forced to live according to their assigned community roles, roles created at the expense of people of color. Hence, Latino/a theology calls for the liberation/salvation of those who suffer under the burden of corporate sin, as well as those who benefit because of it.

## Christology

Mark recounts an incident when Jesus, along with his disciples, left for the villages and towns surrounding Caesarea Philippi (8:27–

30). There was much speculation as to Jesus' identity. Was he a prophet? A reincarnation of Elijah or John the Baptizer? Or was he the Christ, the Messiah? Jesus looked at his followers and put the question succinctly: "Who do you say that I am?" Ever since Jesus posed that question, succeeding generations of Christians have been forced to grapple for an answer, and Hispanics are not exempt. How can a two-thousand-year-old Palestinian Jew be relevant to the present Latino/a experience? How do Latinos/as seek a Christ who knows what it means to be a Hispanic in the United States?

Hispanics recognize Jesus' commitment to the marginalized and their importance in understanding Christ's purpose and mission. Why is it important to see Jesus through the lens of the disenfranchised? Because the marginalized of Jesus' time occupied the privileged position of being the first to hear and respond to the gospel. Hispanics understand a Jesus who willingly assumes the role of the ultradisenfranchised. While biblical scholars may disagree about Jesus' supposed marginality, insisting that as a carpenter he may have belonged to the "middle class," Latinos/as claim that Jesus' life was one of poverty, which creates a strong bond between the disenfranchised in this culture and the Divine based on the fact that Jesus knew what it means to be poor. Latina/o theologians are quick to point out that Jesus was born into, lived, and died in poverty. According to the scriptural text, Jesus was born to a poor family, for Mary made use of the biblical provision for the poor and brought two doves as an offering for her purification (Lev. 12; Luke 2:24). Throughout his ministry Jesus lived in privation, having "nowhere to lay his head" (Luke 9:58). He wandered without money in his purse (Matt. 17:22–27; Luke 20:20–26) and relied on the charity of others (Luke 8:1–3). At Jesus' death, his earthly possessions consisted only of what he wore, which was partitioned among the soldiers (Matt. 27:35).

Besides emphasizing Latino/a solidarity with Jesus' economic station, Hispanics also relate to Jesus' suffering. The Euroamerican quest to understand the presence of suffering in human existence raises the theodicy question. How can an all-good and all-powerful God allow evil to exist? Either God is not all-good, or God is not all-powerful. The Christ Latinos/as worship offers God within that suffering. A perusal of Hispanic art depicting the Crucifixion reveals a Christ in all the gory brutality of suffering. The bloody

Christ repels, if not repulses, all who fail to understand the interpretation from a Hispanic context of Christ's suffering. Surely the Divine can redeem the world through a more civilized and less violent process. Yet, Christ is presented as a bruised, blood-streaked victim of human hatred who struggles in anguish with death. This Christ suffered freely, not as a price demanded by God, but as the price of a world that suffers, a suffering and violence that spill over into the Divine.

Such depictions of Christ portray the ultimate tragic victim who dies, as do the innumerable oppressed victims of the dominant culture's institutionalized violence. But God manifests God's presence, not as a transcendent power standing triumphantly over against earthly injustice, but as the self-negating Christ who surrenders his life in the struggle against the political injustices of his day. Through Christ's unjust death, he is made the King of life, drawing all to him as he is "lifted up" (John 12:32). Yet, his agony does not end with the cross but continues to exist within the daily afflictions of all who suffer unjustly. First demonstrated to a particular oppressed group of his time, Christ's crucifixion extended his reconciling power to embrace all oppressed groups of all times. Today we find hope for immortality in the Divine's self-negation manifested as a love praxis leading always toward justice. Those who, like Christ, suffer injustice are now called to the mission of reconciliation to a hostile and estranged world. They take up the way of the cross, both ritually in Holy Week devotions and in attitudes and actions as they seek to follow the resurrected Christ who suffered.

While the cross is a sacred space, we must avoid the temptation of romanticizing it. A Jesus who only suffers cannot liberate. The understanding of the cross must move us beyond a narrow devotion to suffering toward a redemptive solidarity with the oppressed. The solidarity forged in the shadows of the cross requires more than just establishing fellowship in suffering. Beyond Christ's suffering lies the realization of his salvation, liberation, and reconciliation, for to suffer solely for the sake of suffering disconnects the disenfranchised with Christ's purpose. Those who struggle against corporate sin by following the example of the Suffering Servant will discover that they are accompanying Christ in his mission. To claim the comfort of Christ while rejecting his way is to advocate a false Christianity.

The cross benefits not only humanity but also God. At the cross, God is able to experience the human condition and the consequences of oppression. God learns total abandonment, for Christ was betrayed by his friend, deserted by his followers, convicted by the elite in his Father's name, and condemned by the community that praised his entrance into Jerusalem a few days earlier. The cross becomes a place that allows the Divine to become one with those residing on the underside of U.S. society.

## Salvation

For all Christians, the gospel message is a message of salvation (although admittedly there are different concepts of salvation). *Soteriology* is precisely the theological attempt to understand how individuals and communities obtain salvation. If a typical Protestant believer (in a broadly evangelical and theologically conservative tradition) was asked how to obtain salvation, she or he would likely recite John 3:16. For many, the entire message and purpose of the Bible can be reduced to this verse: "For God so loved the world that he gave his only Son, so that everyone who believes in him may not perish but may have eternal life." In fact, it is not unusual to find someone holding a poster at a televised sporting event with simply "John 3:16" written upon it.[7]

While most Hispanics do not deny the importance of John 3:16, they also view Luke 4:18–19 as playing a major role in their understanding of salvation. This passage recounts Jesus' first proclamation concerning his mission. After his baptism, forty days in the desert, and temptation by Satan, Jesus returned to the place where he had been brought up. On the sabbath he attended synagogue. There he opened the scroll to the Book of Isaiah and chose a passage to describe his earthly commission:

> "The Spirit of the Lord is upon me,
>   because he has anointed me
>     to bring the gospel news to the poor.
> He has sent me to proclaim release to the captives
>   and recovery of sight to the blind,
>     to let the oppressed go free,
> to proclaim the year of the Lord's favor."

So angered were those who heard this message that they sought to kill Jesus.

Many Hispanic Christians see a Jesus who links salvation with the praxis of liberation. They remember the words of Jesus recorded by Luke, "Every tree therefore that does not bear good fruit is cut down and thrown into the fire" (3:9). Such an understanding of salvation subverts the dominant culture's reduction of the salvific act to the recitation of a proclamation of belief. Influenced by Luther, Euroamericans, specifically Protestants, insist that salvation can never be earned but is a gift from God. Through God's grace, not works, we are saved. Although Latinas/os agree that salvation begins as a love praxis from God, they insist that the works of the believer are an outward expression of an inward conversion.

Jesus tells his followers how salvation will be dispensed through the parable of the "sheep and the goats" as recorded in Matthew 25:31–46. In this story, Jesus divides the saved and the unsaved by what they did, or failed to do, for the hungry, the thirsty, the alien, the naked, the sick, and the incarcerated. Salvation was determined, not by one's belief in doctrine (orthodoxy) or one's church affiliation, but rather by what one did or did not do to "one of the least of these." Hispanics link salvation with the treatment of those who are oppressed. To ignore the plight of the disenfranchised is to ignore Christ's message of salvation, a message synonymous with liberation. To be saved is (1) to be liberated from the sins of the individual through the acceptance of a new life in Christ; (2) to be liberated from the oppressive economic, political, and social conditions that constitute corporate sin; and (3) to take control of one's own destiny. In the deepest sense possible, liberation is salvation.

## The Body of Believers

*Ecclesiology* is the study of how the church understands its own existence and its faithfulness to its historical development. Beyond this formal understanding, Hispanics are aware that, within their contexts, Catholics and Protestants have had different trajectories in their formal ecclesiologies. This is naturally the case as Hispanic theologies seek to be articulated from within the contexts of specific U.S. Latina/o communities. However, one cultural com-

monality that affects all Hispanic understanding of ecclesiology is
the concept of *familia*.

For Latinos/as, *familia* (family) is the archetype of the church
and also an important aspect of Hispanic culture. The common
modern Euroamerican concept of the nuclear, or immediate, family
composed of father, mother, and 2.4 children is too narrow to fit
the U.S. Hispanic ethos. *Familia* embraces a broader extended family: cousins, uncles, aunts, parents, grandparents, nieces, nephews,
and siblings living either together or in close proximity. *Familia*
is not limited to blood ties, for the concept of *padrinos/madrinas*
(godparents) binds different clans together. *Compadres/comadres*
(coparents) are united at the baptismal sacrament of the child, assuming joint responsibility for that child's welfare and creating new
family bonds. Catholic in origin, the concept of godparents has
transcended religious borders as Protestants who insist on "believers' baptism," that is, the baptism of adults, have baby dedication
services with the equivalent of *padrinos* and *madrinas* serving as
witnesses.

Through the extended family and the binding together of different families through the social institution of *compadres/comadres*,
Hispanics enlarge and strengthen the social institution of *familia*.
Hispanics stand ready to offer a healing alternative to insidious
individualism. Compassion, a will to sacrifice, and an ability to sus-
tain each other are crucial elements in a healthy *familia*. They serve
as a counterbalance to a "survival of the fittest" mentality. Such a
cutthroat environment, while sought after in the North American
marketplace, still undermines the gospel message of sacrificial love.
*Familia*, as an example for churches, becomes a much needed theological perception for Euroamericans. Yet, with sadness, Latinos/as
are discovering that in all too many cases the Euroamerican model
is beginning to prevail within their *comunidad*, as members of the
*familia* begin to adopt Euroamerican paradigms that supposedly
lead to economic success.

The church, as a *familia* of believers, becomes the basis for
how Latinos/as understand ecclesiology. The importance of the
*familia* or *comunidad* of believers in doing theology creates a
churchcentric understanding of theology that subverts the indi-
vidualistic theology of Euroamericans. The ideal model under
which Latinas/os attempt to create this churchcentric approach to

theology is called a *pastoral de conjunto* (collaborative pastoral ministry).

The reemergence of the concept of *pastoral de conjunto* originated from pastoral experiments in Latin America in the 1960s and 1970s. Latin American Catholic bishops, meeting in Puebla in 1979, adopted it as the preferred pastoral strategy to meet the exigencies of evangelization. This strategy called for full participation by every level of the faith community. The goal, according to the bishops, was for the church to learn "how to analyze reality, how to reflect on this reality from the standpoint of the Gospel, how to choose the most suitable objectives and means, and how to use them in the most sensible way for the work of evangelization."[8] In the United States, *pastoral de conjunto* came to prominence through the three national meetings of Hispanic Catholics known as Encuentro Nacional de Pastoral (1972, 1977, 1985). Through those meetings, U.S. Hispanic Catholics appropriated the concept of *pastoral de conjunto*. According to Ana María Pineda, this collaborative pastoral ministry "invites the people of God to commit themselves actively to continue the work of Jesus by entering into the cultural, religious, and social reality of the people, becoming incarnate in and with the people."[9]

U.S. Latinos/as are developing a process that attempts to understand the Divine from within the social location of Hispanics. Such a process analyzes their reality, a reality tied to a theological perspective that demands a sociopolitical response to oppression, both internal and external. A relationship has developed between oppressed Latinas/os and theologians or intellectuals aware of the structural crises Hispanics face in the United States. *Pastoral de conjunto* connects the pastoral work done by both Catholic and Protestant ministers and the academic work done by intellectuals with those within the local Hispanic congregation. These ministers and scholars attempt to learn from the disenfranchised while serving them as organic intellectuals, that is, intellectuals grounded in the social reality of the people, and acting in the consciousness-raising process of the faith community.

For the Hispanic community, such a task attempts to heal the brokenness of lives. Many Latinas/os living in this country are disjointed from the culture of their heritage and the culture in which they reside, outsiders and foreigners to both, all the while creating and living within a distinct third cultural sphere. *Pastoral de conjunto* seeks mending for a broken existence through the rich diversity found among Latinas/os, who are a multiracial and multi-cultural people. Although Hispanics are multifarious, a holistic collaborative spirit emerges when they gather to share the Word of God and their stories of suffering and pilgrimage in the diaspora. Succinctly stated, *pastoral de conjunto* is the construction of a collaborative theology based on the reflection of Hispanics who struggle in understanding their faith and vocation as these are contextualized in their lives and struggles. An example of this process are conferences held by theologians, across denominational lines, for the purpose of discussing a theological question or dilemma. The product of these conversations usually concludes with a collection of essays appearing in book form.

## Evangelism

The mission of the church, especially for evangelicals, is the proclamation of the gospel message of salvation that is found in Christ Jesus. This Great Commission is based on Matthew 28:19: "Go therefore and make disciples of all nations, baptizing them in the name of the Father, and of the Son, and of the Holy Spirit." For most evangelicals, Christian discipleship encompasses the responsibility of witnessing the message of salvation to unbelievers so that they too can hear, be converted, and gain eternal life.

Latino/a *evangélicos*, like their Euroamerican counterparts, understand the Great Commission to be Christ's appointment of the believer to go and convert the world to the message and lordship of Christ. Yet, an assumption is made by some churches that because they hold the "truth," and the unbeliever lives in darkness, the unbeliever must change and assimilate to the evangelist's worldview. Unfortunately, in many cases, the evangelist's cultural traditions are confused with the biblical message.

Ironically, *evangélicos*, who exist on the margins of U.S. religiosity, have historically been bombarded to assimilate to the Euroamerican evangelical norm. Thus, Hispanic *evangélicos* know what it means to be seen as the ones who must convert from understanding the gospel through their own cultural symbols to understanding through the "purer" Euroamerican symbols, which has led to greater sensitivity in understanding evangelism. Rather than questioning how the unbeliever must change to become part of the church, they ask how the church must change to welcome the outsider. A careful reading of the early church's mission, as recorded in the Book of Acts, revealed that the church did not conceive of its mission on the day of Pentecost; rather, it was an ongoing process. As the church went about fulfilling its mission of solidarity with Christ, it discovered how that mission was to be fulfilled. The original church was forced to die to its traditions in order for God's ministry to begin. As Loida Martell-Otero points out, "The church is being made to convert, even as it seeks converts."[10]

## The Spirit

Human life and the world are sustained by God through the Spirit. The study of the Spirit of God, *pneumatology*, examines how God's presence is made real within each epoch of human history as well as within specific Christian communities. Through the Spirit, the will of God achieves fulfillment through humans by transforming their society in each and every ensuing generation. Life in the Spirit for many Latinos/as means a greater sense of identity, freedom, and community in which the various callings of women and men find expression and, thereby, affirmation and empowerment by God's Spirit. Furthermore, the charismatic revival among various religious traditions has produced among the Latino/a faithful a liberative theological response to their disenfranchisement. Eldín Villafañe attempts to explain how Hispanics understand the working of the Spirit. Interpreting Galatians 5:25, Villafañe maintains that to live in the Spirit (a theological self-understanding) is to also walk in the Spirit (an ethical self-understanding). The Spirit's historical project is to participate in the reign of God, that is, a reign concerned with the establishment of justice by restraining evil and fostering conditions for an ethical moral order. Through the power of the Spirit, structures of sin and evil are challenged and confronted as disenfranchised congregations receive charismatic empowerment and the spiritual resources to encounter social struggles.[11]

Hispanics contribute not only to the understanding of the function of the Spirit but also to the role the Spirit plays within the Trinity. Several Latino/a theologians understand the relationship existing within the Trinity, between Father, Son, and Holy Ghost, as the pattern for humanity. They view the Trinity, not as a cosmic puzzle in need of a solution, but rather as a paragon to be emulated. Father, Son, and Spirit do not exist in a hierarchy; rather, all three share equally in substance, power, and importance. To believe in the Trinity is to follow the model set. Trinity represents a Godhead whose very existence is that of a sharing Being, co-equal in power, awe, and authority.[12] Hence, structural poverty within North America is at odds with the doctrine of the Trinity as understood by Hispanics.

## Marianism

The Virgin Mary plays a profound role among Latinas/os, especially those who are Catholic. Devotional representations of European origin of the Virgin Mary have adherents in the Americas, but her manifestation in the Americas has also taken shape in the form of those oppressed, which allows a biracial Mary to affirm all aspects of the Hispanic culture. In particular, for Mexicans, Mexican Americans, and other Latinos/as, the story of La Virgen de Guadalupe, also known as *La Morenita* (the little brown lady), defines their spirituality. According to tradition, in 1531 on a hill of Tepeyac (on the outskirts of Mexico City), La Virgen de Guadalupe appeared to an Amerindian named Juan Diego. Within seven years of La Virgencita's apparition, over eight million Amerindians were baptized into the Catholic Church. For many Catholic theologians, the impact and influence are such that she has been called the "Evangelizer of the Americas." Virgilio Elizondo describes the events of Tepeyac as having the most "revolutionary, profound, lasting, far-reaching, healing, and liberating impact on Christianity" since Pentecost.[13]

What La Virgen de Guadalupe represents to Mexicans, La Virgen de Caridad means to Cubans. According to the traditional Catholic version, around 1610, two Taíno native brothers, Juan and Rodrigo de Hoyos, along with a black slave boy named Juan Moreno, went rowing on Nipe Bay in search of salt. Nipe Bay is not far from the copper mines of Cobre on the northwestern tip of the island. At about 5:30 in the morning, while rowing their canoe, they came upon a fifteen-inch carved statue of the Virgin Mary, floating on a piece of wood. Miraculously, the statue was dry. At her feet was the inscription "I am the Virgin of Charity." She was, in effect, *la primera balsera* (the first rafter) to be rescued.

Las Virgenes de Guadalupe and Cobre affect and inform how Hispanics do theology. A return to the Virgencita reclaims her as an important symbol for Latinos/as, characterizing the hopes and aspirations of many Hispanics, regardless of national ethnicity or religious affiliation. For many, these manifestations of the Virgin Mary provide meaning, reconciliation, and a resource for daily life. First, both manifestations of Mary symbolized the birth of a new racial/ethnic identity. Ceasing to be a European white figure, she appeared in the form of a bronzed woman of color, a color symbolizing life (the color of the new Latin American race). Second, she gave dignity to the oppressed. Rather than appearing to the religious leaders, she identified with the economic and racial outcasts by appearing in the color of oppression. A *virgen* appearing as a woman of color severs the bond between inferiority and nonwhiteness, as she assumes the color and cause of those oppressed. Her presence allowed the indigenous witnesses of her appearance — and, with them, all Hispanics — to become *compañeros/as* (companions) with the Divine. Not surprisingly, La Virgen's earliest devotees were the Amerindians and slaves. Finally, her gender provides hope to women against machismo by providing a feminine space within the Divine. As the ultimate mother, she represents God's motherly love, a love that calls all of her children to reconciliation.

Yet, how do Latino/a Protestants come to terms with Marianism? Although Las Virgencitas represent one of the most important symbols within Hispanic popular Catholicism and Mary as the Mother of Jesus is highly respected by *evangélicos,* nevertheless, for many Latino/a Protestants, particular devotion and veneration of Mary are viewed with suspicion at the very least. They insist that such veneration should solely be offered toward God. Furthermore, as a result of Protestant understandings of Christ Jesus being the mediator between God and humanity, there is little room for Mary as any type of mediator for the majority of Latino/a Protestants. More theologically conservative Protestants go further and claim that such roles and devotions border on idolatry. Yet, to argue that devotion to Mary is some sort of idol worship is a reductionist tendency that misses the option of a deeper theological significance of this Hispanic symbol. Several Latino/a Catholic theologians have suggested that devotion to La Virgencita is not necessarily a veneration of the historical Mary of Nazareth, Jesus' mother; rather, Marianism is a pneumatological issue. In other words, these manifestations of the Virgins in Latin America are seen as acts of the Holy Spirit and not the historical Mary. The encounter between the marginalized people of the land and La Virgencita is an experience of "God-who-is-for-us." These images become the authentic language by which the Holy Spirit communicates grace to the oppressed, grace to confront the reality of daily oppression and dehumanization.[14]

The Virgencitas and patron saints throughout Latin America become bearers of Latino/a cultural identity and as such serve as a rich religious source of empowerment. However, for many Hispanic Protestants, especially Latino/a Pentecostals, these various pneumatological roles are said to be experienced through direct contact with the Holy Spirit. As Latino/a Protestants reassess their understandings of the role of Mary in the plan for salvation, these points will be some of the most difficult to negotiate. Notwithstanding that difficulty, in the United States there are some Hispanic Protestants, for example, some Episcopalian communities, who have adopted perspectives more akin to Latino/a Catholics and have openly brought Mary into the devotional life of their congregations.

## The Last Days

*Eschatology* is the study of "the last days," an exploration of the destiny of the whole cosmos. Among theologically conservative Euroamerican Christians, one particular approach is known as *dispensationalism.* Dispensationalists create charts based on so-called hidden biblical clues that forecast how and when the world will end; some Hispanic Christians also participate in this religious worldview. Others, however, look at the liberative meaning of the last days, which assures victory to the believer within the defeats and struggles of living in the underside of North American culture.

In spite of structural and individual oppression, hope resonates within the Latino/a that a day will come when all, as one body, will eat and drink at the table of the Lord. The celebration of such a day is expressed in what was earlier discussed as a "sacred fiesta." Fiesta is more than just a party; it encompasses the eschatological hope of inevitable liberation.

Hispanic theologians reiterate the message of Jesus that the kingdom of God (or reign or kin-dom) is within us.[15] God's establishment of justice is not limited to a transcendent reality, some "pie-in-the-sky" hope for fairness. Rather, the eschatological hope for a "here-after" justice is a directive to be established in the here and now. Jesus' eschatological pronouncements are to be instituted in the present reality. While perfect justice remains the ultimate hope of God's eventual reign, such justice serves as a touchstone for Christian praxis in the quest for God's will, hence encompassing both the last and present days.

## The Complexity and Challenge of Latino/a Theology

In this chapter, we have reviewed some of the basic theological concepts formulated by Latinos/as to simply introduce the reader to a rudimentary appreciation of Hispanic thought and its contribution to the overall theological discourse. In addition to the freshness and complexity of these theological perspectives, Hispanic life and thought have also affected larger theological discussions. Additionally, Hispanic theology, like many other theologies from the margins, has shown itself to be fully conversant with Euroamerican theological discourses. The reverse is less frequent. The realities of the social and cultural contexts are that Latinas/os in theology, as in other areas of life, are multilingual and multicultural and, therefore, multicompetent. Even when the dominant theological discourse fails to value Hispanic theological perspectives, Latino/a communities continue to develop, articulate, and cherish them. Latina/o theologians and scholars of religion draw upon these community-based theologies as the source of their theological development, while simultaneously mastering theological information from other communal traditions. As Hispanics in the United States increasingly become a larger part of the church, the challenge exists for theologians from other communities to become theologically multicultural also.

So far, we have seen how the social location of Hispanics contributed to the development of Latina/o theological concepts and briefly discussed some of those concepts. In the next chapter, we begin to make a closer examination of the historical development of Hispanic theologies, the different manifestations that arose within the Latino/a community, and the different theologians who participated in articulating the diversity found within these multicultural theologies.

# Chapter 3 Study Questions

## Definition Question

Define the following terms: epistemology, praxis, *teología de conjunto*, anthropology, hermeneutics, *imago Dei*, Christology, soteriology, ecclesiology, *pastoral de conjunto*, missiology, pneumatology, eschatology.

## Essay Questions

1. What contributions have Hispanic theologians made to the field of epistemology? Why is praxis important? Can praxis be reconciled with the normative Euroamerican Protestant notion of being "saved" solely by grace, not works?

2. What does it mean to read the Bible through the "eyes of Hispanics"? Is such a reading objective or subjective? Can any biblical interpretation be objective? What problems, if any, exist in reading the Bible through Latina/o eyes? Can Euroamericans be accused of reading the Bible with Eurocentric eyes? If so, why? Does it make a difference if the Bible is read in Spanish instead of English? If so, what difference?

3. What is the significance of Jesus' being from Galilee? How do Hispanics see Christ? Why do Hispanic theologians insist on the poverty of Jesus? How does God, according to Latinos/as,

reveal Godself to humanity? Why is the brutal crucifixion of Christ emphasized?

4. What is sin? How does the Hispanic understanding of sin differ from the Euroamerican understanding? What is the difference between individual and corporate sin? Which one do Euroamericans emphasize and why? How and why is this different from how Latinas/os understand sin?

5. On what ideal is the Latina/o church based? Does this differ from Euroamerican church communities? If so, how? What is required from the church's center to reach the margins?

6. How does the Hispanic understanding of the Trinity inform how the community should be structured? What is significant about La Virgen de Guadalupe and La Virgen de Caridad to the Latino/a community?

7. What are some of the differences existing between the theological perspectives of Latino/a Catholics and Protestants?

## Chapter 4

# Historia: Reflections on the Latino/a Story

The stereotypical fabrication of the Latino/a identity by the dominant culture vacillates between exotic dream and dangerous nightmare. In many respects, Hispanics are perceived through the imaginations of non-Hispanics. Throughout the history of the United States, a collective identity of Latinas/os has been forced upon them. How then do Hispanics recall their history apart from the imagery imposed upon them by the gaze of the dominant U.S. culture? Among the first acts of empowerment for any group seeking to liberate themselves from how they are seen by others is the telling of their own stories. Reclaiming Latina/o history from the underside of U.S. history challenges the dominant culture to come to terms with Hispanics as real human beings rather than distancing Latinos/as as a stereotyped footnote to Euroamerican history.

Like any human community, Hispanics have many stories to tell. One of the shared characteristics is opposition to any imposed epic story that attempts to collapse everything into a simple tale. The fact is that many stories make up Latino/a theologies. Depending upon where one chooses to begin, a history can be told with a variety of story lines. It is not that one is wrong or another inauthentic but rather that many authentic stories run concurrently, with some going in different directions, while others feed into themselves.

Many historical stories converge in clusters that flow into the reality of Latino/a theologies. These clusters include the forerunners of Latino/a theologies and their present-day emergence, with the latter concentrating on Catholics, Protestants, Latina women, and organizations. We will briefly investigate these clusters formed by the Hispanic story, cognizant that history cannot be narrated. Some stories are told here. Some are told only in part. There are hints of other tales, and other details and stories wait for another day to be told.[1]

## Forerunners of Hispanic Theologies

Although Hispanic theologies emerged in the last half of the twentieth century, they did not appear out of thin air. Latino/a perspectives are rooted in the acts of resistance to the oppression of colonial Christendom established during the European conquest of the indigenous people of the Western Hemisphere. In fact, the argument can be made that as long as Latinos/as lived under oppression, resistance existed. Perhaps one of the earliest antecedents of Latina/o theology in the United States can be seen in the work of Father Antonio José Martínez of Taos, New Mexico. Known as *el cura de Taos*, he was accepted as a respected civic and religious leader among the New Mexican clergy and people. Unfortunately, Martínez was not equally well regarded by the French cleric Jean Baptiste Lamy, who was appointed Roman Catholic bishop (and later archbishop) to Santa Fe in 1851. Prior to the Mexican-American War, the Catholic parishes in what was to become the southwestern United States were under the jurisdiction of the Mexican Catholic Church. As a result of the war, the predominately Mexican Catholic parishes found themselves under the jurisdiction of the U.S. Catholic Church. This tension can best be examined through the conflict that developed between Martínez and Lamy.

The theologically conservative Lamy, who served under the diocese of Baltimore, quickly clashed with Father Martínez, who among other things openly rejected celibacy. Martínez advocated an understanding of Catholic Christianity that allowed for the continued practice of popular religion, a position that Archbishop Lamy opposed. Additionally, Martínez questioned the directional flow of tithes from his parish toward Lamy's offices, an act Martínez considered immoral because it was tantamount to taking money from the poor and giving it to the rich. Martínez also challenged what he perceived to be prejudicial attitudes and actions of the official church against local Catholics. Eventually Father Martínez was excommunicated and removed in 1857. The traditional practices of New Mexican Catholics were strongly discouraged by the new clergy, which resulted in a greater rift between the official church and local communities of faith. Nonetheless, local New Mexicans' understandings and practices of Christianity persisted into the twentieth century.

Another important antecedent of Hispanic theology is the *Tejano* Catholic community centered in San Antonio, Texas. The struggle of the *Tejano* community and its commitment to its own understanding of faith helped prepare the ground for Latino/a theology, both Catholic and Protestant. Even before Mexico became independent of Spain in 1821, the region of northern Mexico known as *Tejas* (Texas) developed a cultural identity that provided resources to resist assimilation to Euroamerican religion and culture. The role of public celebration and ritual was a key factor in this resistance and maintenance of identity. Although oppression and suppression of local understandings of Christianity came from a variety of sources, nevertheless, elements that preserved and promoted a culturally relevant understanding of Christianity that was *Tejano* in its essence persisted. Even as Euroamericans came to dominate the social and political spheres of San Antonio, especially in the nineteenth and first half of the twentieth centuries, alternative understandings of the Christian faith persevered in the family and in the barrio, thereby planting seeds that were destined to produce greater fruit at a later time. Timothy Matovina, a historian of Hispanic religiosity, writes of the development of local initiatives in religious affairs as San Antonio came under different sovereignties. Local traditions and feasts persisted through the years, despite a growing sense of separation from Mexico as Euroamericans moving to Texas surmounted the social structures of power and privilege.[2]

Soon after the turn of the twentieth century, other developments in religious life and theological thought also had a profound effect on the later development of Hispanic theologies. As the United States expanded its worldwide possessions, Puerto Rican Juan L. Lugo (1890–1984) found himself in Hawaii with other Puerto Rican immigrant laborers. There, in 1913, he was converted to Pentecostal Christianity. After a period of ministry in San Francisco, California, Lugo returned to the city of Ponce in Puerto Rico in 1916, bringing with him a Pentecostal understanding of the gospel. Lugo's influential ministry led to the establishment of Hispanic congregations in Puerto Rico, California, and the northeastern United States. Through the establishment in 1937 of the Instituto Bíblico Mizpa (later Colegio Pentecostal Mizpa), Lugo left his mark on grassroots Hispanic theological education, as students came not only from Puerto Rico but from throughout Latin America.[3]

Elsewhere in the borderlands between the United States and Mexico, Mexican-born Pentecostal church leader Francisco Olazabal (1886–1937) was preaching the gospel and ministering to Spanish-speaking people. Olazabal was an important Pentecostal evangelist who influenced many through his ministry, not only in the borderlands context of revolutionary Mexico but also throughout the United States. Both Olazabal and Lugo were key in the establishment of grassroots theologies and institutions among various groups of Hispanics early in the twentieth century. After serious difficulties with the Euroamerican-dominated Assemblies of God, Olazabal established the independent Latin American Council of Christian Churches in 1923. Both Olazabal and Lugo ministered in New York City and at certain times collaborated in their ministries. They also worked together in Texas, California, and Puerto Rico. Such cooperation helped foster a broader Latino/a Pentecostal understanding that transcended local or regional identities. Although many Roman Catholics and historic mainline Protestants, both within the dominant culture as well as among Latinas/os, considered early Hispanic Pentecostalism to be marginal and theologically deficient, it nevertheless exercised a lasting influence on other expressions of Hispanic Christianity in the United States.

Some contemporary Hispanic Pentecostal groups have a very negative understanding of both particular denominations and of the concept of "denomination" in general. These Latina/o Pentecostals, who maintain that the denominations have been unfaithful to the gospel message of Christian unity, try to avoid anything that may give the appearance of replicating denominations, which does not mean that these groups are all independent congregations that have abandoned all ecclesiastical connections. Very often, these alternative ecclesiastical connections or cooperative affiliations come under the name of *concilio* (council).

An individual whose influence exceeded Pentecostal circles, both as a noted woman minister and as a precursor to a Hispanic theology rooted in the community, is the Reverend Leoncia Rosado, better known as Mama Leo. Born in Puerto Rico in 1912, Mama Leo was converted and underwent the baptism of the Holy Spirit in 1932. Shortly thereafter, she entered the ministry. Together with her husband, the Reverend Francisco Rosado, she founded and pastored the Iglesia Cristiana Damasco and the Damascus Youth Crusade in New York City.[4] A significant part of Mama Leo's ministry was to people on the margins of society, including drug addicts and alcoholics, in effect advocating a Christian social engagement, a type of option for the marginalized.

Mama Leo was not the only Latina woman forerunner to Hispanic theology. Latina women in various roles and callings had always been the backbone of Hispanic churches in the United States. They served as religious workers and were involved in the educational ventures of congregations and parishes. While most Latino Protestant evangelists and pastors were male, their wives were more than simple companions. They were real partners in the ministry, participating in preaching and articulating the faith, even though conventions of the time among most groups would never have publicly recognized what they did as preaching. In some Protestant traditions women were recognized as pastors and evangelists in their own right. One such woman within the Church of the Nazarene was Santos Elizondo. A native of Mexico, Elizondo was converted in 1905 and soon after entered the ministry. She did evangelistic work in El Paso, Texas, and Juárez, Mexico, ministering in that borderlands context until her death in 1941. There Pastor Elizondo, who founded a school, orphanage, and women's society and in addition worked as a nurse and midwife, was the focus of opposition from other Protestant missions, not only over Nazarene doctrine, but also over the fact that she was a woman in ministry.[5]

For the majority of U.S. Christian history, church hierarchies placed pressure upon Latino/a congregations of all denominations, including Roman Catholic, Methodist, Baptist, and Disciples of Christ, to assimilate to the Euroamerican norm. Against this denominational push were countercurrents of local initiatives to understand and practice Christianity. In 1939, the Catholic archdiocese of New York directly appointed non–Puerto Rican Redemptorist clergy to minister to Puerto Ricans in East Harlem. Later, in the 1950s, this ministry was expanded to include diocesan priests who attempted to create unified parishes instead of the norm of parishes characterized by language and ethnicity. An Americanist impulse that had been present in the overall U.S. Roman Catholic Church was again operative, the assumption being that while a parish might have an English-language and a Spanish-language congregation in the short run, through assimilation the Puerto Rican culture and the use of Spanish would fade away. This latter expectation did not materialize, creating tensions between English-speaking congregations and Spanish-speaking Puerto Ricans.[6]

In New York City, Spanish-speaking congregations did not fade away, partly due to the Cursillo movement, one of the most significant expressions of grassroots religious understandings and practices. *Cursillo,* literally "small or little course," is a renewal movement within the Catholic Church that originated in Spain in 1947. This three-day retreat eventually spread to the United States, where it quickly crossed denominational borders as Protestants attended these retreats to seek deeper spiritual lives. Among Latinos/as, specifically Puerto Ricans in New York City, the Cursillo, combined with a creative practice of Hispanic Catholicism, allowed for Spanish-language liturgies and cultivated lay leadership.[7]

Another example emanating from New York City was the Reverend Santiago Soto Fontánez, longtime pastor of the Central Baptist Church in Brooklyn, New York. A professor of literature at Brooklyn College, Fontánez served as pastor from 1945 to 1959 and from 1966 to 1972. Emphasizing an understanding and practice of the Christian faith that was relevant to the social context of the community, he influenced generations of laity and clergy in his ministry.

Although a more detailed and formal articulation of Hispanic theology did not emerge until the 1960s, these accounts indicate the presence of themes that would eventually be articulated and developed. In many locations and at different times, the various Latina/o communities were active and creative in their own understandings of Christianity amid very distinct (and often difficult) contexts. Although many of these Hispanic expressions of Christianity were disregarded, ignored, or held in low esteem as theologically deficient, even by their own denominations, these negative responses do not indicate a lack of theological and pastoral reflection before the 1960s. In fact, these very negative attitudes from the larger Euroamerican denominations toward those who were theoretically part of the same communion or tradition helped create the tension that contributed to the emergence and articulation of distinct Latino/a theologies. Against very difficult odds, Hispanics in the United States were able to put into words and cultivate understandings of Christian life and ministry that were sensitive to their communities' needs.

## Emergence of Hispanic Theology

In their scholarship of U.S. Latino/a religious realities, Ana María Díaz-Stevens and Anthony Stevens-Arroyo speak of a Hispanic religious resurgence that started after 1967. Their research focuses mainly on Hispanic Roman Catholicism; however, this religious resurgence also influenced Protestantism. These sociologists of religion note that while there had always been a Latina/o presence in the United States, especially after 1848, it was not until the mid-twentieth century that certain events converged to mark the beginning of new forms of Hispanic religious life, expression, and engagement with the wider society. Noteworthy characteristics of this religious renaissance include its national scope, efforts toward a broader coalition, creation of sophisticated organizations, and a style of leadership that was collegial, connected to local communities, and engaged with contemporary social and political realities. Díaz-Stevens and Stevens-Arroyo also perceived several consequences of this Latina/o religious resurgence. These included implicit and explicit challenges to church establishments that maintained unsympathetic attitudes and approaches to Hispanic ministries. Additionally the Latino/a religious resurgence was characterized by the pivotal development of grassroots groups. These groups developed religious and theological thoughts more contextual to urban life. Moreover, the resurgence facilitated the reality of a pan-ethnic commonality across church barriers, and it also advocated a wider role for women in church leadership and ministry.[8]

For most of the nineteenth and twentieth centuries, efforts in Hispanic ministry by many denominational hierarchies were characterized by paternalism and assimilationism. However, with the social changes and upheavals of the 1960s, including the civil rights movement and a new sense of La Raza (the Race), came a shift toward a more formal articulation of Hispanic theology in the years 1966–68. This was the era of the Mexican American labor leader César Chávez (1927–93) and the United Farm Workers' labor union. In 1968 Chávez led a nationwide boycott of California grapes with the goal of obtaining fair labor contracts for agricultural workers. The year before, 1967, brought riots in Spanish Harlem, the takeover of a county courthouse in Tierra Amarilla, New Mexico, and the appearance of the poem "I Am Joaquín/Yo Soy Joaquín" by the Chicano Rudolfo "Corky" Gonzáles, all major cultural landmarks. This was a time when Chicano/a and Puerto Rican activism emerged. These and other events point to a significant shift in Latina/o consciousness, which in turn affected religious understandings and actions.

During the 1960s, a younger generation of pastoral leaders, educators, and laity sought to make connections between their faith, culture, and their times. Early efforts toward the forming of theological responses to the particular conditions of Hispanics included the work of two early Roman Catholic organizations: PADRES (Padres Asociados para Derechos Religiosos, Educacionales y Sociales; Priests for Religious, Educational, and Social Rights) and Las Hermanas. Founded in 1970, PADRES was initially a Mexican American/Chicano organization of Roman Catholic clergy advocating a more intentional effort to address the ministry needs of the Chicano/a community. PADRES later broadened its Latino/a membership.

In 1971 the organization Las Hermanas (Sisters) was founded. Although the initial leadership consisted of Mexican American religious women, from its start membership was open to all Latina women in religious orders, and later to lay women. In one of its founding documents it declared that

*Hermanas* is an organization that wants to keep itself aware of the suffering of our Hispano people. By reason of our heritage, and in response to the mind of Vatican II and the encyclical *Populorum Progressio,* we feel obliged to be faithful to the Christian message of hopeful creation for a Christian humanism within the context and culture of the Hispano community.[9]

An important series of events also contributed greatly to the historical development of Latino/a theologies in the United States. National conferences of Hispanic lay and religious leaders were conducted under the name of Encuentro Nacional Hispano de Pastoral (National Hispanic Pastoral Encounter). Sponsored under the authority of the National Conference of Catholic Bishops, the Encuentros (held in 1972, 1977, 1985, and most recently 2000) were major efforts to address the Hispanic cultural and pastoral realities that confront the U.S. Roman Catholic Church. Encuentro 2000 addressed the religious and faith traditions, not only of Latina/o Catholics, but also of all Catholics in the United States. To the extent that Hispanic Protestants and Catholics were in dialogue in the development of Hispanic theology and ministry, the Catholic Encuentros had an impact far beyond Roman Catholic circles.

## Catholics

An important center for Hispanic Catholic theology and ministry is San Antonio, Texas, which moved from being a center of *Tejano* religion toward providing broader leadership in the overall Hispanic church. By 1970, Patricio Flores became the Catholic auxiliary bishop of San Antonio. Additionally, Father Virgilio Elizondo served as rector at San Fernando Cathedral in his hometown of San Antonio, where his pastoral ministry developed against the background of *Tejano/a* religiosity. Elizondo, together with other Mexican American Catholic clergy and laity, founded the Mexican American Cultural Center (MACC) in 1972 to focus on the spiritual, temporal, and educational needs of the Mexican American Catholic community in the United States. MACC offered culturally focused studies in pastoral ministry, language studies, and research. Elizondo advocates a culturally relevant Catholicism that seeks to bring the Good News to all situations of life. In an early book, *Galilean Journey* (1983, rev. ed. 2000), Elizondo connects the Latino/a identity of *mestizaje* with the marginality of first-century Christianity. Central to this approach is mining the theological and cultural riches found in popular religiosity, especially the devotion to the Virgin of Guadalupe. Elizondo developed a connection between *mestizaje* and popular religiosity and combined this theological perspective with his ministry as rector at San Fernando Cathedral and his work at MACC to forge pastoral and religious leadership that empowered Hispanic ministry.

Another Catholic theologian and priest, Allan Figueroa Deck explored the role of liturgy in Mexican American culture in his early written works. Deck later published the influential *The Second Wave* in 1989, in which he explored the implications of a "new wave" of Catholic immigrants from Latin America. He deemed necessary a new pastoral approach for Hispanics. Any such approach must take seriously the North American contexts of U.S. Latinas/os and avoid both a replication of earlier assimilation-type models and methods or unmodified adoption of Latin American initiatives.[10]

A connected development in Hispanic theology was the founding in 1988 of the Academy of Catholic Hispanic Theologians of the United States (ACHTUS). ACHTUS is an organization of Roman Catholic scholars who focus on Latina/o theological understandings at yearly colloquiums. The mission statement of ACHTUS includes the following objectives:

1. Accompany the Hispanic communities of the United States, helping to critically discern the movement of the Spirit in their historical journey.

2. Give expression to the faith experience of the people within their historical, socioeconomic, political, and cultural contexts.

3. Encourage interdisciplinary scholarly collaboration.

4. Create resources, instruments, and a professional network to develop a U.S. Hispanic *teología de conjunto*.

5. Support Hispanics currently engaged in theological research and studies.

An important outgrowth of ACHTUS is the *Journal of Hispanic/ Latino Theology* (*JHLT*), whose first issue appeared in 1993 with a grant from the Lilly Endowment. *JHLT* is a quarterly, refereed journal with both Latino/a and non-Hispanic authors from a wide variety of denominational affiliations.

## Protestants

Among Protestants, the Cuban-born United Methodist minister Justo González is a historian of the early church and a leader in the development of Hispanic theology. González's 1969 work, *The Development of Christianity in Latin America*, is an early example of how he ties his work in Christian history and theology to important concerns of Latina/o theology.[11] González was the founding editor of *Apuntes*, an ecumenical journal of Hispanic theology that first appeared in 1981. *Apuntes* was the first regularly published theological journal that addressed the Latino/a religious contexts. Articles address theological, pastoral, and cultural concerns and are printed either in English with a Spanish summary or in Spanish with an English summary. Hispanic Catholics, mainline Protestants, evangelicals, and Pentecostals all publish in *Apuntes*, making it an important forum for developing *teología en conjunto*, a vehicle for the public discussion of Hispanic theology, and an entry into ecumenism.

The late Orlando E. Costas was also an influential leader at all levels of the Hispanic theological movement, from the grass roots to the academy. As a scholar, Costas was formally a missiologist, but the range of his interests and the issues he addressed were quite expansive and therein lies part of his significance in the development of Latino/a theology. Costas was a Puerto Rican Protestant who spent some time as a minister in Latin America, where he engaged liberation theology and North American evangelical theology. He crafted his own understanding of the nature of the Latina/o church and its mission. Always connected to but also critical of his evangelical heritage, Costas remained ecumenical in his work and his outlook. Costas published a number of works in English and Spanish. Two of his first books in English were *The Church and Its Mission* in 1974 and *The Integrity of Mission* in 1979, making Costas one of the earliest Hispanic theo-

logians in print in the United States.[12] After being the first director
of the Hispanic Program at Eastern Baptist Theological Seminary
in Philadelphia, Costas was named dean at Andover Newton Theological School, a position he held until his untimely death in 1987.
Costas had a tremendous impact upon Latino/a Protestant pastors,
teachers, and activists that continues to the present day.

## Latina Women

Often silenced, the voices of Latina women comprise another invaluable contribution to Latino/a theology. Although it ought to
be obvious that the U.S. Hispanic *comunidad* contains a majority of women who, both today and throughout history, provide
leadership in all areas of life, this is seldom recognized by official
leadership structures or within the institutional church. Latinas in
the United States must contend with deep-rooted paternalistic and
sexist ascriptions, from Latin American cultures and the dominant
U.S. American culture, from within the church and without. From
the very beginning of the emergence of Hispanic theologies, Latina
women have played significant leadership roles in its growth, as we
have noted with individuals like Rev. Leoncia Rosado (Mama Leo)
and Santos Elizondo.

Historically, sexism has always been a social construction that
assumed men to be inherently superior to females, and hence the
very structures by which society and the church function are arranged to perpetuate this assumption. Operating from this premise,
some Christian traditions teach that God made "man" in God's
own image while the woman is a deficient copy, made in the image
of man, thus giving men divine authority to rule over women. As
an elite group, men insist on their superiority and justify their right
to dominate and domesticate those they consider to be inferior,
often to enhance their own social standings. Laws, traditions, and
church doctrines, established mostly by men, reinforce these societal assumptions about the nature of gender in order to establish
a power structure that becomes normative and legitimate in the
minds and hearts of the community, including women abused by
the system. In fact, many of these women learn to perceive reality
through the eyes of men (a type of false consciousness) and at times
become the most vocal defenders of the status quo, thereby inter-

nalizing their oppression. Yet, despite these oppressive contexts, many Latin American women and Latina women in the United States have developed alternative understandings and strategies of survival that coexist covertly with dominant paternalistic and patriarchal interpretations.

To listen to the voices of Hispanic women is to hear a concern for issues and actions that affect the daily existence of the entire *comunidad,* especially the lives of women. Latina feminist theologies seek to correct the harm done by androcentric (male-centered) approaches and theories that in the past ignored women, who represent the majority in Latino/a faith communities. Women are often in the forefront of the difficult and sometimes unrecognized work of sustaining and maintaining family, community, and church. As Gloria Inés Loya has stated, Hispanic women are frequently the *pasionarias* and *pastoras,* that is, the spiritually passionate and pastoral leaders of Hispanic communities.[13] Whether or not they are given official titles, Hispanic women are engaged in ministries within the context of the struggle for survival. These Latina women contend daily with negative and oppressive stereotypes.

Latina women still contend with situations of oppression and discrimination. If women are employed to do the same jobs as men, it is usually for less pay. However, the absence of fair wages is only part of the oppression; the limitation on the types of work available to Latina women is another part. Latina women must deal with the internal sexism of the community as manifested in machismo. Increasingly Latina women are heads of households and, with their children, are more likely to be living in poverty. Yet these spiritual, familial, and community leaders are quite literally the backbone of the Latino/a church. Their daily reality requires Hispanic theology to address fully their needs in the future, rather than merely to make the necessary "politically correct" statements that provide a facade of inclusiveness but mask the absence of a thorough investigation into how the Latina perspective affects every aspect of theological discourse.

Although Latina feminist theologies have been critical of North American feminists, especially in the area of race and class analysis, they still share some general characteristics. Both feminist theologies are primarily concerned with (1) a genuine respect for the personhood and well-being of all women, (2) an emphasis on social location, (3) an unmasking of the traditional understandings of humanity, and (4) a valuing of women's experience as a source and lens for the critique and construction of theologies. In addition, U.S. Hispanic feminist theologies enable Latina women to understand multiple oppressive structures, to identify their preferred future, and to confront internalized oppression. Furthermore, Latina feminist theologies identify the importance of female leadership, even in the midst of oppression, in maintaining the health and life of the *comunidad.*

One of the most prominent approaches in Latina feminist theology is *mujerista* theology (from the Spanish word for "woman," *mujer*) as articulated by Ada María Isasi-Díaz, a Cuban and one of the earliest developers of Hispanic theology in the United States. Elements of what later developed into *mujerista* theology can be discerned in her writings as early as 1977.[14] By 1988, together with Yolanda Tarango, Isasi-Díaz published *Hispanic Women: Prophetic Voice of the Church.* In this book, the authors seek to represent the beliefs and understandings of the women they interviewed.

Isasi-Díaz states that *"feminista hispanas* [feminist Hispanics] have been consistently marginalized within the Euroamerican feminist community because of our critique of its ethnic/racial prejudice and its lack of class analysis."[15] *Mujerista* theology is a particular way of identifying and examining Latina understandings of faith and its function in the struggle for life and liberation. It is an intentionally different theological perspective seeking new approaches to the issues of sexism, ethnic prejudice, and economic oppression. *Mujerista* theology identifies Latinas' explanations of their lives and faith and how the two are connected in the struggle for liberation. Isasi-Díaz explains:

> Because of the centrality of religion in the day-to-day life of Hispanic women, our understanding of the divine, and about ultimate meaning, plays a very important role in the process of giving significance to and valuing our experience. It is imperative for us, therefore, to comprehend better how religious understandings and practices impact our lives. In order to do this, we need to start from what we know, ourselves, our everyday surroundings and experiences.[16]

Such an emphasis becomes a means of empowerment for Latina women. While originating in the Latina social-religious reality, it is concerned not just with Latina women but with the well-being of the entire *comunidad*.

Another important developer of a Latina feminist theology of liberation is María Pilar Aquino, a professor at the University of San Diego. Critical of both Latin American liberation theology for its initial male-centeredness and of North American feminism for not addressing issues of race and class, she also distinguishes her approach from the *mujerista* theology of Isasi-Díaz. Like other Latina feminist theologians, Aquino, of Mexican descent, emphasizes the importance of the sociocultural context of Latinas, particularly the multilayered reality of oppression in which "theological reflection must take into account their multiple interests as believers, as poor, and as women, together with their religious and cultural values."[17] In the midst of multilayered oppression, Latina women live life in a holistic fashion in which their Christian faith permeates all aspects of life. A realistic understanding of these contexts, in which women are the primary actors for putting the gospel into practice, becomes an important ingredient in determining liberating practices for the present and the future. An important aspect of the context is the historical setting. Aquino states that

> For us indigenous women, *mestizas,* or Afro-Caribbean women, it is radically impossible to disregard the fact that we sprang from a conquered and colonized continent. Our ways of looking at life, understanding our own existence, and interpreting our faith experience are all indelibly marked by this fact, regardless of whether it results in the perpetuation of an oppressive reality or brings forth emancipating experiences.[18]

With this recognition, Aquino calls for Latina American feminist approaches that are engaged in a search for women's autonomy and human integrity within their particular social and historical contexts. Aquino sees women as both the subjects and the objects of a theological enterprise of hope and emancipatory praxis that engages the sociocultural and socioeconomic realities of Latinas/os in the United States and Latin America. As Latinas and Latin

American women do theology, they bring to the task their unique points of view as they continue to participate in the *comunidad*.

Another important voice in Latina feminist theology in particular and in Hispanic theology as a whole is Ana María Pineda, who was born in El Salvador and migrated to the United States. Pineda is a member of the Sisters of Mercy order, has worked in the earlier Encuentros, and for a number of years was the director of the Hispanic Ministries Program at the Catholic Theological Union in Chicago, before moving to Santa Clara University in California. Writing from the theological perspective of pastoral work, Pineda explores the connections between identity, culture, and faith. Additionally, in her theological work, Pineda draws on the religious and theological depth of the Latina/o in a way that speaks to the wider Christian church. One example of her ability to make connections is how Pineda explores a theology of welcome that is practiced within Hispanic communities, such as in the ritual of Las Posadas. Pineda states that through this annual Advent ritual, which re-creates the story of Mary and Joseph searching for a place for Jesus to be born, Latinas/os "ritually participate in being rejected and being welcomed, in slamming the door on the needy and opening it wide. They are in this way renewed in the Christian practice of hospitality, the practice of providing a space where the stranger is taken in and known as one who bears gifts."[19] In this way, persons who may themselves be strangers in the United States act out their popular religion with a deep awareness of the Christian faith's call for hospitality.

While numerous approaches taken by Latina theologians have found expression in *mujerista* and Latina feminist theologies, the differences that exist are partly a result of different perspectives and methodologies brought to the study of Latinas in their communities. Each approach addresses the roles race, ethnicity, and class play in the lives of their communities, as well as in the formal articulation of systematic theologies. However, the issues facing Latina women are so pressing and the stakes so high that differences in approaches may be an indication of the complexity of the issues faced in the struggle for the greater common good of Latina women in particular and the U.S. Hispanic community as a whole.

While other Latina theologians have emerged since the late 1960s, Aquino, Pineda, and Isasi-Díaz continue to influence the nature of Latina feminist theological discussions. These interdisciplinary discussions run in many directions. As noted earlier, the work of Ana María Díaz-Stevens is significant. Other Latina theologians and scholars of religion include Elizabeth Conde-Frazier, Leticia Guardiola, Rosa María Icaza, Daisy L. Machado, Loida Martell-Otero, Lara Medina, Nancy Pineda, and Jeanette Rodríguez.

## A Short History of the New Ecumenism

Like the rest of Christian theology, Latino/a theology can be studied by historically tracing the development of perspectives and traditions of theological interpretation. Nevertheless, due to the multiple connections and influences within Hispanic theologies, it is not yet clear if one can speak of definite schools of thought. Indeed, one of the hallmarks of Latino/a theologies is a certain type of ecumenical awareness and solidarity that crosses traditional denominational and interpretive boundaries. Reflecting an intentional effort to do theology together as the whole household of God in Christ, this new ecumenism of Latino/a theologies emerged in the late 1960s and the early 1970s, cognizant of the mixed histories of the U.S. National Council of Churches and the World Council of Churches. The new ecumenism of Hispanic theologies developed along alternative paths with a profound sense of the various Latino/a communities, to which many Hispanic theologians and scholars of religion felt an ongoing responsibility and commitment.

One place where this Latina/o theological ecumenism has been most apparent is within organizations that have taken on roles as de facto Hispanic ecumenical institutions. Two of these, the Hispanic Summer Program (HSP) and the Hispanic Theological Initiative (HTI), have their roots in an earlier organization known as the Fund for Theological Education (FTE). The HSP and the HTI are different but closely connected, particularly through an overlap of constituencies. In November 1993, the Pew Charitable Trusts, a major underwriter of the FTE, began to contemplate a change in the funding priorities, prompting a reevaluation of the structure and the funding of the HSP. Taking the initiative and leadership, Justo González invited accredited seminaries and schools of theology within the Association of Theological Schools to enter into a new type of partnership. At the reorganization meeting of the "new" HSP held at Princeton Theological Seminary in June 1995, the attending seminary representatives expressed their commitment to this new initiative in theological education in North America. While conceptually rooted in the HSP, the HTI is a distinct program that provides grants for Latinos/as pursuing degrees in theological education for ministry. Established in 1996, the HTI was funded by the Pew Charitable Trusts with the initial goal of increasing the number of Latino/a faculty in North American seminaries, schools of theology, and universities.

The Academy of Catholic Hispanic Theologians of the United States (ACHTUS) is one of the major ways Hispanic theology has become institutionalized. Although its regular membership is composed of Roman Catholic scholars, ACHTUS is also an important contributor to the new ecumenism through its work in the *Journal of Hispanic/Latino Theology*. Another organization that has played an important role within the Latino/a scholarly community is the Asociación para la Educación Teológica Hispana (AETH, Association of Hispanic Theological Education). One of AETH's primary goals is to encourage and strengthen theological education for Latinas/os. From its inception, AETH's membership has been open to all theological educators at all levels who are engaged in some way with Hispanic religious contexts, including historic mainline Protestants, Roman Catholics, and Pentecostals. However, the majority of its members are Protestant, and indeed AETH has been perceived by some as a Protestant equivalent of ACHTUS. AETH has established regional chapters and is a growing publisher of works in Hispanic theology, both in English and Spanish.

Finally, ad hoc consultations and meetings have figured prominently in the historical development of Latino/a theology and the new ecumenism. These include the October 1991 national ecumenical conference on Hispanic theology at Union Theological Seminary in New York City titled "La Fe Que Hace Justicia" ("Faith Doing Justice"). This conference prepared the ground for cooperative initiatives that were to follow, such as the interdenominational conference titled "Aliens in Jerusalem: The Emerging Theological Voice of Hispanic Americans," at Drew University in Madison, New Jersey, in 1994. A final joint ecumenical project is worth mentioning. The "Hispanic Churches in American Public Life" program examines the impact of Catholic, Pentecostal, historic mainline Protestant, and new religious communities on civic engagement in politics, education, business, social programs, and community activism in the Latino/a community. The two directors of this study are Jesse Miranda of the National Alliance of Evangelical Ministries (AMEN) and Virgilio Elizondo of the Catholic Mexican American Cultural Center (MACC) with Gastón Espinosa as project manager.

## A Concluding Reflection

The presence of Latinos/as in the United States is a long-standing one and is not simply or solely the story of recent arrivals. Therefore, from one perspective, we can speak of the origins of Hispanic theologies by focusing on the community understandings that developed in San Antonio or among the Hispanos of New Mexico or amid the rapidly developing Pentecostalism in the social borderland areas in the early twentieth century. Latino/a theologies are an expression both of an immigrant church and, in some areas, of long-established faith communities engulfed by larger religious, social, and political entities and forces. Clearly, local Hispanic theologies existed before there was something more formally designated as Latino/a theology, but telling a strict chronological story is difficult. Like subterranean roots and shoots, Hispanic theologies have multiple connections spreading in various directions.

## Chapter 4 Study Questions

### Definition Question

Define the following terms: *Tejano/a, mujerista* theology, *concilio,* Cursillo, PADRES, Las Hermanas

## Essay Questions

1. Explain the importance of and the relationship between (*a*) Antonio José Martínez and Jean Baptiste Lamy; (*b*) Juan L. Lugo and Francisco Olazabal; and (*c*) Leoncia Rosado and Santos Elizondo.

2. What events during the 1960s contributed to the articulation of Latina/o theologies?

3. What early theological perspectives were developed by Hispanic Catholic theologians in the 1960s and 1970s, and what contribution did they make to the initial articulation of Latino/a theologies? Also, what early theological perspectives were developed by Latina/o Protestant theologians in the 1960s and 1970s, and what contribution did they make to the initial articulation of Hispanic theologies?

4. How does sexism manifest itself, specifically within the church? What challenges do Latina women face that differ from the challenges of Euroamerican women? Explain several approaches developed by Latina women to address the sexism they face. What are some differences between Euroamerican feminism and Latina feminism? What can Euroamerican feminists learn from Latinas?

5. Describe ecumenism within Hispanic theologies. How has this ecumenism expressed itself institutionally?

## Chapter 5

# Popular Religion and Alternative Traditions

Within institutional churches, established faith communities communicate the historical teachings and dogmas of their traditions. While a Catholic priest or a Protestant minister attempts to guide the congregation toward the purity of the faith, shielding and protecting them from heresy, Latina/o parishioners, usually untrained in systematic theology, may perceive the workings of the Divine quite differently than their spiritual leaders do. In many cases, parishioners' understanding of God's movement within humanity clashes with what church officials designate as theological truth. This chapter explores these differences by addressing a broad range of views and issues held by the ordinary folk sitting in the pew that affect the development of the overall Latino/a theological perspective. Special attention will be given to the different ways in which Hispanic communities express their faith and spirituality, giving voice to varying types of religious realities among Latinos/as in the United States. Some are direct sources for Hispanic theology, while others remain indirect sources. Some of these expressions, as in the case of *curanderismo, espiritismo,* or Santería, are not necessarily considered Christian in their outlook or practice, yet they form parts of the U.S. Latina/o reality. Consequently, this chapter concentrates on Latino/a popular religion, the religiosity of Hispanics of faith, and non-Christian religious traditions, all of which inform, shape, and influence Latina/o theological perspectives.

## What Is Popular Religion?

Not limited to Christianity, popular religion is a phenomenon that appears in many different religious traditions and contexts. In a

117

Christian context, popular religion is primarily those religious expressions found outside the institutional church that address the more affective aspects of religious spirituality in a holistic way. This viewpoint equates popular religion with "unofficial religion" and often contrasts it with the "official religion" of a particular church establishment. However, such a strict division between "official" and "popular" religion is open to criticism. Oftentimes the designation of "official religion" gives an impression of respectability and normalcy to dominant institutional expressions of religiosity. From such a perspective, institutional or official religion becomes the standard against which popular religion is measured, and, therefore, by implication popular religion deviates from the norm. In such a comparison popular religion inevitably appears to be lacking or insufficient in some way.

Orlando Espín has focused much of his work on understanding Latino/a popular religion. As Espín states, "I insist that the people's faith be taken seriously as a true *locus theologicus* [religious social location] and not solely or mainly as a pastoral, catechetical problem."[1] In other words, Hispanic popular religion is not a curious, exotic, theologically backward, or even inferior oddity of an eccentric, voiceless monolithic people. Rather, Latino/a popular religion is a shorthand way to refer to a vibrant, creative, and fundamental theological and cultural mother lode of diverse groups of peoples. Through popular religion, Latina/o peoples voice and act out their own theological and spiritual understandings of the Divine, themselves, and the world. Espín further states that without an honest appreciation of what he refers to as "the faith of the people," one has an impoverished understanding of the entire Hispanic reality. Its importance is such that he sees at work

> an epistemology of suffering (and of living) for most Latinos. I am not blind to its numerous shortcomings. I do believe, however, that too much of the Latino universe is understood and shared through the popular religious network to have it easily dismissed (in Latino and Euro-American scholarship) as ultimately irrelevant.[2]

Several Hispanic theologians are beginning to follow the lead of Espín and others who emphasize that the religion of the people should not be automatically devalued but rather ought to be taken seriously on its own terms. Popular religion as "the faith of the people" includes the religious understandings and accompanying practices that flow from the majority and form part of their everyday lives, whether or not they are sanctioned formally by institutional, academic, or ecclesiastical authorities. Popular religion has profound theological significance, pastoral importance, and cultural relevance. Additionally, the religion of the people or community is not necessarily always and everywhere at odds with "official religion." Popular religion may or may not be consistent with institutional understandings of faith or religion. Indeed, many times popular religion has had such a force of appeal that institutional religion has been known to adjust itself accordingly by incorporating elements of popular religion into its formal faith.

When defining "popular religion," Espín insists that the term "popular" does not refer to popularity in the sense of a widespread practice of the religion. Instead, he focuses on the sociohistorical reality. The religion is "popular" because the disenfranchised are responsible for its creation, making it a religion of the marginalized. The emphasis is on *el pueblo* as opposed to the elite. Popular religion becomes the expression of the creativity of the popular classes.[3] It is dynamic. The majority of its practitioners are, not religious professionals, but the laity in the true sense of the word *populus*, "the people, the whole people." More specifically, the reality of Latina/o popular religion as the religion of the people contests any understanding of religion that sees a clear and neat division between what is sacred and profane, which is not to say that there is a confusion or even fusion between what is "holy" and what is not. Rather, it is to say that the "holy" (however understood) is present in the everyday.

## Popular Religion and Material Religion

Our consideration of popular religion begins with a brief review of what has been termed by scholars "material religion." The study of material religion is simply a focus on the physical objects and related themes associated with the practice of religion in particular communities. The material dimensions of religion include physical aids to religious practice such as candles, photographs and pictures, special mementos, printed music, statues and statuettes, palm leaves, prayer handkerchiefs, church buildings and special locations, medals, and prayer cards. Material religion includes whatever physical items are used within a religious community and viewed by that community as carrying some sort of significance. Colleen McDannell asserts that in the study of religious communities, some observers overlook the material dimension:

> People build religion into the landscape, they make and buy pious images for their homes, and they wear special reminders of their faith next to their bodies. Religion is more than a type of knowledge learned through reading holy books and listening to holy men. The physical expressions of religion are not exotic or eccentric elements that can be relegated to a particular community or a specific period of time.[4]

The material dimensions of religion are part of a particular community's everyday life and knowledge. The material elements of religion, one type of currency for popular religion, are vehicles for the expression and transmission of the religion of the people. By taking note of the material elements, we can better understand the popular religion of a community.

### Hispanic Popular Religion

With these theoretical considerations as a base, we can now turn our full attention to Latino/a popular religion. In one sense, Hispanic popular religion is something that has always been there; it is not a new invention or concept. Nonetheless, in recent years it has been specifically recognized, studied, and discussed. Latina/o popular religion, religiosity, or spirituality, as it is sometimes referred to in Protestant contexts, incorporates discernible practices that may or may not use particular objects for communicating with God and the spiritual realm. Also, it assists in the Latino/a understanding and interpretation of ordinary life, both its joys and struggles. Through Hispanic popular religion the so-called natural and supernatural realms become closely intertwined.

Hispanic popular religion may be public or private, practiced by individuals, families, or whole communities. In many contexts, women, and especially older women, are the de facto community elders serving as facilitators, leaders, innovators, educators, and keepers of the popular religion. These women, in turn, pass on what is important to succeeding generations of women: mother to daughter, grandmother to granddaughter, aunt to niece. In such community settings, the *abuelitas* (grandmothers) become the wisdom figures for all, not just for the immediate family. Since Hispanic popular religiosity is not restricted to any particular economic class, it appears anywhere and everywhere. We encounter it in homes, during worship in church buildings, or at makeshift sites, such as roadside memorials to those lost in automobile accidents. Latinos/as bring their important personal devotions and wisdom sayings into all circumstances of their lives.

An important characteristic of Hispanic popular religiosity is its grassroots practices that inform and shape theology and in turn affect devotional and spiritual practices. Another feature is that it draws heavily upon indigenous Amerindian and African beliefs and practices, depending on specific local contexts. Since popular religion is a dynamic reality, these various sources are worked and reworked within specific contexts. Examples of expressions of Latina/o popular Catholicism include devotional practices such as the celebrations of feast days of patron saints, family devotions and the keeping of a home altar, pilgrimages, and special devotions to a particular saint.

Historically, the formal exploration of popular religion within the field of Hispanic theology first occurred within the Catholic context. Theologian C. Gilbert Romero described popular religion from within the Hispanic Catholic system as "a form of popular devotion among Hispanics based more on indigenous cultural elements than on official Roman Catholic worship patterns."[5] Jeanette Rodríguez, in her study of Mexican American women and their devotion to the Virgin of Guadalupe, defines popular religiosity as a complex folk faith system that consists of "spontaneous expressions of faith which have been celebrated by the people over a considerable period of time." They are spontaneous in that people celebrate because they want to and not because they have been mandated by the official hierarchy, in this case the Roman Catholic tradition. Rodríguez sees Hispanic popular religiosity rooted in sixteenth-century Catholicism as a distinct identity and an authentic expression of Roman Catholicism. Additionally, Rodríguez views popular religiosity as a "source of power, dignity, and acceptance" for the "poor and marginalized." As such, popular religiosity was conceived, not for static speculation, but as an encouragement for people to put their faith into practice and, in turn, narrate, act out, and represent "the people's own history."[6]

María Pilar Aquino asserts that a purposeful communal decision has been made in order for popular religion, or the faith of the people, to be central in the daily life experiences of Hispanics. Aquino argues that U.S. Latino/a theology must honor the communal choice and

> take *this* faith and not another as the starting point for theological reflection as organizing principle of our theologizing. It could be argued that, as understandings of the faith, all theologies presuppose and imply faith. But what Latino/a theology emphasizes is that the faith of the people is the faith lived and expressed primarily and fundamentally within the concrete reality of popular Catholicism.[7]

What Aquino says about U.S. Latino/a theology and popular Catholicism can also be applied to the reality of popular Hispanic Protestantism.

Another Latino theologian who has explored the richness of Hispanic popular religion in a Catholic context is Roberto Goizueta. Like others, Goizueta notes the vital role popular religion plays in the historical, cultural, social, and congregational contexts of Latinos/as. In considering this central function, Goizueta states:

> What remains unchallenged and often taken for granted is, first, the fundamentally sacramental character of the U.S. Hispanic way of life, wherein physical existence is seen as intrinsically related to the supernatural, transcendent realm of the sacred. Secondly, U.S. Hispanic theologians assume the crucial significance of this sacramentality for the theological task, i.e., any theology done from the perspective of U.S. Hispanics cannot ignore this fact and still remain rooted in the experience of U.S. Hispanics.[8]

The focus on popular religion, on the faith of the people, challenges U.S. Latino/a theology to put its principles into practice by always going back to the community.

From a historical perspective Hispanic Catholic explorations of popular religion or religiosity prompted the formal study of Hispanic Protestant popular religion. Some of the key features identified in popular Latina/o Catholicism, such as the characteristics that Jeanette Rodríguez articulates, also seem to be present in Latino/a Protestant popular religion. Nevertheless, while many Catholic Latina/o scholars assert the importance of popular religion as a source of theology and revelation within Latino/a popular Catholicism, Hispanic Protestants do not make a similar claim about the centrality of popular religion within their denominations. This is not to say that there are no popular religious devotions and practices within Hispanic Protestantism, that the impulse of popular spirituality is somehow muted, nor that popular religion does not inform Hispanic Protestant theology. Rather, it is to acknowledge the distinctive settings of the two traditions and Protestants' own understandings of being both Latino/a and Christian. Within Protestant contexts are several additional distinctive elements, including the heritage of the Protestant Reformation and the central role of the Word of God, both read in the Bible and spoken through sermons and testimonies.

The almost sacramental emphasis on the Word strongly influences the nature of Latino/a Protestant popular religion. Furthermore, among Hispanic Protestants, especially in those communities influenced by Pentecostalism, a profound emphasis on the Holy Spirit and the experience of the Spirit shapes the expressions and practices of the faith of the people. Added to this mix is the historical aversion of many Hispanic Protestants to overt elements of Latino/a popular Catholicism, specifically praying to saints or lighting candles. These factors combine to produce different expressions of popular religion, even while some underlying shared characteristics of Protestants and Catholics can be identified.

Elizabeth Conde-Frazier perceives Hispanic Protestant spirituality as displaying four prominent characteristics that serve as both interrelated expressions and resources, namely, doctrine, discipline, liturgy, and personal action.[9] Given that Latina/o Protestant popular religiosity or spirituality reflects its Protestant context, alternative material symbols emerge that are deemed theologically acceptable. These might be a plain, empty cross in a church sanctuary or a verse from the Bible in a prominent place in the church building or, interestingly enough, the common portrayal of a northern-European-looking Jesus. Beyond these material expressions Hispanic Protestant popular religion is verbally expressed and acted on through *testimonios* (testimonies), daily devotions, Christian service, prayer vigils, *coritos* or *estribillos* (choruses), and community worship. Within all of these material dimensions the study and exposition of the Bible plays an important role.

## Alternative Expressions and the Faiths of the People

As previously noted, popular religion is a widespread phenomenon that finds expression in many settings. If, as has been suggested, U.S. Latino/a theology uses as a major starting point and resource the lived faith of the people, then it must be admitted that the faith of the U.S. Hispanic peoples takes on a wide variety of forms and expressions. Not all U.S. Latinos/as are Christians. Other Hispanic institutional and grassroots religious practices and devotions do not fit under the rubrics of either Roman Catholicism or a particular expression of Protestantism. Some of these draw more heavily and directly upon indigenous Amerindian traditions or African sources. These alternatives are also manifestations and expressions of the grassroot faiths of Hispanic peoples. Through these other ways, Hispanics find routes of knowledge and understanding, pursue ways toward health and healing, and find accessible paths that furnish a sense of holistic balance in life.

Some of the better-known alternative expressions and practices include *curanderismo* (a Mexican American path of folk healing and medicine), different types of *espiritismo* (spiritism), and Cuban Santería. In addition to the above options, a growing number of Latinos/as in the United States are affiliated with Judaism and Islam, joining the historically small number of U.S. Hispanic members of those traditions. Furthermore, some Latinas/os connect with several traditions simultaneously and see no contradiction or mutual exclusion in their multiple allegiances. This last occurrence has a direct impact on Latino/a Catholic and Protestant popular religion.

Many persons in Hispanic communities are in touch with all or part of these alternatives and still view themselves as members of Christian communities. Indeed, they view these multiple avenues as complementary and acceptable combinations for faith and life. For example, Carlos Cardoza-Orlandi relates the story of a Dominican family in New York City who were members of a Protestant church Cardoza-Orlandi pastored. When their child was gravely sick, the family asked the Protestant congregation for prayer and visited a *santero* (healer). The child regained health. Cardoza-Orlandi relates, "In a moment of confusion and surprise, I asked the father, 'Whose miracle is it? Is it your *orisha?* Is it Jesus Christ?' The father, puzzled by the question, looked at me and said, 'It was God, pastor, it was God. It is your problem to decide whose miracle it is, not my problem.' "[10]

## Curanderismo

Mexican American or Chicano/a *curanderismo* is a dynamic and fluid combination of indigenous Mesoamerican and Spanish popular religious outlooks and orientations to the physical world and spiritual realms that finds a particular expression in healing and health practices. The name finds its roots in the Spanish verb *curar,* meaning "to heal, cure." Its origins predate the conquest of Mexico by the Spaniards. *Curanderismo* has developed into an extensive health-care system that assumes sickness has a natural or supernatural cause and therefore may require a natural or supernatural cure, or even a combination of both. Luis León describes *curanderismo* as

> a wide variety of community-based healing movements organized around somatic techniques of power; from home remedies such as herbal teas and ointments, to spiritual or symbolic open heart surgery, and other spiritual operations conducted to heal cancer for example. Social ills and family problems are also addressed in *curanderismo.*[11]

*Curanderismo* is an extensive collection of rituals and customs, explanatory stories and myths, and a complex symbolic system that seeks to understand life on its own terms. The practice of *curande-*

*rismo* is quite extensive within Mexican American and Chicano/a communities in the United States, whether they are in Los Angeles, south Texas, Dallas, Chicago, or New York City.

*Curanderos/as* (both men and women) are specialized healers who are from the people but also are recognized as having received a special gift (*el dón*) for healing. The healers inherit and pass on many of the ancient ways and knowledge, including the remedies for a variety of sicknesses, physical complaints, and injuries. Although to the casual outside observer this health system appears to be composed of independent agents, each healer is really part of a sophisticated alternative worldview with a hierarchy of healers.

Reflecting the different approaches to healing within *curanderismo*, the major categories of healers include first the *señora/ abuela* (a woman, a grandmother), then the *yerbero* (herbalist), the *sobador* (a type of massage therapist), and the *partera* (midwife). The final referral is made to a *curandera* or *curandero*. As the ultimate specialist, a *curandero/a* is the healer who can treat *mal puesto*, illnesses caused by an evil spell or a hex, usually as the result of the work of a *brujo* or *bruja* (witch). Anyone who suspects that he or she is a victim of *brujería* (witchcraft) will seek a *curandero/a* for help. Spiritual interpretation is important to the people who come to *curanderos/as;* thus, it is not uncommon for the local Roman Catholic priest to be the second choice of a person for consultation. Catholic pastoral workers vary in their attitudes toward *curanderismo,* whereas widespread opposition exists among Latino/a Protestants against *curanderismo* as the work of the devil.

The way *curanderismo* treats illness and healing is evidence of a complex interplay between the material and immaterial worlds. Illness, *mal de ojo* (the evil eye), and *susto* (loss of spirit and deep profound discouragement and hopelessness) are considered afflictions on several levels: material, spiritual, and mental.[12] The physical symptoms of an illness are often believed to have supernatural or spiritual causes. The *curandera* may prescribe an herbal remedy or conduct a religious ritual. The cure may employ a type of countermagic, herbal remedies, potions, or rituals, depending on the illness, and may use ordinary religious symbols, such as the crucifix, rosary, or holy pictures.

## Espiritismo

*Espiritismo*, also known as Kardecism or spiritism, was considered a scientific movement when it became the rage throughout Latin America during the nineteenth century. It originated in France, founded by an engineer named Hippolyte Rivail, who wrote under the pseudonym Allan Kardec. His writings spread throughout Europe and North America during the latter part of that century. Around 1856, *espiritismo* appeared in the Spanish and French Caribbean and in Central and South America, including Portuguese Brazil. As this movement took root in different nation states, cultures, and regional groups, it developed unique manifestations. The *espiritismo* practiced in Puerto Rico differed considerably from that practiced in Mexico or Argentina or Brazil. In fact, even within the same country, different social classes or races practiced *espiritismo* differently. Class and race deviations affected the practice's cultural content.

Not originally considered a religious movement, *espiritismo* was a combination of scientism, progressivist ideology, Christian morality, and mysticism. Rivail hoped to subject the spiritual world to human observation and then, from these observations, develop a positive science. As the movement spread through the Western Hemisphere, it generally took the form of small groups of mediums assisting their clients in communicating with the spirits of the dead. A group of believers would gather at someone's home, sit around a table, make specific invocations, fall into a trance, and allow a medium to become a bridge to the spirit world. They insisted their practice was not ritualistic; rather, it was pure experimental science in which the practitioner verified the experience by speaking with the dead through the medium, who provided immediate solutions to what ailed them. Hence they were called *científicos* (scientists).

Among the first to be attracted to this movement were the middle and upper classes, who founded periodicals to discuss and promote *espiritismo*. It spread from the Creole middle and upper classes to other urban groups of less power and privilege, eventually reaching the rural countryside. The poorer segments of society turned to *espiritismo* for help and guidance with the struggle of daily life, specifically in areas of material deprivation and health problems. In the Spanish Caribbean, specifically in Cuba and Puerto Rico, which were still under Spain's colonial yoke, *independentistas* (freedom fighters) found in *espiritismo* an alternative to the Catholic Church, which they perceived to be in league with the Spanish monarchy. With the suppression of political organizations that challenged the colonizer's authority, *espiritismo* served as a political space for liberal ideas to flourish.

Among the lower classes and rural poor who considered themselves Catholic even though they seldom visited a church or a priest, the practice of *espiritismo* did not appear to conflict with their religious worldview. Others, including those who objected to the church's conservative dogma, found in *espiritismo* a progressive ideology that advocated science, modernity, and democracy. Still others found a connection to their pre-Christian past of ancestral spirits that encouraged different religious practices historically repressed by the official church, like *curanderismo* and Santería. In most cases, *espiritismo* absorbed into its practice elements of Spanish folk religion, specifically herbalism, African religious practices, and Amerindian healing practices. In short, *espiritismo* became one of the elements Hispanics used to resist assimilation by the dominant culture.[13]

## Santería

Santería is a religious expression whose roots are African. In reality, several religious-cultural structures, all originating in Africa, live within the overall Latino/a culture. They are the *palo monte* of Congo origin; the *regla Arará* of Ewe-fon origin; the Abakuá Secret Society containing Ejagham, Efik, Efut, and other Calabar roots; and the *regla de Ocha* of Yoruba. The latter, in the form of Santería, is the most popular among Hispanics. Santería, the "worship of saints," also known as the Lucumi religion, is the product of a religious space created by those who were subordinated to the arbitrary exercise of power imposed by Catholic Spaniards upon their African slaves. Santería's components consist of European Christianity expressed as a Spanish folk Catholicism, African *orisha* worship as practiced by the Yoruba of Nigeria, and nineteenth-century Kardecan spiritualism as popularized in the Caribbean.

Santería recognizes the existence of a supreme God. Olodumare, the supreme being, is a transcendent world force or "current" known as *ashe*. This sacred energy becomes the power, grace, blood, and life force of Olodumare and nature, embracing all mystery, all secret power, and all divinity. *Ashe* is absolute, illimitable, pure power, nondefinite, and not definable. *Ashe* is a nonanthropomorphic form of theism.[14] *Orishas* are quasi deities serving as protectors and guides for every human being, regardless of the individual's acknowledgment of the religion. They were the first to walk the earth, and from them all humans are descended. Hence, the *orishas* are the first ancestors. Created by Olodumare, they are the specific parts, forces, or manifestations within Olodumare. *Orishas* govern certain parts of the universe, for Olodumare is an absentee ruler. Because the universe is so vast, Olodumare has no time to become directly involved in the affairs of humans. Consequently, when an animal is sacrificed to Babalu-Aye (who governs the sphere of illness), the practitioner is worshiping the part of Olodumare exemplified in this particular *orisha*. Olodumare created the *orishas* to allow the divine form and will to be manifested to humanity via nature. Although the Yoruba system lists over seventeen hundred *orishas*, only a few became renowned within the Latino/a culture.

*Babalawo*, the "Father of mystery," a high priest in Santería, is not to be confused with a *santero/a*, who serves as priest. Each *santero/a* is consecrated to a specific *orisha*, becoming the representative of that specific divine force, which reflects the era when the inhabitants of each Yoruba city-state served as "priest" to a sole *orisha*, the one who protected that individual city. The elaborate belief system of the Yoruba became part of the Latin American culture when colonial Cuba began to import African slaves to develop the urban centers and work the mines and sugar estates. These Africans were not ignoble savages captured in the slavers' nets; instead, most were patricians and priests who had rebelled at the ascendancy of new rulers, specifically in the kingdoms of Benin and Dahomey and the city-states of Yoruba. The vicissitudes of monarchic power struggles resulted in those opposing the new hegemony becoming enslaved and expatriated, especially within the Yoruba city-states. Tragically torn from their ordered religious life, Africans had no time to ponder a spiritual response to their tragedy. They were compelled to adjust their belief system to the immediate challenges presented by colonial Cuba. This transition created a nascent state for Santería, where a Yoruban ethos survived by manifesting itself through Spanish Catholicism.

Santería was legally recognized as a legitimate religion on June 11, 1992, when the United States Supreme Court ruled that the practitioners of Santería had a constitutional right to sacrifice animals in connection with their rituals. Although it is impossible to document the exact number of *orisha* worshipers, some scholars estimate that about five million persons in the United States are identified with *orisha* worship.[15] Even when Latinos/as reject Santería and insist solely on their Christianity, they still may observe the adage, "Tenemos que respetar los Santos" (We have to respect the Saints). Clearly, Santería can be classified as a "popular religion" and, as such, cannot be ignored.

### Christianity vs. Curanderismo, Espiritismo, and Santería?

Due to persecution, many practitioners of *curanderismo, espiritismo,* and Santería maintained an outward appearance of belief in the dominant social religion (in most cases Roman Catholicism). For example, *orishas* in Santería can appear as male or female: Changó (the male warrior) may appear as St. Barbara and Obatalá (the father of the *orishas*) as Our Lady of Mercy. Over time, the official faith traditions began to share quite similar sacred spaces with these unorthodox religious expressions. Some in the Catholic Church see these expressions as an authentic search on the part of believers to grasp the reality of the Divine; they view the priest's role to be one of gently correcting practitioners of the unofficial religion so that they can enter the official faith of the church. Others voice harsher criticism, claiming that *curanderismo, espiritismo,* and Santería adulterate the purity of Catholicism.[16] For Protestants, specifically Pentecostals, these religious expressions represent satanic cults. For those attempting to assimilate to the Euroamerican culture, they become a source of embarrassment, appearing both backward and primitive.

Christians usually portray *curanderismo, espiritismo,* and Santería as the dialectical product of an indigenous belief system and Iberian Roman Catholicism, in which a "confused" and idiosyncratic merging of the traditions occurred. Throughout the Americas, the phenomenon of cultural groups simultaneously participating in two diverse, if not contradictory, religious systems is widespread. Christianity, when embraced under the context of colonialism or slavery, creates a threat to the indigenous beliefs of the marginalized group, which, to resist annihilation, must adapt to the new dominant religion. For example, unique hybrids developed as the religious traditions of Yoruba slaves took root on Caribbean soil. The vitality of the Yoruba belief system found expression through Catholicism as Voudou in Haiti, Shango in Trinidad and Venezuela, Candomble in Brazil, Kumina in Jamaica, and Santería in Cuba.

The official Catholic or Protestant church places itself above the "unofficial" popular religion of the people and seeks to reduce *curanderismo, espiritismo,* and Santería to the sphere of ignorance and impurity. The official religion exercises power in the way it "sees" the unofficial religion from the margins. "We" (read official religion) operate from doctrinal knowledge; "they" (read unofficial religions) are confused. "Our" beliefs are pure; "theirs" are impure. "Our" task is to correct their confusion. Seeing the Other as "confused" relegates them to an inferior social position while elevating official religion to an authoritative location from which paternal correcting can originate.

Yet followers of these unorthodox religious expressions do not consider themselves "confused" in their beliefs. For example, it is not uncommon for practitioners of Santería who were raised in homes where this religious expression flourished to consider themselves as good and faithful Catholics. Such persons may have been initiated into Santería, yet they still have attended parochial school, have participated in receiving first communion, have been confirmed by the church, and practice weekly confession. Nevertheless, at night crowds would still visit their home to consult the *orishas.* In these cases the participants have no internal "confusion" as to the difference between what was done at the Catholic church down the street and what was done in their home. Different practices take place in different settings. For the participant of Santería, the rituals they practice could not be revealed to the *curas y monjas* (priest and nuns) because *they* are "confused" about how God works. In most cases, *santeras/os* do not renounce their Catholic faith. Many declare, "Somos católicos romanos, y apostólicos, creemos a nuestra manera" (We are apostolic Roman Catholics; we believe in our own way). While both religions share the same sacred space, there is no confusion among those practicing Santería, or *curanderismo* and *espiritismo* for that matter, concerning the differences between them and *los curas y monjas*.

Are *curanderismo, espiritismo,* and Santería popular forms of Christianity? Some Latino/a theologians who advocate the exploration of popular religion believe these three religious manifestations of the people are not Christian; that is, they are different from Christianity. Nevertheless, is a Christian categorization needed for them? They have reached sufficient maturity to discard the synthetic label. While such a label may help elucidate their genesis, it hinders understanding them as a present-day transcultural phenomenon. As genuinely popular religious expressions, rooted in the violent contact of separate religious faiths, they contribute to a U.S. Latino/a theological view on their own terms. As their own defined sacred space, the truth content of *curanderismo, espiritismo,* and Santería can neither be comprehended nor communicated through traditional Christian religious and theological models but must be recognized as a unique phenomenon bound to cultural life through its historical development. They need to be understood on their own terms.

## Judaism and Latino/a Jews

The impact of medieval and early modern Iberia upon the Americas is undisputed among historians. Therefore any discussion of Hispanic Jews in the United States must profile the significance of the Jewish *conversos* (converts). Throughout much of the Middle Ages, Iberia, the region now consisting of Spain and Portugal, was the home to a large and culturally thriving Jewish community. As the Christian kingdoms of Iberia embarked on a campaign of *reconquista* (reconquest) of lands under Moorish (Muslim) control, Jews within those lands often faced conversion, expulsion, or worse. Many tried to escape persecution in Spain by going to the "Indies" (the Americas). Some changed their names to circumvent the royal decree that Jews could not immigrate to the new lands. Nevertheless, the Inquisition pursued them into the New World.

The records of the Inquisition in New Spain (Mexico), Peru, and New Granada (Colombia, Venezuela, and Panama) show the surnames of *conversos* who were tried for relapsing into Judaism. Several *conversos* fled to the north into what is now California, Texas, New Mexico, and Arizona, where many of their descendants still live. For descendants of these exiles from Latin America, Judaism has been an uninterrupted faith, while for many others it has been a well-kept but persistent secret in family histories.

In recent years, particularly in the U.S. Southwest, Hispanics who have followed Catholicism for generations are investigating their possible family heritage as Jews from Spain or Portugal. Many times clues in the popular religiosity of a family prompt searches for roots and a spiritual home. For instance, a particular dialect of Spanish used in devotions is discovered to be actually Ladino, the common language of Sephardic Jews. Or Latino/a members of a family realize that they have never owned a crucifix despite their tradition of Roman Catholicism. Some families have the tradition of never eating shellfish or pork. A grandmother might teach her daughters to light candles on Friday nights. Another person remembers that a grandfather may have had the habit of going off to a remote location with other men for weekly prayers. There are reports of grandmothers telling a granddaughter that the family had always been Jewish.

Family rites, rituals, stories, objects, all the elements of popular religiosity, are the clues that some Latinas/os are following to rediscover their Jewish heritage. Once the family secret becomes known, some Hispanics have decided to lay aside the religion in which they were raised in favor of the religion of their ancestors. As they seek a new place in their community, these Latino/a converts find opposition from Jews who believe that they are not authentically Jewish, while some Christians charge them with abandoning their faith.

In addition to those reconnecting with their Jewish heritage, other Latin American communities have been openly Jewish and have always struggled as a marginalized people. Some of their members have come to the United States and become part of Hispanic communities, bringing their religion and popular religiosity with them. For example, throughout its history Cuba has been a major site for settlement of Jews who were refugees from persecution. Spanish and Portuguese Jews arrived either with the conquering Spaniards as *conversos* and crypto-Jews (secret Jews) or in later migrations from the island of Curaçao, the center of Sephardic culture in the Caribbean. Later, in 1898, as a consequence of the United States military presence on the islands of Puerto Rico and Cuba, there was a migration of U.S. American Jews. Some European Jews migrated to Latin America prior to World War II as they sought to escape the coming Holocaust in Europe, although in 1937 a ship called the *St. Louis,* carrying 937 Jewish refugees from Germany, was turned away from both Cuba and the United States. Today, a large Cuban synagogue composed of Cuban Jews (known as Jubans by the Miami exilic community) exists in Miami Beach. Throughout Latin America, small Jewish communities were supplemented by later arrivals from Eastern Europe after World War II. Many Jews from Eastern Europe settled in Argentina, Bolivia, Brazil, Colombia, and Mexico, bringing their cultural influences to the Latin American mix.

## *Islam*

An additional manifestation of the faith of the Latino/a people is Islam, which includes both historical echoes and the more recent embracing of Islam by Hispanics in the United States. The formal presence of Islam in Iberia, lasting nearly eight hundred years, left a profound and sometimes forgotten influence on Spanish and Portuguese culture. This imprint was transferred to the Americas with migration and is an element in the *mestizaje* of Latin America and the United States. Spanish literature, music, and thought are filled with African and Islamic themes. In fact, a Moorish influence persists in Mexican American *curanderismo.*

Just as some Hispanics are exploring the possibility of Jewish roots, others are finding a connection with their Muslim heritage from Spain. In recent years a small but growing number of Latinos/as are converting to Islam. According to a 1999 article in the *Los Angeles Times,* an increasing number of Hispanics have been embracing Islam during the past two decades.[17] Sizable communities of Latino/a Muslims exist in Chicago, Los Angeles, Miami, New York City, and Newark, New Jersey. Estimates of Latino/a Muslims in 1999 vary widely from a low of fifteen thousand to over one hundred thousand. New York City's El Barrio serves as home to Alianza Islamica, a mosque and community center attracting Puerto Ricans, Dominicans, and Panamanians. Puerto Rican converts to Islam who wanted to express their faith and their culture founded the mosque in 1975.

## Conclusion

All the theological perspectives of Latinos/as cannot be classified solely as Christian. In many cases, they compose a mixture of Christianity and other religious traditions, ones usually opposed by the "official" religious institutions. Yet, for the disenfranchised, these religious expressions attempt to provide an immediate remedy for the struggle of daily life, a life laid heavy with institutionalized oppression. A common feature of the religion coming from marginalized spaces is the perception of a world that experiences a vibrant interaction between what has been called the natural and supernatural. Although at times at odds with the official orthodox faith of Christian institutions, popular religious expressions become a sacred space by which to understand God's movement in people's lives. As such, any exploration of Hispanic theological perspectives requires an understanding of the interaction between "official" and "unofficial" religion.

## Chapter 5 Study Questions

### Definition Question

Define the following terms: popular religion, material religion, *locus theologicus,* faith of the people, *curanderismo, espiritismo,* Santería, *el dón, conversos.*

## Essay Questions

1. What are the differences between popular religion and the official religion of the church? What tensions are created because of these differences? Do Euroamerican churches have expressions of popular religion? If so, give some examples. What are some of the material dimensions of Euroamerican religions?

2. What role do women have in Latino/a popular religion? From which sources does Hispanic popular religion usually draw? Where is it practiced? Who participates in it?

3. How is Latino/a Catholic popular religion different from or similar to Hispanic Protestant popular spirituality?

4. What are some of the religious practices of *curanderismo, espiritismo,* and Santería? How do these religious expressions conflict with or complement Latino/a Protestantism and Catholicism?

5. Are *curanderismo, espiritismo,* and Santería Christian? Are they satanic? Are they the primitive religious expressions of a confused people? Explain your answer.

6. How did the Jewish and Islamic presence develop among U.S. Latinos/as? What impact did they have, and are they having, on Hispanic theological perspectives?

## Chapter 6

# Emerging Theological Concepts

Theology, as a reflection of the experiences of a specific community, is a vibrant and fluid discipline. Theological perspectives of the last century, or last millennium, will forever be rooted in the prior commitments and thoughts of those expressing that theology. Theologies of the past were not immune from the ideological tendencies of the era from which they sprang nor from the socioeconomic status of the one (usually male) writing the theology. Because those theologians constructed their "studying of God" from within their own cultures, biases, customs, and traditions, they were more apt to provide us with information as to who they were rather than who God is. While these past theologies may be informative, a connection with the present community may be lost due to the passage of time or a shift in culture.

We find ourselves at the start of a new millennium, cognizant that the Latino/a community of today is different in many respects from the Hispanic community of the last fifty or even twenty-five years. While this present generation of Hispanics still faces many of the old struggles, Latinos/as of today exist in a different world than did their parents or grandparents. If theology is indeed a grassroots process tied to the local faith community, then it stands to reason that as the social situations of Hispanics change, new theological perspectives will develop to give voice to those changes.

If theology is to remain an active, relevant component of the lives of Hispanics, revealing how the Deity makes Godself known to a people, then theological views must be updated to include the changing ethos of Latinas/os. Gustavo Gutiérrez, often credited for being among the first to articulate Latin American liberation theology, said it best during the 1996 conference of the American Academy of Religion in New Orleans. He said he did not believe in

137

liberation theology; rather, he believed in Jesus Christ. And while all theologies are born to die, a theological voice from the margins will always exist. Specifically, he wrote,

> In the past few years we have been witnesses to a series of economic, political, cultural, and ecclesiastical events, both in the international arena and in Latin America. This might cause one to think that important aspects of the time that birthed and developed the reflection of what we call liberation theology since the late 1960s have come to an end. Undoubtedly, the convulsive events within that period of Latin America were stimulating and creative, while at the same time, tense and conflicted. Faced with new situations, many of the statements and discussions of that period of time do not respond to today's challenges.[1]

This chapter will endeavor to peer into the immediate future by examining the changing ethos of today's Latina/o community. It does not list every conceivable challenge the Latino/a community will face. Obviously, many Hispanics will insist that some of the items mentioned are not as important as others that were not included. This chapter is not a book of prophecies, nor does it aspire to chart the course Hispanic theologies should take. Rather, based on the changes occurring within the Latino/a community, we attempt to identify the emerging perspectives that are being constructed to meet these new challenges.

## A New Ecumenism?
## Catholic/Protestant Dialogue and Dilemma

One of the simultaneously exciting, challenging, and sometimes frustrating features of Hispanic theology is the conversations and collaborations between Roman Catholics and Protestants. Latino/a Protestants and Catholics are reading each others' works and cooperating in some local ministry efforts in different parts of the country. The very fact that any of this occurs at all is remarkable, given the checkered history of contacts between Protestants and Catholics in Latin America and the United States. This fluid reality is seen by some as an expression of a new ecumenism that is developing in the U.S. Hispanic community. To date, the relationship between Hispanic Catholics and Protestants has primarily taken the form of formal dialogue on common matters of theology and pastoral concerns. In several conferences, Catholics and Protestants have sought together to further explicate and understand Latina/o theology. For example, in 1991 a symposium hosted by the Mexican American Program at the Perkins School of Theology in Dallas, Texas, focused on the five hundredth anniversary of the *encuentro* (encounter) of 1492 between Europeans and Amerindians. Catholic and Protestant theologians from the United States and Latin America presented papers on the subject. Another important interdenominational consultation was "Aliens in Jerusalem: The Emerging Theological Voice of Hispanic Americans," which was held in 1994 at Drew University in Madison, New Jersey. This ecumenical conference (whose papers appear in the volume *Hispanic/Latino Theology: Challenge and Promise*) examined three broad areas of Latino/a theology: sources (the Bible, history, cultural memory, literature, oral tradition, Pentecostalism); contexts (urban communities, the experience of exile, the complex case of Puerto Ricans, feminist perspectives); and examples (*mujerista* theology, popular religiosity).

A great deal of theological discussion, influence, and cross-fertilization of ideas and perceptions has taken place, particularly as Latinos/as have sought to carve out a theological space for themselves within the church in the United States. Individuals like Virgilio Elizondo (a Catholic priest) are a resource for Hispanic Protestant theologians, while, simultaneously, Protestant minister Justo González is a source for the theological work of Latina/o Catholics. Catholics María Pilar Aquino and Jeanette Rodríguez are engaged in cooperative common projects on Latina feminist theology with Protestants Daisy Machado and Nora Lozano-Díaz. And today, with a foundation of at least three generations of contemporary Hispanic theological scholarship, senior Hispanic scholars are mentoring younger Latinas/os. This mentoring takes place across traditional denominational barriers as Catholics mentor Protestants and Protestants, Catholics.

One result of this new ecumenism is that a number of collaborative institutions have been established in which Latinos/as engage

each other across denominational boundaries. One such collaborative institution is the Hispanic Summer Program, the graduate
seminary program that is hosted by a different seminary each
summer, as well as the Hispanic Theological Initiative, housed at
Princeton Theological Seminary, both of which owe much to the
vision and leadership of Methodist Justo González. Another important collaborative effort is the groundbreaking work of the
Program for the Analysis of Religion among Latinos (PARAL)
at the City University of New York under the leadership of
Roman Catholic Anthony Stevens-Arroyo. Ongoing dialogue with
a broader scholarly scope takes place within the U.S. Latino/a
Religion, Culture, and Society Group, which is part of the American Academy of Religion. These institutional expressions have
proven to be highly successful and richly productive centers of
new ecumenism between Protestants and Catholics. This ecumenism is broader than is usually realized, as scholars of religion,
both Latino/a and non-Hispanic, without any particular religious
commitment participate in exploring Hispanic religion and culture.

   Although the new ecumenism between Latina/o Catholics and
Protestants is indeed remarkable, it has not occurred without struggle, disappointments, and ongoing frustrations. Though commonly
discussed in private, these frustrations are rarely brought into the
open for ecumenical discussion and resolution. They remain part
of the present and future challenges of Latino/a theology. A common concern among both U.S. Latino/a Catholics and Protestants
is deeply held doctrinal differences. Nevertheless, many Protestants and Catholics share a desire for a greater and more effective
Christian witness within U.S. Hispanic communities.

   One area of challenge is that cordial and collaborative relationships between Hispanic Catholics and Protestants are more
common among theologians, scholars, and denominational officials than among people at the congregational level. Among the
grassroots faith communities, mutual suspicion persists, as old
stereotypes of "heretic" and "papist" continue to wield their
power. Attitudes formed in the colonial period and during the nineteenth century continue to be drawn upon. One way this has been
and continues to be addressed is through relationships formed by
theological students preparing for the ministry who participate in
initiatives like the Hispanic Summer Program.

However, even with years of building trust, misunderstandings are still great. For example, a continuing sore point for Protestants is the reference to them as members of "sects" by some Catholics. Within Protestant contexts, the term "sects" has a specialized meaning, referring only to non-Christian groups. A related, but distinct, concern is that Hispanic Protestants are not monolithic, but at times some Catholics view Protestants as an undifferentiated whole. There are many profound and long-standing historical, theological, and cultural differences at work in the Protestant traditions.

An ongoing concern of many Latino/a Catholics regarding Protestants falls under the label of "sheep stealing," that is, the proselytizing or conversion of Catholics to Protestantism. This practice reflects a lingering anti-Catholicism among some Protestants. Furthermore, it is related to real differences in an understanding of the nature of evangelization by Catholics and Protestants. How can these differences be resolved? Certainly this will take time and intentional effort. Different perspectives on evangelism and evangelization are among other issues that need extended discussion in ecumenical forums.

## An Evolving *Mestizaje*

Columbus's journey to the so-called New World included a crusade to make the Americas Spanish and Christian. The first "thanksgiving" in what was to be called the United States was conducted, not by Protestant Pilgrims at Plymouth Rock, but by Spanish Catholics in 1526 at a settlement named San Miguel near the site where Jamestown would be founded nearly a century later. What would become the southern United States originally fell under the jurisdiction of the bishop of Santiago de Cuba. From the Chesapeake Bay to the San Francisco Bay, colonies, cities, and missions dotted the landscape. The decline of the Spanish Empire, and the consequential rise of the empire of the United States, contributed to the expulsion, marginalization, and disenfranchisement of Latinas/os residing within U.S. territories. The goal of making the Americas Spanish and Catholic gave way to Manifest

Destiny by the United States and its understanding of Protestant Christianity.

Yet, some of the advances made by Manifest Destiny are now being reversed. In 1992, salsa outsold ketchup as America's favorite condiment. This minor change in taste is symbolic of the transformation the United States is undergoing. In the past, Latinos/as faced the danger of assimilation in the Euroamerican culture. Now, Euroamerica is in so-called peril of assimilating to Hispanic culture. The end of the twentieth century witnessed the creation of a new people through the Latino/a *mestizaje* in the United States, which seems to indicate a reversal and healing of the consequences of the Euroamerican venture of making the continent white and Protestant. The rapid increase of Latinos/as within U.S. territory has set in motion a reversal of Manifest Destiny, a Latinization of the dominant Eurocentric culture's concept of expansion. With the Latino/a population growing at seven times the rate of the general population, Hispanic influence will be even greater in the twenty-first century. Contrary to general opinion, this growth is not due to "illegal" immigration; rather, it is fueled by natural causes — births outweighing deaths. This increasing Latino/a presence is leading to a reaction among North American whites, arising as a defense against the perceived danger of a Hispanic *comunidad* struggling to become empowered. Hence, xenophobic laws like multiple "English-only" referendums or the newly virulent rhetoric demanding walls along the Mexican–U.S. border represent desperate attempts to stunt the growing Latina/o presence.

The rapidly increasing U.S. Hispanic population has not gone unnoticed by the business world. *Generation Ñ* is the title of a recently published glossy magazine marketed to young Latinas/os coming of age in the United States. The construction of Generation Ñ among the Hispanic young serves as a counterpart to the Euroamerican Generation X. Latinos/as create their own space because little if any room exists for them within the dominant culture. What differentiates them from Generation Xers is their attempt to simultaneously live within two worlds, one Hispanic and the other Euroamerican, without losing anything in the "translation." Ñs are bicultural in the fullest sense of the word, largely bilingual, more often fluent in English. Many are well educated and possess economic clout in the marketplace. This helps explain why "salsa" music is used by advertisers who hope to tap into this rapidly growing market. Predominately in their twenties and thirties, Ñs, unlike the aging Euroamerican baby boomers, are getting younger and younger.

Ñs are challenging the historically negative images of Latinos/as in the United States. Unlike some of their elders who attempted to assimilate into the dominant culture for the sake of survival, Ñs have learned to say *¡Basta!* (Enough!). They have learned how to "be" U.S. American when needed but can easily revert to being Hispanic when desired. In effect, they are flaunting, not hiding, their Latino/a roots, telling the dominant culture that they will live and succeed in the United States on their own terms. In fact, the danger Ñs pose to the dominant Euroamerican culture is Latinization, as more Euroamericans move to Ricky Martin and Gloria Estefan, cheer for Oscar de la Hoya and Sammy Sosa, read Junot Diaz, Sandra Cisneros, and Christina Garcia, and succumb to Latino/a food, music, and art.

As we have seen, Hispanics in the United States are still predominately Catholic, and in this respect, the Ñs are no different. As cultural Catholics, they honor and respect Catholic traditions without necessarily practicing them. Their practices, or lack thereof, are beginning to affect Latino/a theology, which attempts to "do" theology from the grassroots. As their voices are added to the dominant Hispanic theological conversation, they are asking questions avoided in the past, are being more critical of older Hispanic theologians who have yet to interact with this rapidly growing contingency, and are moving away from some of the basic assumptions made of the Latino/a culture that have not been updated to encompass the changing reality of Latinos/as. The Generation Ñ phenomenon has contributed to the dismantling of the romanticization of the oppressed, has facilitated the assimilation to Euroamerican mores for a privileged segment of Hispanic culture, and has resisted the pan-ethnic Hispanic identity many scholars attempt to construct.

Romanticizing the oppressed has always been a pitfall for those doing a liberationist form of theology. God's preferential option for the oppressed has at times created an attitude of spiritual superiority due to the eventual assurance of liberation. While many Hispanic theologians maintain that God "takes sides" with those subjugated by the dominant culture's unjust structures, several have raised concerns about Hispanics participating in their own forms of institutionalized violence. While Latino/a theologians search for a more egalitarian community to foster liberation, many Hispanics are finding their liberation through capitalism. Generation Ñ represents the ethos of a younger generation of Latinos/as who may seem not as committed as the previous generation to the creation of an economically just society.

For those Hispanics who are light-skinned enough, possess middle-class status, or have cultural capital, acceptance by Euroamericans could cause problems. Greater opportunities exist for these "acceptable" Latinas/os, contributing to an intra-Hispanic power structure. As "successful Hispanics" rise within the community structures, intra-Hispanic power structures develop between them and those Latinos/as who still suffer economic oppression. The growing appeal among these Latinos/as for conservative political action groups, groups historically hostile to the Hispanic presence, indicates the emergence of a new Latina/o identity. Generation Ñ is one manifestation of a new cultural identity that is neither fully Latina/o nor fully Euroamerican. In some respects, it has become a space for Hispanics who are not "too dark" nor "too poor." Yet, this space may itself be a transitional stage. Latina/o children regard becoming "American" (i.e., United States definition) as highly desirable. To become an "American" is a choice made by the individual but also indicates acceptance by the national community if the child is "white" enough and has sufficient middle-class status. As a result, some Hispanic children face an entirely different set of circumstances that contribute to an ambiguous alignment with the dominant culture.

For example, a recent survey reveals that Cuban youth preferred speaking English. Also, they seldom identified themselves by their national origin. Of those surveyed, only 3 to 6 percent of youths in private schools thought of themselves as Cuban, as opposed to 17 percent of those in public schools. The conclusion of the study showed that those with greater socioeconomic advantages and ambitions (translated as light-skinned with higher economic status) adopted a more mainstream identity, while those with fewer advantages continued to identify themselves as Cuban. Not surprisingly, light-skinned Latinas/os are least likely to report experiencing discrimination, even less than European or Canadian whites.[2] While these studies focus on the children of exilic Cubans, a similar argument can be made for Mexicans, Puerto Ricans, and Central and South Americans who possess middle-class status and/or lighter skin pigmentation. One question before the next generation of Hispanic theologians is how to continue a grassroots theology when a segment of the grass roots is adopting Euroamerican values detrimental to their darker and poorer compatriots. How will these children identify with a second-class "Hispanic-other" when their "honorary whiteness" and class privilege allow easy incorporation within the dominant culture? In short, what happens to our theological perspectives when those who were formerly oppressed do not make a preferential option for the oppressed?

## Challenge of New "Undocumented" Immigrants

When the subject of Latin American immigration arises in conversation, the image that often prevails in the popular imagination is that of a flood of "illegal" Mexicans crossing the border at night. In fact, this scene was used in television ads by Bob Dole's presidential campaign of 1996 to show the ineffectiveness of then-President Bill Clinton in "controlling the borders." This discriminatory image is common in the rhetoric of some divisive politicians, particularly at election time, who seek to establish blame for a whole host of social ills, concerns, and anxiety. The simple cry "Build a wall along the border, and build it high" unites some Euroamericans against a common enemy. "Undocumented" immigrants become the scapegoat to explain conveniently the causes of downsizing faced by "real" Americans. Such rhetoric of fear and distortion is part of the impetus of a number of acts that restrict services to immigrants, most notably in California, which in 1994 passed Proposal 187 making illegal immigrants ineligible for public assistance, including health care, public schooling, and other social services.

    Although a flow of Mexican immigrants continues, the last part of the twentieth century saw increasing numbers coming to the

United States from other parts of Latin America. Many Central Americans, especially Salvadorans and Guatemalans, settled in urban areas of Los Angeles, Washington, D.C., and New York City. Dominicans are a growing presence in the northeastern part of the United States. Nicaraguans began to arrive in large numbers as a result of the war in that country in which the United States funded rebel forces. As the war in Nicaragua dragged on, spilling over to neighboring countries, it generated a Honduran migration to the United States. Mayans from Guatemala, who can be found in Florida and in Houston, Texas, show the complexity of these recent migrations. Having maintained their preconquest cultural identity, Mayans speak Spanish as a second language, if they speak it at all. Others of the newer Latin American migrants in the 1970s and 1980s included political refugees from the life-threatening oppression of the regime of General Augusto Pinochet in Chile. From northern South America, Colombians, Ecuadorans, and Peruvians also settled in the United States. Portuguese-speaking Brazilians have migrated to the United States in the last quarter of the twentieth century, pushing the limits of what it means to be Latino/a. Additionally, an increasing number of Mexican and U.S.-born individuals with Mexican origins are migrating to nonmetropolitan and agricultural areas in the United States. Some researchers suggest various reasons for this settlement, including the desire to re-create traditional agricultural activities and economic patterns.[3]

The infusion of a Hispanic presence throughout the United States is partly fueled by these new waves of immigrants and has produced scenes that some thought they would never see in their part of the country. Latino/a day workers line up in places like the commuter town of Mamaroneck outside New York City, hoping to be hired for the day in gardening or small construction jobs. North Carolina has begun to be aware of a growing Hispanic population within its midst as some cease being migratory agricultural workers on tobacco farms and become year-round residents working on dairy farms or in local restaurants.

All these diverse groups contribute in different ways to the constantly shifting U.S. Latino/a identity, but not without internal difficulties beyond the challenges of settling in a new land. This new land throws these various groups together. Chileans and Argentines in Chicago continue the long-standing disputes

that existed between the two nations in South America. Various
Spanish-speaking groups sneer at the way Spanish is spoken by
members of another group. Stereotypes of national groups that
would not be tolerated if spoken by the dominant Euroamerican
culture become acceptable ways by which one Hispanic group
refers to Latinos/as with different national origins. When there is a
shared sense of Latino/a identity, some groups are judged as being
insufficiently Hispanic. For example, tensions arose between recent
arrivals and "established" Mexican Americans who supported the
anti-immigration propositions of California.

The challenge for Hispanic churches and Latino/a theologies is
how to respond to this constantly changing and multileveled diversity consistent with theirs internal theological understandings.
Is it possible for local congregations to embrace both the recent arrivals and the third-generation Chicanas? If the popular religious
devotions and practices of the people are sources for U.S. Hispanic
theology, which practices are to be accepted? Who does the choos-
ing? How are ethnic differences to be negotiated to achieve some
sort of common identity? Is that even a desired and legitimate
goal? Pastors, pastoral agents, ministry workers, and congregations must decide the ultimate standard by which they determine
their response when they are called to minister to people who may
have fled for their lives and may be undocumented immigrants and,
therefore, are considered "illegal aliens" by the U.S. government.

## Intra-Hispanic Oppressive Structures

During the early years when Latino/a Christian theology began to
be voiced, it faced the constant threat of being torn apart by differences existing among distinct national groups. A conscious decision
seems to have been made by Hispanic theologians to minimize
those differences and, instead, concentrate on areas of commonality. Pan-ethnic unity was sought at all costs, masking those areas
that threatened to tear Latinos/as apart.

Unfortunately, the desire of Latino/a theologians to evoke a pan-
ethnic unity diminishes the reality of how sexism, racism, and
classism are alive and well within the social space occupied by
Hispanics. Casting Latinas/os solely as victims of the dominant cul-

ture obscures the dubious role they can also play as victimizers. In respect to a theology of liberation, several Latino/a theologians are beginning to insist that Hispanics are simultaneously both the oppressed and the oppressors, a fact that is inconvenient and sometimes ignored by those who would lump us all together as solely victims of U.S. hegemony. Traditionally disenfranchised groups usually construct well-defined categories as to the perpetrators and the victims of injustices. All too often, Hispanics tend to identify the oppressive structures of the dominant Eurocentric culture while overlooking repression originating within their own communities. Within the marginalized space of the Latino/a community, structures of oppression exist along gender, race, and class lines, creating the need for an initiative to move beyond the rhetoric of blame.

The rise of the exilic Cuban community in Miami witnesses the emergence of intra-Hispanic oppressive structures. During the early 1960s, the United States media broadcast numerous stories of penniless Cubans rising from adversity to success. These stories stereotyped Miami's Hispanic community as "the Cuban success story."[4] By lumping exilic Cubans with Mexicans, Puerto Ricans, and other Latin Americans under the term Hispanic, Latinos/as mask the power and privilege that come with lighter racial composition and upper- and middle-class status. The success Cubans found in Miami resulted from the demographics of those who immigrated, rather than from any particular characteristics intrinsic to Cubans.

The social background exilic Cubans brought to the United States affected the construction of Cuban ethnicity once in this country and set them apart from the minority reality of other Latinas/os. Suzanne Oboler's social-scientific work shows how middle- and upper-class college-educated Hispanics integrate into the dominant culture. Like previous southern and eastern European immigrants, these Latinos/as are seen as "white," thus enhancing their ability to reach "first-class" citizen status relatively quickly. Because the first two waves of Cubans (1959–73) consisted mostly of white, middle-class Cubans with some level of education, they were able to define their ethnic identity along the predominant ethnic and racial classifications of the United States.[5]

While discrimination against exilic Cubans is a reality and is reflected in the distribution of income, still exilic Cubans, more than any other Hispanic group, earn higher average incomes and more frequently occupy professional-level jobs. Within one generation, this group, unlike any other ethnic group arriving on U.S. shores, captured the political, economic, cultural, and social structures of a major U.S. city. Several Cuban theologians have begun to address the exilic Cuban theological location within the context of power in the Miami community, attempting to unmask race, class, and gender oppression existing within their own space. Latino/a theologians are beginning to scrutinize these spaces where former oppressed Hispanics mount the social structures without dismantling the inherent systems of oppression. The Miami reality may serve as a paradigm of what to avoid for other Hispanic groups who gain some forms of political clout.

## Complexity of the U.S. Colonialization of Puerto Rico

Puerto Rico and Puerto Ricans provide a unique challenge for Hispanic theology and its future development in the life and ministry of the Christian church in North America. Since 1898, when it was acquired from Spain as booty in the Spanish-American War, Puerto Rico has been a colonial possession of the United States. Almost immediately, the United States embarked upon a process of Americanization of the people and culture. Under U.S. rule the first few governors of Puerto Rico were appointed Euroamericans. Even the spelling of the island's name was changed to "Porto Rico" in order to be more friendly to Euroamerican patterns of pronunciation. By 1911, English was made the official language, and United States patterns of government and education were imposed.

This radical shift in political sovereignty also affected the religious life of the island. Roman Catholicism had been formally established in Puerto Rico in 1511. Over the centuries the Puerto Rican Catholic Church became diverse along urban and rural lines as it struggled with a scarcity of qualified ministers, an inadequate distribution of resources for ministry, and only sporadic interest from Spain. Reflecting its rich indigenous, African, and European heritage, popular religion included devotions to Our Lady of Monserrate, La Virgen Negra (the Black Virgin). The institutional church, which favored an urban elite, had an ambivalent relationship with rural society.

With the coming of the U.S. rule, state sponsorship of the church ended, and many Spanish Catholic clergy and religious workers under the Spanish colonial authorities departed. Euroamerican religious workers and clergy arrived to "missionize" a land that had already had a Christian presence for four hundred years. During much of the early period of U.S. sovereignty, institutional Catholic efforts partook in the Euroamericanization drive, and until the 1960s the Catholic bishops of Puerto Rico were Euroamericans.

Simultaneously, although there had been a small Protestant presence during the Spanish period, many Protestant denominations from the United States saw an opening for evangelism and sent missionaries to work in Puerto Rico. The North American Protestant mainline churches entered into a *comity agreement,* which recognized delineated areas of respective ministries so that they would not directly compete with one another (a process also implemented in Cuba). Many viewed this effort to Protestantize the island as the natural complement of Euroamericanization. Meanwhile, virtually undetected by either Roman Catholics or mainline Protestants, Pentecostal Protestant Christians began their work in Puerto Rico, an act particularly significant for the phenomenal growth of Pentecostalism on the island.

With the official acquisition of Puerto Rico by the United States in 1898, the migration of Puerto Ricans from the island to the U.S. mainland began. By 1917 the U.S. Congress had granted all Puerto Ricans U.S. citizenship. This new status allowed Puerto Ricans to be drafted into the armed forces for service in World War I. Although there had been a constant flow of Puerto Rican migrants to the mainland since 1898 (with an accompanying reverse migration), it was really after World War II that a combination of factors brought about the great migration of Puerto Ricans to the United States. Initially, the majority settled in the northeast, with New York City a major point of entry.

As new Puerto Rican communities established themselves in various cities, the response of churches was inconsistent and sometimes tepid. In some locations, Puerto Rican migrants seized the initiative and leadership, replicating island traditions in new urban settings. Initially, many church leaders, both Catholic and Protestant, viewed Puerto Ricans as an alien and problematic people. Given the void of institutional church neglect, many Pentecostal and conservative Protestant ministries made their initial gains among newly arrived immigrants, some of whom carried their new faith back to Puerto Rico with them.

Since the 1960s, civil rights activism and new theological perspectives began to change institutional church perceptions and approaches to Puerto Ricans, both on the mainland and on the island. Hispanic theology must deal with the fact that, unlike many other Hispanics, Puerto Ricans, whether on the island or the mainland, are U.S. citizens living in a society that treats them as illegal aliens.

To a certain extent, all Puerto Ricans are multicultural Latinos/as. There are Puerto Ricans in the United States whose primary language is not Spanish and who, if they visit the *isla* at all, do so only to see relatives. Their only experience of a Puerto Rican community is Humboldt Park in Chicago, La Park in Hartford, El Barrio in East Harlem, or El Bronx in New York. Attitudes of Puerto Ricans *de la isla,* who question the authenticity of Puerto Ricans from *afuera* (from "the outside," a common Puerto Rican island idiom for the mainland United States), create tensions and challenge Latino/a theology.

Additionally, despite more than a century of U.S. possession, Puerto Rican culture and the Spanish language persist. This popular resistance is especially astonishing when one compares what happened with Hawaii, another island acquired by the United States in 1898. The complicated and somewhat ambivalent attitude of Puerto Ricans toward the United States presents another dimension of the challenge facing Hispanic theology. Periodically this tense relationship erupts into the open, as recently happened with the island of Vieques.

Vieques is a small island and township off the east coast of Puerto Rico, which was appropriated by the federal government in 1941. Most of Vieques has been used as a target site for the U.S. Navy. On April 19, 1999, a civilian security guard, David Sanes, was killed, and others were injured, due to a tactical error in bombing. As a result of these events, a coalition of Protestant and Catholic churches, civic organizations, and political groups, both in Puerto Rico and on the mainland, sought to force the U.S. Navy to terminate all military training and bombing on Vieques. Some of these ecumenical protesters camped on Vieques until they were removed by federal authorities. Catholics erected a protest camp in front of the capitol building in San Juan. For some, the Vieques protest has become a rallying point for advocating independence for Puerto Rico. Others seize it as proof that Puerto Rico must become the fifty-first state in the Union in order that Puerto Ricans will be treated equally and receive all the benefits enjoyed by Euroamericans. For some Puerto Ricans on the mainland, Vieques has provided an opportunity to connect with their island roots. The question before Christian churches is how they will think and act theologically in this situation. How will these events challenge Hispanic theology?

## Chicanos/as vs. Mexicans

When Californians voted on propositions that were detrimental to the more recent Mexican immigrant community, passage occurred with the help of Chicanos/as, who arrived decades earlier. Throughout the Southwest, South, and Midwest tensions exist between the older and better-established Mexican American community and the more recent arrivals. From the rural agricultural fields to the meatpacking plants to the sweatshops, incidences of Chicanos/as taunting new arrivals with insults like "wetbacks" are common. Likewise, recent immigrants refer to the Chicanas/os with the derogatory term *pocho*. As children, Chicanos/as had to endure shame from a dominant culture that scorned them for not speaking English correctly. Now as adults, they are mocked by the newer arrivals for not speaking proper Spanish. They may be *la raza* (the race), but more recent arrivals question if they are *la gente* (the people).

These tensions mask questions concerning class, levels of U.S. acculturation, and generational differences marked by when entry into the United States took place. Not limited to those of Mexican descent, these tensions had similar manifestations in Miami during the 1980s between the established Cuban community and the new arrivals, who were pejoratively labeled *Marielitos*. These intranational tensions also exist among Puerto Ricans, with those who reside in the United States looking down on their cousins on the island, as well as among Dominicans in New York and the various Central American communities. As these tensions play out within local congregations, Latino/a theologians are forced to deal with the creation of intra-Hispanic forms of prejudices and discrimination. As a newer generation of Hispanic scholars enters the discourse, these issues will be brought to the forefront.

## The Changing Social Location of Latino/a Theologians due to Education

Many Latino/a scholars pride themselves on being "organic intellectuals." In other words, they operate as agents within the social location of disenfranchised Hispanics to raise critical consciousness about oppression. No doubt, the majority of these scholars were born into and arose from these economically depressed spaces. Yet, with education comes privilege, "cultural capital." A dilemma arises between the "organic intellectuals" grounded in the local community of faith and the college-educated theologians who possess cultural capital. Are their voices truly from the margins even though their new professors' salaries afford them the privilege of not having to live in the barrio? While some Latino/a theologians choose to continue living among and with the poor, physically accompanying them in their struggle for existence, others opt for the security of the suburbs. Can a Hispanic theologian who no longer lives with the disenfranchised be able to be a voice for them? Does the security of a job and the safety of a middle- or upper-class home disconnect a Latina/o theologian who "escaped" from those still trapped in the economic oppression of the barrio? As more Hispanics obtain their doctorate in theology, religion, or biblical studies and enter the ranks of the middle- and upper-class intelligentsia, questions like these will require greater deliberation.

Additionally, a liberal education may produce theological graduates that are more to the religious "left" than their congregation. While many Hispanic congregations express a conservative religious worldview, much of the scholarship being written by Latino/a theologians avoids some of these perspectives. This raises questions and concerns. Are Hispanics voicing the theology being created by the faith community, or are they imposing their own views, influenced by a liberal theological education, upon the congregations hoping to lead them toward the theologians' views, which are then equated with "raised consciousness"? Can the educated Latina/o theologian be part of *la comunidad* when suspicion still exists within the faith community toward those with degrees?

## Postmodern Thought

In academic settings, postmodern and postcolonial conversations affect every discipline of higher education. Briefly stated, postmodernity is a philosophical concept that claims absolute truths are constructed by a given society within a particular time period. Therefore, assertions of objectivity in truth or knowledge are untenable. Any objective claims to universality are basically an exercise in power. In short, postmodernity is a skeptical inquiry into all claims of authority.[6]

A few Hispanic theologians and scholars of religion have embraced postmodern theory, while others have responded to this dialogue with suspicion and skepticism. Fernando Segovia makes use of a postmodern methodology in what he calls a "theology of the diaspora." Segovia envisions such a theology as deeply rooted in the theoretical contexts of postmodernism and liberation theology. Diaspora theology is defined as

> a postmodernist theology ... theology that argues for a multitude of matrices and voices, not only outside itself but also within itself, and regards itself as a construct, with thorough commitment to self-analysis and self-criticism as a construct; a postcolonial theology ... a theology that is grounded in the margins, speaks from the margins, and engages in decolonization both within and from the center; and a liberation theology ... theology that seeks to re-view, reclaim, and re-phrase its own matrix and voice in the midst of a dominant culture and theology. It is also a theology with exile, flesh-and-blood exile, at its heart and core.[7]

As a postmodern theology, Segovia's theology of the diaspora attempts to celebrate the radical diversity of the Hispanic ethos rather than the so-called objective universality of the European theologies. One challenge facing Latinos/as using a postmodern approach is to construct ethical initiatives that are different from the value imperatives of the dominant Euroamerican culture. Some theologians, such as Roberto Goizueta, call for a type of reason that goes beyond modernity *and* postmodernity, where, from the perspective of popular Catholicism, theological truth is encountered not in clear distinct ideas but in relationships; not in universal, abstract concepts but in particular, concrete sacraments or symbols; not through observation but through participation.[8]

For some Latinos/as who do use a postmodern methodology within their theology, the call for liberation does not reduce their theology to one interesting perspective among a multitude of possible perspectives. They claim, instead, that Hispanic theologies do contain universal truths that are not solely restricted to Hispanics or other oppressed groups. Thus, postmodernity is used to understand oppressive social structures and not as a complete worldview. What remains to be seen is whether such postmodern perspectives will be welcomed by Latina/o theologians or if they will continue to be viewed with suspicion.

## Emerging New World Order

Latino/a theologies have developed in a way considerably different from liberation theologies in Latin America. These differences occur as U.S. Hispanics continuously formulate their own contextual approaches. Generally speaking, economic and political analysis of the society is one major emphasis of Latin American liberation theology. Class struggle and its political ramifications are central to the creation of a theology rooted in the life struggles of the poor, which provides an avenue for them to secure justice in their situation. There is no dispute that the use of these social and theological analyses greatly influenced the development of U.S. Hispanic theologies. However, the overall emphasis this side of the border has been on the historical and cultural dimensions in addition to a socioeconomic critique. The story of U.S. Latinos/as who face ethnic discrimination, dehumanizing social norms, and a history of oppression influenced the main analytical methodologies employed. This is not to say that socioeconomic analysis is abandoned totally in favor of culture analysis. Several U.S. Latino/a theologians also consider the economic and political roots of oppression, as they recognize that racial/ethnic discrimination in the United States is closely tied to economic factors, adapting the option for the poor to a North American context.

Within Hispanic theology, the option for the poor is not solely limited to economics; it also addresses the sociopolitical conditions of the barrios. Commenting as an outside observer, Mexican theologian Ruy G. Suárez Rivero has noticed that for U.S. Latino/a theology, "one must infer that the most profound meaning of the ethical-political option of the poor is not sociopolitical transformation alone, but the hopeful transformation of every dimension of everyday (social, familial, individual) human life."[9] Increasingly, Latino/a theologians are expanding their understandings of the call of the gospel and the nature of oppression to be addressed. For example, Harold Recinos speaks of a "hard-hitting Jesus" at the center of what Recinos calls a "new barrio Christianity," which includes the assurance of abundant life as well as social critique of the amassing of wealth.[10] As the applicability and appropriateness of social, economic, cultural, and political critique and engagement are constantly debated, perhaps here is one point of difference between (1) formal systematic theologians and other scholars of religion and (2) the pastors and pastoral agents at the grassroots level. Nevertheless, they are instances of faith-based Latino/a Christian efforts to merge theological convictions with social engagement.

With the retreat of socialism in the late twentieth century and the aggressive assertion of market-based economies throughout the world, some theologians experienced aimlessness caused by the end of "utopias," as some theologians concluded that capitalism had "won." A so-called New World Order created a global economy that extends and strengthens economic oppression between the rich "First World" and the poor "Two-Thirds World." The emergence of this New World Order is rapidly changing how international structures of oppression operate. These quickly shifting circumstances pose a whole new set of challenges for Latino/a theologians. For example, the North American Free Trade Agreement (NAFTA) between Canada, Mexico, and the United States provides for the removal of all trade barriers between those countries, tying their economies even closer together. This has increased a movement of goods and capital as well as people. U.S. companies dominate the *maquiladora* industries along the U.S.–Mexico border. These industrialized concentrations have attracted workers, a large percentage being women, not only from Mexico but from Central America as well, all working in poor conditions. How should Hispanic theology address the moral issues raised by trade agreements like NAFTA or the economic hardships created by multinational corporations for Latinos/as on both sides of the Mexican border?

Likewise, although by no means ignored, the role of the economic oppression of Latinas/os by Hispanics has not been fully considered. How does the Hispanic presence in the United States become complicit with global structures of oppression? For example, while U.S. Hispanic theologians make a "preferential option for the poor," are the poor making a "preferential option for McDonalds"? Drinking a cup of coffee or enjoying a double cheeseburger increases demand for coffee beans and beef. Such a demand makes it profitable for multinational corporations in Latin America to cultivate coffee beans and raise cattle as export commodities. Vast tracts of land in Central and South America previously plowed by indigenous people to grow their own food or acres of forest are now diverted for the production of coffee beans and beef for North American consumption, including that of Latinos/as. The cost of drinking a cup of inexpensive coffee or eating a cheeseburger by U.S. Hispanics is subsidized with the blood of dispossessed *campesinos* (land peasants) who need just land reform. Eating and living within the United States food-production system, Latinas/os also contribute to the exploitation of fellow Hispanics. How widespread is the awareness that buying a head of lettuce for under a dollar is due to the backbreaking work of agricultural laborers in California? What is the response of the church to the lives and working conditions of Hispanic temporary workers in beef-packing plants in Kansas or poultry farms in Arkansas, Georgia, North Carolina, and Maine?

Additionally, global pressures influence the movement of the powerful and privileged elite of Latin America to the United States, specifically south Florida. From the year 1999 to mid-2000, an estimated two hundred thousand people from Argentina, Colombia, Ecuador, and Venezuela left the political turmoil and insecurity existing in their country for the United States. Many of these new immigrants are not the traditional uneducated poor; rather, they are middle- and upper-middle-class professionals. As globalization advances, and the economic status of Latin American immigrants changes, U.S. Latino/a theologians will need to refocus on economic and political analysis to reevaluate the effects of the emerging New World Order upon U.S. Hispanics. A greater balance between the cultural and historical source of Latina/o theology and the economic and political realities of the communities seems to be evident as theologians struggle to give voice to the changing structures of world oppression.

## Gay and Lesbian Issues

A conversation is beginning to occur among Latino/a theologians on the issue of homosexuality. The Hispanic bias against gays differs from the homophobia of the dominant U.S. culture. Hispanics do not fear the homosexual; rather, homosexuals are often held in contempt as men who choose not to prove their manhood. Among Euroamericans, two men engaged in a sexual act are both called homosexuals; among Latinos/as, only the one that places himself in the "position" of a woman is gay. In fact, in several Hispanic cultures, the man who is in the dominant position during the sex act, known as *bugarrón*, is able to retain, if not increase, his machismo. Also missing from any Hispanic theological analysis is the space occupied by lesbians. While gays constitute a "scandal" as men forsaking their manhood, lesbians are usually ignored due to the overall machismo of a society that grounds its sexuality on the *macho*'s desires, repressing feminine sexuality. Tolerance of lesbians is partly due to their unimportance to the *macho*'s construction of sexuality. They simply have no space in the dominant construction.

Even though several Hispanic theologians are gay or lesbian, the adage "Se dice nada, se hace todo" (Say nothing, do everything) remains an accepted norm of the Hispanic theological community. A review of theological literature reveals the prevailing silence of Hispanics on this issue, an issue with considerable impact on the dominant theological discourse. However, the silence is beginning to be broken. During a 1999 panel discussion of the Hispanic American Religion Group of the American Academy of Religion, the sexual orientation of the seventeenth-century theologian Sor Juana Inés de la Cruz was raised, yet no connection was made as to how this orientation might affect today's Latina/o theological discourse. One of the Hispanic group sessions during the 2000 Academy of American Religion dealt with issues of homosexuality and transexuality; however, not one of the presenters was Latino/a, and few Hispanics attended the session. Another discussion occurred through the Hispanic Theological Initiative in March 2001. Yet, it still remains to be seen if Latina/o theologians are ready for such a discourse and if younger theologians will add their voices to dismantle this conspiracy of silence.

## The Environment

The first chapter of this book argued that Latinas/os are more likely to live with pollution than any other U.S. minority group. Figure 7 of that chapter compares the percentage of Hispanics living with pollution with Euroamericans and African Americans. The table revealed that Hispanics have a greater chance of living in environments that are ecologically hazardous to their health. Why do they live in areas that are ecologically unsound? Because various types of waste-disposal plants are placed in Latino/a neighborhoods. Throughout this nation's cities, the geographic space normatively relegated to Hispanics becomes the same space where the city's refuse centers are usually located. Latinas/os are forced to live with odorous, unhealthy air and water. Under the pretense that such plants would create employment opportunities, plants that contribute to higher levels of pollution are usually located in economically depressed areas, areas predominantly occupied by people of color. The consequences of these actions are greater health concerns, further aggravated by poor medical health coverage. Yet, ecological concerns are not presently a major topic of discussion among Hispanic theologians, and challenging city planning has not been a major concern. However, as theologians begin to dig deeper to the root causes negatively affecting Latinos/as, we can expect more discourse along the lines of ecological concerns.

## Conclusion

A younger Hispanic population with a median age of twenty-six years, almost a decade younger than the dominant culture, and un-precedented growth in numbers have positioned Latinos/as within reach of redefining what it means to be a citizen of the United States. If future demographic forecasts are correct and Hispanics represent one-quarter of the United States population by 2050, their traditions and customs may move from the margins toward the mainstream. What we call Hispanic or Latino/a theologies may cease to be an "interesting perspective" and become, instead, one of the central voices within North American theological discourse. As Latinas/os move from society's margins, and as changes occur within their socioeconomic locations, their theology, a reflection of how they understand the Deity from their space, can also be expected to change.

The future of Latino/a theology depends on the vitality of its grassroots foundation. All theologies remain a reflection of a cer-tain people within a certain time period. By remaining faithful to the preferential option for those oppressed, Hispanic theology can develop and mature along with the changing ethos of the people. No doubt, with the beginning of the new millennium, Hispanic theological perspectives are poised to accompany the people as they struggle with their understanding of the Deity and of the Deity's will for their life, their *familia*, their *comunidad*, and the nation in which they find themselves residing.

## Chapter 6 Study Questions

### Definition Question

Define the following terms: Generation Ñ, Chicanos/as, *pocho*, NAFTA, postmodernity.

## Essay Questions

1. How are the changing demographics of the United States affecting the Latina/o community, and how are these changes affecting theological perspectives?

2. What are some of the issues preventing ecumenism between Catholic and Protestant Hispanics?

3. Who belongs to Generation Ñ? How do they differ from the "new undocumented immigrants"? What challenges do these groups present to Latino/a theologies?

4. How does intra-Hispanic oppression manifest itself? How does oppression exist within a marginalized group as opposed to the oppression generated from the dominant culture? How is the intra-Latino/a oppression masked? As the Latino/a population increases, what challenges exist in dismantling intra-Hispanic racism, classism, and sexism?

5. How does the New World Order affect Hispanic theologies? What differences exist between Latina/o theologies and Latin American liberation theology? What role do you think the economy should or should not play in constructing theological perspectives? Do economic concerns affect Eurocentric theologies?

6. What should the U.S. policy be toward its "possession" of the Puerto Rican island? What challenges have Puerto Ricans faced that differ from the challenges of other Latinos/as? What should the political future of the island be? Why?

7. How do Hispanic theologians view the postmodern discourse? What are some of the problems Latina/o scholars have with postmodernity? Do all Hispanics reject postmodernity? If not, how do they use its methodology within their theological perspectives?

# Notes

## Introduction

1. Eldín Villafañe, *The Liberating Spirit: Toward an Hispanic American Pentecostal Social Ethic* (Grand Rapids: Eerdmans, 1993), 70–71; Orlando E. Costas, *Christ outside the Gate: Mission beyond Christendom* (Maryknoll, N.Y.: Orbis Books, 1982), 115–16.

2. "New Lights of the Spirit," *Time* (December 11, 2000): 84–85.

3. The concept "theological specialist" is similar to what Isasi-Díaz and Tarango have referred to as the "theological technician," as opposed to the "grassroots theologian." See Ada María Isasi-Díaz and Yolanda Tarango, *Hispanic Women: Prophetic Voice in the Church: Toward a Hispanic Women's Liberation Theology* (San Francisco: Harper & Row, 1988), 104–9; and Ada María Isasi-Díaz, *En la Lucha: A Hispanic Women's Liberation Theology* (Minneapolis: Fortress Press, 1993), 176–79.

## 1. U.S. Hispanics: Who Are They?

1. Fernando F. Segovia, "Two Places and No Place on Which to Stand," in *Mestizo Christianity: Theology from the Latino Perspective*, ed. Arturo J. Bañuelas (Maryknoll, N.Y.: Orbis Books, 1995), 31.

2. Exilic Cuban Lourdes Casal captures the difficult task of constructing the Hispanic ethnic identity in the poem "For Ana Veldford," in *Bridges to Cuba*, ed. Ruth Behar, trans. David Frye (Ann Arbor: University of Michigan Press, 1995), 24:

> This is why I will always remain on the margins,
> a stranger among the stones,
> even beneath the friendly sun of this summer's day,
> just as I will remain forever a foreigner,
> even when I return to the city of my childhood
> I carry this marginality, immune to all turning back,
> too *habanera* to be *newyorkina,*
> too *newyorkina* to be
> — even to become again —
> anything else.

3. Edward Murguia, "On Latino/Hispanic Ethnic Identity," *Latino Studies Journal* 2 (September 1991): 11.

4. Christine Granados, "Hispanic vs Latino," *Hispanic Magazine* (December 2000): 40–42.

5. U.S. Bureau of the Census, *1990 Census of Population and Housing Data Paper Listing* (CPH-L-133); and Summary Tape File 3C.

6. Andres Viglucci, "Hispanics Now Equal Blacks in Population," *Miami Herald* (March 8, 2001): 1A.

7. Margaret L. Usdansky, "Old Ethnic Influences Still Play in Cities," *USA Today* (August 4, 1992): 9A; and "The Number Game," *Time* (fall 1993): 13–14.

8. Marlita A. Reddy, ed., *Statistical Record of Hispanic Americans* (New York: International Thomson Publishing Company, 1995), xxxvi.

9. U.S. Bureau of the Census, *Statistical Abstract of the United States, 1998*, table 22, pp. 22–23.

10. U.S. Bureau of the Census, *Projections of the Hispanic Population: 1983–2080*, Series P25-995; and *Population Projections of the United States, by Age, Sex, Race, and Hispanic Origin: 1992 to 2050*, Series P25-1092.

11. Reddy, *Statistical Record of Hispanic Americans*, xxxvi–xxxvii.

12. U.S. Immigration and Naturalization Service, *Statistical Yearbook of the Immigration and Naturalization Service, 1993*, 156.

13. U.S. Bureau of the Census, *Estimates of the Population of States by Race and Hispanic Origin: July 1997*, Series PE-64, PE-65, PPL-110, PPL-111, and PPL-112.

14. U.S. Bureau of the Census, *State and Metropolitan Area Data Book, 1997–98*.

15. U.S. Bureau of the Census, *County and City Data Book, 1994*; and "The Number Game," *Time Special Issue: The New Face of America* (fall 1993): 14–15.

16. Nora Hamilton and Norma Stolz Chinchilla, "Central American Migration: A Framework for Analysis," in *Challenging Fronteras: Structuring Latina and Latino Lives in the U.S.*, ed. Mar Romero, Pierrette Hondagneu-Sotelo, and Vima Ortiz (New York: Routledge, 1997), 81–100.

17. Reddy, *Statistical Record of Hispanic Americans*, xxxvii.

18. U.S. Bureau of the Census, *Current Population Reports: Money Income in the United States, 1998*, Series P60-206.

19. United States Bureau of Labor Statistics, *Employment and Earnings*, January 1998; U.S. Bureau of the Census, *Current Population Reports: Money Income in the United States, 1998*, Series P60-206; *The Hispanic Population in the United States: March 1997*, Table 7.2; and Reddy,

*Statistical Record of Hispanic Americans,* 223, 510, 589, 653, 762, 868–69.

20. While discrimination against exilic Cubans is a reality and is reflected in the distribution of income, still exilic Cubans, more than any other Hispanic group, earn higher average incomes and more frequently occupy professional-level jobs. Dade County, Florida, containing a large concentration of exilic Cubans, has become the only area in the United States where first-generation Latin American immigrants have become dominant in city politics. The ascension of exilic Cubans to positions of power is a relatively new phenomenon and will be discussed in greater detail later.

21. Reddy, *Statistical Record of Hispanic Americans,* xliii.

22. Paul Shepard, "Rights Group's Study Links Justice and Race," *Grand Rapids Press* (May 7, 2000): A-5.

23. Amnesty International U.S.A., *Police Brutality in Los Angeles, California, United States of America* (June 1992).

24. Robert Suro, "Pollution-Weary Minorities Try Civil Rights Tack," *New York Times* (January 11, 1993): A-1.

25. Environmental Protection Agency in Reddy, *Statistical Record of Hispanic Americans,* 465.

26. Reddy, *Statistical Record of Hispanic Americans,* 465.

27. Dana Canedy, "Often Conflicted, Hispanic Girls Are Dropping Out at High Rate," *New York Times* (March 25, 2001): A-1.

28. The results of the Barna Research Group can be found on their web page: http://216.87.179.136/cgi-bin/PagePressRelease.asp?PressReleaseID= 78&Reference. A total of 4,038 Latina/o adults were interviewed in a series of four nationwide telephone surveys, selected through the use of a Random-Digit Dial sample.

29. The different understandings of what is "evangelical" or "fundamentalist" and the lack of universal agreement on what these terms mean indicate the difficult task of classification.

30. For further development of barrio theology, see Harold J. Recinos, *Who Comes in the Name of the Lord? Jesus at the Margins* (Nashville: Abingdon Press, 1997), 48–55.

31. Manuel Jesús Mejido, "U.S. Hispanics/Latinos and the Field of Graduate Theological Education," *Theological Education* 34 (spring 1998): 51–71.

32. Joseph M. Murphy, *Working the Spirit: Ceremonies of the African Diaspora* (Boston: Beacon Press, 1994), 2–4.

33. Often this fusion is referred to as "syncretism"; however, we deliberately avoid this term in recognition of its possible negative connotations. An analysis of folk or popular religion and so-called syncretized traditions will occur in chapter 5.

34. David Stoll, *Is Latin America Turning Protestant? The Politics of Evangelical Growth* (Berkeley: University of California Press, 1990), 3–10, 335–38. Elsewhere Stoll projects that if present trends continue, "Latin Americans claiming to be *evangélicos* could still become a quarter to a third of the population early in the twenty-first century." David Stoll, "Introduction: Rethinking Protestantism in Latin America," in *Rethinking Protestantism in Latin America,* ed. Virginia Garrard-Burnett and David Stoll (Philadelphia: Temple University Press, 1993), 2.

35. Virgilio P. Elizondo, *The Future Is Mestizo: Life Where Cultures Meet* (Oak Park, Ill.: Meyer-Stone Books, 1988), x.

36. Aurora Levins Morales and Rosario Morales, *Getting Home Alive* (Ithaca, N.Y.: Firebrand Books, 1986), 50. Used with permission.

37. Luis N. Rivera, *A Violent Evangelism: The Political and Religious Conquest of the Americas* (Louisville: Westminster/John Knox Press, 1992), 55–62.

## 2. Common Cultural Themes

1. Virgilio P. Elizondo, *The Future Is Mestizo: Life Where Cultures Meet* (Oak Park, Ill.: Meyer-Stone Books, 1988), 44–45.

2. James Clifford, *The Predicament of Culture: Twentieth-Century Ethnography, Literature, and Art* (Cambridge, Mass.: Harvard University Press, 1988), 173.

3. Sydney E. Ahlstrom, *A Religious History of the American People* (New Haven: Yale University Press, 1972), 845, 877–78.

4. *Speech of John Quincy Adams, May 25, 1836* (Washington, D.C.: Gale and Seaton, 1838), 119.

5. Ulysses S. Grant, in *Personal Memoirs* (New York: Charles L. Webster & Company, 1885), 1:54–56, wrote:

> The occupation, separation and annexation [of Texas] were, from the inception of the movement to its final consummation, a conspiracy to acquire territory.... Even if the annexation itself could be justified, the manner in which the subsequent war was forced upon Mexico cannot. The fact is, annexationists wanted more territory than they could possibly lay any claim to, as part of the new acquisition.... The Southern rebellion was largely the outgrowth of the Mexican War. Nations, like individuals, are punished for their transgressions. We got punished in the most sanguinary and expensive war of modern times.

6. As quoted in Samuel Solivan, *The Spirit, Pathos, and Liberation: Toward an Hispanic Pentecostal Theology* (Sheffield: Sheffield Academic Press, 1998), 138–39.

7. Harold J. Recinos, *Who Comes in the Name of the Lord? Jesus at the Margins* (Nashville: Abingdon Press, 1997), 38.

8. Joan W. Moore and Harry Pachon, *Hispanics in the United States* (Englewood Cliffs, N.J.: Prentice-Hall, 1985), 68.

9. Frank D. Bean and Marta Tienda, *The Hispanic Population of the United States* (New York: Russell Sage Foundation, 1987).

10. Michael Omi and Howard Winant, *Racial Formation in the United States: From the 1960s to the 1980s* (New York: Routledge, 1986), 62.

11. Virgilio P. Elizondo, *Galilean Journey: The Mexican-American Promise*, rev. ed. (Maryknoll, N.Y.: Orbis Books, 2000), 111.

12. David T. Abalos, *Latinos in the United States: The Sacred and the Political* (Notre Dame, Ind.: University of Notre Dame Press, 1986), 59.

13. Jack D. Forbes, "The Hispanic Spin: Party Politics and Governmental Manipulation of Ethnic Identity," *Latin American Perspectives* 19 (1992): 64.

14. Martha E. Giménez, "U.S. Ethnic Politics: Implications for Latin Americans," *Latin American Perspectives* 19 (1992): 7–17.

15. Virgilio P. Elizondo, foreword to *Mañana: Christian Theology from a Hispanic Perspective*, by Justo L. González (Nashville: Abingdon Press, 1990), 17.

16. Andrew Greeley, "Defection among Hispanics," *America* (July 30, 1988): 61–62; Barry A. Kosmin and Seymour P. Lachman, *One Nation under God: Religion in Contemporary American Society* (New York: Crown Trade Paperbacks, 1993), 137–41.

17. Allan Figueroa Deck, "Hispanic Catholic Prayer and Worship," in *¡Alabadle! Hispanic Christian Worship*, ed. Justo L. González (Nashville: Abingdon Press, 1996), 30.

18. Elizabeth Conde-Frazier, "Hispanic Protestant Spirituality," in *Teología en Conjunto: A Collaborative Hispanic Protestant Theology*, ed. José David Rodríguez and Loida I. Martell-Otero (Louisville: Westminster/John Knox Press, 1997), 137.

19. Justo L. González, "Hispanic Worship: An Introduction," in *¡Alabadle! Hispanic Christian Worship*, ed. Justo L. González, 20–21.

20. Daniel Ramírez, correspondence to Edwin David Aponte, December 16, 1997, based on Bell's concept of contextual ritualization. See Catherine M. Bell, *Ritual Theory, Ritual Practice* (New York: Oxford University Press, 1999).

21. Rina Benmayor, Rosa Torruellas, and Ana L. Jurabe, "Claiming Cultural Citizenship in East Harlem: 'Si Esto Pueda Ayudar a la Comunidad Mía...,'" in *Latino Cultural Citizenship: Claiming Identity, Space, and Rights*, ed. William V. Flores and Rina Benmayor (Boston: Beacon Press, 1997), 182.

22. Gustavo Gutiérrez, *The Power of the Poor in History*, trans. Robert R. Barr (Maryknoll, N.Y.: Orbis Books, 1984), xiii.
23. *Random House Dictionary*, s.v. "righteous."

## 3. Theological Perspectives

1. Justo L. González, *Santa Biblia: The Bible through Hispanic Eyes* (Nashville: Abingdon Press, 1996), 19, 28–29.
2. Jean-Pierre Ruiz, "The Bible and U.S. Hispanic American Theological Discourse: Lessons from a Non-Innocent History," in *From the Heart of Our People: Latino/a Explorations in Catholic Systematic Theology*, ed. Orlando O. Espín and Miguel H. Díaz (Maryknoll, N.Y.: Orbis Books, 1999), 115.
3. Ada María Isasi-Díaz, *En la Lucha: A Hispanic Women's Liberation Theology* (Minneapolis: Fortress Press, 1993), 46, 74, 153.
4. Gustavo Gutiérrez, *The Power of the Poor in History*, trans. Robert R. Barr (Maryknoll, N.Y.: Orbis Books, 1984), xi. For Gutiérrez, reading the text from the perspective of those residing within the underside of history reveals two implicit themes. The first is the universality of God's love. The second is God's preferential option for the poor. See *The God of Life*, trans. Matthew J. O'Connell (Maryknoll, N.Y.: Orbis Books, 1991), 116.
5. Luis G. Pedraja, *Jesus Is My Uncle: Christology from a Hispanic Perspective* (Nashville: Abingdon Press, 1999), 47–48, 85.
6. Penitentes are a confraternity or brotherhood of devout Hispano Catholic men in New Mexico (the term "Hispano" is a self-designation by the Latinos/as of New Mexico). The brotherhood traces its roots back to the Spanish colonial period. While drawing on a stream of popular religiosity in northern New Mexico, the Penitentes formally emerged as a distinct group in the nineteenth century. They annually commemorate the sufferings and death of Jesus Christ during Holy Week. Their use of self-flagellation during devotions was opposed by the institutional Roman Catholic Church. These Penitentes demonstrate a strong sense of religious autonomy particularly as expressed in their initiative and creativity to structure their expressions of faith, especially in the face of occasional neglect and opposition from the Church.
7. It is important to note that such soteriological understanding is not prevalent among "mainline" Protestant traditions. U.S. Protestantism is diverse, reflecting sundry theological perceptions on how salvation occurs.
8. *Puebla and Beyond: Documentation and Commentary*, ed. John Eagleson and Philip Scharper (Maryknoll, N.Y.: Orbis Books, 1979), no. 1307.

9. Ana María Pineda, "Pastoral de Conjunto," in *Mestizo Christianity: Theology from the Latino Perspective*, ed. Arturo J. Bañuelas (Maryknoll, N.Y.: Orbis Books, 1995), 128.

10. Quoted in González, *Santa Biblia*, 51.

11. Eldín Villafañe, *The Liberating Spirit: Toward an Hispanic American Pentecostal Social Ethic* (Grand Rapids: Eerdmans, 1993), 195.

12. Justo L. González, *Mañana: Christian Theology from a Hispanic Perspective* (Nashville: Abingdon Press, 1990), 113.

13. Virgilio P. Elizondo, *Guadalupe: Mother of the New Creation* (Maryknoll, N.Y.: Orbis Books, 1997), xi.

14. Orlando O. Espín, "An Exploration into the Theology of Grace and Sin," in *From the Heart of Our People: Latino/a Explorations in Catholic Systematic Theology*, ed. Orlando O. Espín and Miguel H. Díaz (Maryknoll, N.Y.: Orbis Books, 1999), 137–41.

15. Isasi-Díaz and Tarango have noted the difficulties with the English expression "kingdom of God," namely, that the word "kingdom" suggests sexist and hierarchical meanings. Isasi-Díaz and Tarango use the term "kin-dom" to avoid the above difficulties and to emphasize that within the community of God all are sisters and brothers. See Ada María Isasi-Díaz and Yolanda Tarango, *Hispanic Women: Prophetic Voice in the Church: Toward a Hispanic Women's Liberation Theology* (Minneapolis: Fortress Press, 1992), 116.

## 4. Historia: *Reflections on the Latino Story*

1. A common way of outlining Latino/a history uses the images of genealogical and/or chronological lineage. This approach attempts to regulate connections between thinkers and concepts. Who is included on such lists, their order of appearance, and the amount of time spent on examining their thoughts may imply an inherent subjectivity of the ones designing such a list. Usually, Hispanic theological thought is imagined in terms of generations of thinkers in which many branches of thoughts stem from a single trunk, which might be seen as the central source or unifying factor. A concern is that such a description may not adequately describe the fluid movement of theological thought. The danger exists that a descriptive category may be seen as more important than a particular point of view. Those theologians grouped closest to the roots or trunk (as designated by the constructors of the schematic) occupy a privileged position and become the focal point for the development and growth of that particular branch. Such a list creates a hierarchical structure that imposes limitations on the movement of theological thought as it attempts to regulate connections between thinkers and concepts. Given the pitfalls of a genealogical tree, an alternative is required. We suggest "rhizomes." Unlike trees with

roots and branches suggesting a unidirectional flow, rhizomes have multiple subterranean stems, spreading in various directions. Rather than one central trunk or root of original "truth," billions of roots exist with none of them being central. Rhizomes manifest themselves in surface extensions or unseen underground tubers where their interconnections compose unregulated networks that randomly connect. While a tree approach stresses an original, foundational beginning that linearly leads to a conclusion, a rhizome model concentrates on surface connections, where stems freely connect to construct additional understanding and knowledge. In other words, the story can never be completely told. For a complete explanation of the rhizomes paradigm, see Gilles Deleuze and Felix Guattari, *A Thousand Plateaus,* trans. Brian Massumi (Minneapolis: University of Minnesota Press, 1987).

2. Timothy M. Matovina, *Tejano Religion and Ethnicity: San Antonio, 1821–1860* (Austin: University of Texas Press, 1995), 39–48.

3. See David Ramos Torres, *Historia de la Iglesia de Dios, M.I.: Una Iglesia Ungida para Hacer Misión* (Río Piedras, P.R.: Editorial Pentecostal, 1993).

4. Eldín Villafañe, *The Liberating Spirit: Toward an Hispanic American Pentecostal Social Ethic* (Grand Rapids: Eerdmans, 1993), 94–95.

5. Rebecca Laird, *Ordained Women in the Church of the Nazarene: The First Generation* (Kansas City, Mo.: Nazarene Publishing House, 1993), 53–62.

6. Ana María Díaz-Stevens, *Oxcart Catholicism on Fifth Avenue: The Impact of the Puerto Rican Migration upon the Archdiocese of New York* (Notre Dame, Ind.: University of Notre Dame Press, 1993), 98, 103, 108–14.

7. Díaz-Stevens, *Oxcart Catholicism on Fifth Avenue,* 115; Anthony M. Stevens-Arroyo and Ana María Díaz-Stevens, *Recognizing the Latino Resurgence in U.S. Religion: The Emmaus Paradigm* (Boulder, Colo.: Westview Press, 1998), 133–35.

8. Stevens-Arroyo and Díaz-Stevens, *Recognizing the Latino Resurgence in U.S. Religion,* 124–25, 149.

9. Sister Maria Iglesias and Sister María Luz Hernández, "Hermanas," in *Prophets Denied Honor: An Anthology of the Hispano Church of the United States,* ed. Anthony M. Stevens-Arroyo (Maryknoll, N.Y.: Orbis Books, 1980), 141. See also Lara Medina, "Las Hermanas: Chicana/Latina Religious Political Activism, 1971–1997" (Ph.D. diss., Claremont Graduate University, 1998).

10. Allan Figueroa Deck, "Liturgy and Mexican American Culture," *Modern Liturgy* 3, no. 7 (1976): 24–26; *The Second Wave: Hispanic Ministry and the Evangelization of Culture* (New York: Paulist Press, 1989).

11. Justo L. González, *The Development of Christianity in Latin America* (Grand Rapids: Eerdmans, 1969).

12. Orlando E. Costas, *The Church and Its Mission: A Shattering Critique from the Third World* (Wheaton, Ill.: Tyndale, 1974); *The Integrity of Mission* (San Francisco: Harper & Row, 1979).

13. Gloria Inés Loya, "The Hispanic Woman: *Pasionaria* and *Pastora* of the Hispanic Community," in *Frontiers of Hispanic Theology in the United States,* ed. Allan Figueroa Deck (Maryknoll, N.Y.: Orbis Books, 1992), 124–33.

14. "Differences, difficulties — they do not divide us. The celebration of the Eucharist makes visible, surfaces what unites us — our value system: friendship, importance of family, sincerity, spontaneity, hospitality, openness, accepting others and, above all, our faith — our common belief. Yes, we are brought together by our faith, a faith we live as we struggle to understand it and which we understand as we live it." Ada María Isasi-Díaz, "The People of God on the Move — Chronicle of a History," in *Prophets Denied Honor: An Anthology of the Hispano Church of the United States,* ed. Anthony M. Stevens-Arroyo (Maryknoll, N.Y.: Orbis Books, 1980), 332.

15. Ada María Isasi-Díaz, *En la Lucha: A Hispanic Women's Liberation Theology* (Minneapolis: Fortress Press, 1993), 3.

16. Ada María Isasi-Díaz, "Mujerista Theology's Method: A Liberative Praxis, a Way of Life," *Listening* 27, no. 1 (1992): 49.

17. María Pilar Aquino, "Perspectives on a Latina's Feminist Liberation Theology," in *Frontiers of Hispanic Theology in the United States,* ed. Allan Figueroa Deck (Maryknoll, N.Y.: Orbis Books, 1992), 36.

18. María Pilar Aquino, "The Collective 'Dis-covery' of Our Own Power: Latina American Feminist Theology," in *Hispanic/Latino Theology: Challenge and Promise,* ed. Ada María Isasi-Díaz and Fernando F. Segovia (Minneapolis: Fortress Press, 1996), 240.

19. Ana María Pineda, "Hospitality," in *Practicing Our Faith: A Way of Life for a Searching People,* ed. Dorothy C. Bass (San Francisco: Jossey-Bass, 1997), 31.

## 5. Popular Religion and Alternative Traditions

1. Orlando O. Espín, *The Faith of the People: Theological Reflections on Popular Catholicism* (Maryknoll, N.Y.: Orbis Books, 1997), 2.

2. Espín, *The Faith of the People,* 169.

3. Orlando O. Espín, "Popular Religion as an Epistemology of Suffering," *Journal of Hispanic/Latino Theology* 2, no. 2 (November 1994): 65–67.

4. Colleen McDannell, *Material Christianity: Religion and Popular Culture in America* (New Haven: Yale University Press, 1995), 1.

5. C. Gilbert Romero, *Hispanic Devotional Piety: Tracing the Biblical Roots* (Maryknoll, N.Y.: Orbis Books, 1991), 2.

6. Jeanette Rodríguez, *Our Lady of Guadalupe: Faith and Empowerment among Mexican-American Women* (Austin: University of Texas Press, 1994), 143–44.

7. María Pilar Aquino, "Theological Method in U.S. Latino/a Theology: Toward an Intercultural Theology for the Third Millennium," in *From the Heart of Our People: Latino/a Explorations in Catholic Systematic Theology*, ed. Orlando O. Espín and Miguel H. Díaz (Maryknoll, N.Y.: Orbis Books, 1999), 28.

8. Roberto S. Goizueta, *Caminemos con Jesús: Toward a Hispanic/Latino Theology of Accompaniment* (Maryknoll, N.Y.: Orbis Books, 1995), 18–19.

9. Elizabeth Conde-Frazier, "Hispanic Protestant Spirituality," in *Teología en Conjunto: A Collaborative Hispanic Protestant Theology*, ed. José David Rodríguez and Loida I. Martell-Otero (Louisville: Westminster/John Knox Press, 1997), 125.

10. Carlos Cardoza-Orlandi, "Drum Beats of Resistance and Liberation: Afro-Caribbean Religions, the Struggle for Life, and the Christian Theologian," *Journal of Hispanic/Latino Theology* 3, no. 1 (1995): 56.

11. Luis D. León, "Religious Movement in the United States–Mexico Borderlands: Toward a Theory of Chicana/o Religious Poetics" (Ph.D. diss., University of California, Santa Barbara, 1997), 187.

12. Robert T. Trotter II and Juan Antonio Chavira, *Curanderismo: Mexican American Folk Healing*, 2d ed. (Athens: University of Georgia Press, 1982, 1997).

13. George Brandon, *Santería from Africa to the New World: The Dead Sell Memories* (Indianapolis: Indiana University Press, 1997), 85–87.

14. Pierre Verger, "The Yoruba High God: A Review of the Source," *Odu: Journal of Yoruba and Related Studies* 2, no. 2 (1966): 36–39.

15. Migene González-Wippler, *Santería: The Religion* (New York: Harmony Books, 1989), 9.

16. Likewise, a movement known as "Yoruba Reversionism" exists among African Americans who attempt to expurgate Spanish Catholicism from Santería. See Gary Edwards and John Mason, *Black Gods: Orisa Studies in the New World* (Brooklyn: Yoruba Theological Archministry, 1985), v.

17. Margaret Ramirez, "New Islamic Movement Seeks Latino Converts," *Los Angeles Times* (March 15, 1999): Metro section, B-1.

## 6. Emerging Theological Concepts

1. Gustavo Gutiérrez, "Liberation Theology and the Future of the Poor," in *Liberating the Future: God, Mammon, and Theology,* ed. Joerg Rieger (Minneapolis: Fortress Press, 1998), 97.

2. Rubén G. Rumbaut and Lisandro Pérez, "Pinos Nuevos? Growing Up American in Cuban Miami," *Cuban Affairs: Asuntos Cubanos* 3–4 (fall/winter 1998): 5.

3. See Victor Garcia and Laura Gonzalez Martinez, "Guanajuatense and Other Mexican Immigrants in the United States: New Communities in Non-Metropolitan and Agricultural Regions," JSRI Research Report no. 47, Julian Samora Research Institute, Michigan State University, East Lansing, Michigan, 1999.

4. The titles of several press articles indicate the construction of the Cuban success story: "Cuba's New Refugees Get Jobs Fast," *Business Week* (March 12, 1966): 69; Tom Alexander, "Those Amazing Cubans," *Fortune* (October 1966): 144–49; and "Cuban Success Story in the United States," *U.S. News and World Report* (March 20, 1967): 104–6.

5. Suzanne Oboler, *Ethnic Labels, Latino Lives: Identity and the Politics of (Re)Presentation in the United States* (Minneapolis: University of Minnesota Press, 1995), 138–41, 162–63.

6. See Jean-François Lyotard, *The Postmodern Condition: A Report on Knowledge,* trans. Geoff Bennington and Brian Massumi (Minneapolis: University of Minnesota Press, 1984), xxiv.

7. Fernando F. Segovia, "In the World but Not of It: Exile as Locus for a Theology of the Diaspora," *Hispanic/Latino Theology: Challenge and Promise,* ed. Ada María Isasi-Díaz and Fernando F. Segovia (Minneapolis: Fortress Press, 1996), 201.

8. Roberto S. Goizueta, *Caminemos con Jesús: Toward a Hispanic/Latino Theology of Accompaniment* (Maryknoll, N.Y.: Orbis Books, 1995), 140.

9. Ruy G. Suárez Rivero, "U.S. Latino/a Theology: A View from the Outside," in *From the Heart of Our People: Latino/a Explorations in Catholic Systematic Theology,* ed. Orlando O. Espín and Miguel H. Díaz (Maryknoll, N.Y.: Orbis Books, 1999), 244.

10. Harold J. Recinos, *Who Comes in the Name of the Lord? Jesus at the Margins* (Nashville: Abingdon Press, 1997), 50.

# Selected Annotated Bibliography

Throughout this book, we have endeavored to provide a basic understanding of and appreciation for theology as done by Latinas/os. Of necessity, we have simplified complex theological concepts. We hope that the reader will not arrive at the false conclusion that theologies from Hispanic perspectives lack depth, that they are not in conversation with other theological perspectives, or that they do not engage in serious scholarship. Fortunately, a growing collection of primary sources exists that reflects the diversity, complexity, and profoundness of Latino/a theological perspectives. Below is a list of published and forthcoming books dealing with Hispanic theologies in all their rich variety. These books were chosen because they deal specifically with the theological perspectives of Hispanics within the social context of the United States or are applicable to this context. The list, obviously, is not exhaustive. However, it includes, in the opinion of the authors, works from within the Latina/o *comunidad* that have made important contributions in expounding how Hispanics do theology. Following each title is a synopsis of the book presenting its overall thesis. The purpose of this selected annotated bibliography is to allow novices to Latino/a theologies to make informed decisions as to which other books they wish to read, study, and explore.

Abalos, David T. *Latinos in the United States: The Sacred and the Political.* Notre Dame, Ind.: University of Notre Dame Press, 1986.

Through his theory of transformation, Abalos provides an understanding of the political choices U.S. Hispanics make. He presents eight patterns of relationships and three "ways of life" to help the reader see and live in a new way. While this theory helps explain the reality of the human situation of Latinos/as, it is applicable to all groups. After presenting the main components of his theory, Abalos develops and explains the perspective of Latino/a life. He conducts a search for the authentic self that underlies the social self and then examines the family as relationships-in-motion, Latino/a organizations, sacred spaces, assimilation vs. liberation, the emerging middle class, and the future of Hispanics.

Aquino, María Pilar. *Our Cry for Life: A Feminist Theology from Latin America.* Maryknoll, N.Y.: Orbis Books, 1993.

Aquino presents a systematic theology from the perspective of Latinas as "actors/subjects" exercising all their rights within society in general and the church in particular. She seeks to correct the sexism and *machismo* existing within liberation theology. While her focus is to promote a collaboration between women and liberation theologians in Latin America, her analysis also holds true for those women located in the United States. Her quest for liberation is not limited to women at the expense of men. Rather, she searches for liberation from the social structures of patriarchy, which produce death for the entire Latino/a community. Her theology seeks new life in Christ for men, women, and children. One important aspect of this book lies in its reflection on what women are saying about their faith and their church, and its impact on the development of theology.

Aquino, María Pilar, Daisy L. Machado, and Jeanette Rodríguez-Holguín, eds. *Religion, Feminism, and Justice: An Introduction to Latina Feminist Theology.* Austin: University of Texas Press, forthcoming in 2001.

This work contains essays written by twelve Hispanic theologians who identify themselves as Latina feminists rather than as *mujerista* theologians. They share a perspective of the U.S. Hispanic community as culturally plural and *mestizo/a*. From this perspective and reality, they analyze and challenge Euroamerican feminism and womanism. Central to the challenge is their desire to move discussions beyond the white/black paradigm that dominates social and religious discourse in the United States. Throughout the book, the issue of justice is of central concern. The first section considers religious practice as the source of Latina thought. The second section takes up Latina feminist methodology by addressing Latina life in the United States, critically engaging current Latina feminism.

Bañuelas, Arturo J., ed. *Mestizo Christianity: Theology from the Latino Perspective.* Maryknoll, N.Y.: Orbis Books, 1995.

This collection of essays by fourteen well-known Hispanics is presented from within the *mestizaje* paradigm of the U.S. experience. The authors, dealing with the themes of cultural and theological identity among Latinos/as, attempt to provide the reader with an overview of some of the major topics discussed within the Hispanic theological community. These authors (Catholics and Protestants) were among the first to participate in the formation of a Latino/a theological perspective. Their articles deal with issues of theology from the perspective of disenfranchisement, methodology, *pastoral de conjunto*, missiology, popular religion, Latina feminism, social ethics, spirituality, and ecumenism.

Casarella, Peter J., and Raúl Gómez, eds. *El Cuerpo de Cristo: The Hispanic Presence in the U.S. Catholic Church*. New York: Crossroad, 1998.

This book is a collection of interdisciplinary studies on religious, cultural, and artistic aspects of Latina/o U.S. Catholicism. The sixteen essays are arranged into three sections, each one relating to the theme "the body of Christ." The first, the "wounded body," covers theology, liturgy, and spirituality. The second part, "the Latino body," explores the church, the family, and ecumenism. The final section, "the extended body," examines how faith generates culture. These essays expose the reader to both the Spanish colonial and Amerindian roots of the Hispanic culture, as well as to the religious depth of contemporary Latina/o Catholics. Almost half of all U.S. Catholics are Hispanic. This book attempts to lead the Catholic Church into the new millennium.

Costas, Orlando E. *Christ outside the Gate: Mission beyond Christendom*. Maryknoll, N.Y.: Orbis Books, 1982.

Writing from within the Latino/a culture, the noted missiologist Costas presents an analysis of issues dealing with mission work, addressing his book, in particular, to the Euroamerican Protestant missionary community. The book is divided into two sections: mission work in the Latin American periphery and mission work in the periphery of American cities. Costas interprets the missionary ventures of the United States from the margin of the dominant Euroamerican culture. In this work, a "theology of the crossroad" emerges, where cultures, ideologies, religious traditions, and social, economic, and political systems converge and confront each other, challenging those involved in mission work to hear the voices from outside the gate.

―――. *The Church and Its Mission: A Shattering Critique from the Third World*. Wheaton, Ill.: Tyndale, 1974.

This work was one of the first books to challenge how Euroamericans do missions. Costas speaks on behalf of Christians from the "mission fields" who have been on the margins of such discussions. He calls for a rethinking of the mentality that mission work is the "bearing of the gospel to heathens." He divides the book into three sections. The first addresses God's mission and the church's nature (its character, calling, and message) as fulfilled in Christ and fulfilled by human praxis. The second section studies God's mission and church growth. Costas's third section examines God's mission and church tensions, specifically the relationship among mission, church, and liberated humans. He concludes his discussion with an appraisal of the challenges facing world missions. In this book, the reader can see some of the earliest developments of what will eventually mature into Protestant Hispanic theological perspectives.

————. *Liberating News: A Theology of Contextual Evangelism.* Grand Rapids: Eerdmans, 1989.

Evangelization from the perspectives of the poor, the powerless, and the oppressed is the central theme of this book. Costas begins his study by examining two biblical paradigms: the story of Esther, who comes to the aid of those living on the margins at great political risk to herself, and Christ, who ministered from the Galilean periphery. These models contribute to the construction of a contextual evangelism based on the communal function of the Trinity. Furthermore, he looks toward the cross to find the new life and hope that are achieved through suffering and death. Salvation ceases to be a single event occurring in time. Instead, it becomes a lifelong transformative process that moves people from hyperindividualism toward communal praxis. In effect, Costas merges evangelism with social action.

Deck, Allan Figueroa, ed. *Frontiers of Hispanic Theology in the United States.* Maryknoll, N.Y.: Orbis Books, 1992.

This collection of essays sets out to (1) demonstrate the range and seriousness of the theological reflection occurring among Latina/o Catholic theologians; (2) develop a dialogue between Hispanic theologians and the academy; and (3) create a bridge between North American churches and Latin American liberation theology. These goals are accomplished by exploring the central themes of Catholic Hispanic theology, specifically issues dealing with popular religion, spirituality, liturgy, feminism, and *mestizaje.* Through this methodology of theological reflection, Latino/a Catholics offer a theology rooted within their culture that challenges both the Euroamerican church and the overall theological community.

————. *The Second Wave: Hispanic Ministry and the Evangelization of Cultures.* New York: Paulist Press, 1989.

As the U.S. Hispanic presence continues to grow, Deck expresses concern that the "cultural evangelization" prominent among Euroamericans, with its overly emphasized individualism and materialism, robs Latinas/os of their rich religious heritage. In fact, he maintains that the so-called evangelizers of the dominant culture are the ones in need of evangelizing. Concentrating specifically on people of Mexican descent in the U.S. Southwest, Deck constructs a Catholic ministerial method that respects, and conducts its approach from within, the Latino/a ethos. The importance of *comunidad* is apparent in his insistence that evangelism must be directed as much to the society as to the individual, striving toward the conversion of oppressive social structures.

Deck, Allan Figueroa, and Jay P. Dolan, eds. *Hispanic Catholic Culture in the United States: Issues and Concerns.* Notre Dame, Ind.: University of Notre Dame Press, 1994.

This is the final volume of a three-part series. The first two books, *Mexican Americans and the Catholic Church* and *Puerto Rican and Cuban Catholics in the U.S.*, use primary and secondary sources to focus on themes affecting specific national groups. This latest volume offers a collection of essays on key issues affecting most Catholic Latinas/os regardless of national origins, regional location, or cultural identity, for example, Hispanic Catholic contemporary history, social identity, church organization, issues affecting Latinas and youth, popular Catholicism, contemporary liturgy, and the challenges presented by evangelicals and Pentecostals. These articles expose the national struggles that Catholic Latinas/os face within the church, overturning previous assumptions that such conflicts were merely local parochial disharmonies.

Deck, Allan Figueroa, Ismael García, Justo L. González, Ada María Isasi-Díaz, and David Maldonado, eds. *Nuestra Teología: A Handbook of Latino/Hispanic Theology.* Minneapolis: Fortress Press, forthcoming in 2002.

These editors compile a bilingual resource handbook with alphabetized entries on a wide-ranging variety of topics that are key to an adequate understanding of Latino/a theology. The authors of this intentionally ecumenical effort come from a wide range of faith traditions, among them Catholic, historic mainline Protestant, evangelical, and Pentecostal. The sponsoring agency for the handbook is the Asociación para la Educación Teológica Hispana (AETH). Each article includes a short summary of traditional views of a topic and then describes the Hispanic theological perspective. Among the topics are the following: the Bible, the church, eschatology, exile/migration/globalization, family, feminist theology, *mestizaje/mulatez*, popular religion, preaching, and the Trinity.

De La Torre, Miguel A. *The Quest for the Cuban Christ: A Historical Search*. Gainesville: University Press of Florida, 2002.

This book argues that Cubans must understand Christ through the historical development of the Cuban culture. Because a Eurocentric Christ is impotent for many Cubans, the author conducts a historical analysis of the Cuban ethos in order to discover God's movement in Cuban history, a history that reveals a Christ who is also Cuban. The Christ of the conquistadores and the imperialists, the apotheosis of José Martí as the ideal Cuban Christ, the black Christ of the African slaves and Santería, the understanding of Christ through Marianism and Cuban feminism, the Christ of the Revolution, the Christ of the *exilio,* and the Christ depicted through Cuban art, both on the island and in the States, are all part of, if not central to, Cuban identity and religiosity. De La Torre reviews these historical representations of Christ to construct what he calls "an *ajiaco* (stew) Christ" rooted within the Cuban experience.

———. *Reading the Bible from the Margins*. Maryknoll, N.Y.: Orbis Books, forthcoming in 2002.

This textbook for undergraduates introduces Christian biblical concepts and interpretations from a variety of perspectives, notably the perspectives of those suffering from race, class, or gender oppression.

Díaz, Miguel H. *On Being Human: U.S. Hispanic and Rahnerian Perspectives*. Maryknoll, N.Y.: Orbis Books, 2001.

Díaz provides an exploration of Hispanic theological anthropology that puts Hispanic theology in conversation with Catholic tradition. This study presents basic understandings of the theological anthropology developed by Virgilio Elizondo (*mestizaje*), Roberto Goizueta (accompaniment), Orlando Espín (popular religion), Ada María Isasi-Díaz (struggle), Alejandro García-Rivera (creatureliness), María Pilar Aquino (patriarchy and oppression), and Sixto García (relationality). Turning to the theological approach of Karl Rahner, Díaz demonstrates how Rahner's understandings of sin, grace, salvation, and the human person mesh with Hispanic understandings.

Díaz-Stevens, Ana María. *Oxcart Catholicism on Fifth Avenue: The Impact of the Puerto Rican Migration upon the Archdiocese of New York*. Notre Dame, Ind.: University of Notre Dame Press, 1993.

Since the late 1940s, Puerto Ricans have been migrating to the cities of the North, particularly New York. In that cold concrete city, far from the mountains and farms of their birth, they are told to assimilate in order to survive. Yet, the oxcart, used in the homeland to bring food, healing, and religion, symbolically becomes the signifier of the Puerto Ricans' longing for the homeland and their heritage. Díaz-Stevens takes the reader on a quest for empowerment and identity free from the limitations of geographic constraints. By examining the impact of Puerto Ricans on the Catholic Church in New York, she shows how identity can be created apart from the homeland in the same way that the religiosity of the Puerto Rican highlands existed and flourished in the absence of the church as an institution.

Durand, Jorge, and Douglas S. Massey *Miracles on the Border: Retablos of Mexican Migrants to the United States.* Tucson: University of Arizona Press, 1995.

*Retablos* (also known as *ex-voto*) are works of plastic art that depict Mexican popular religiosity. Their origins predate the 1500s. These small votive paintings, usually done on tin, were left at religious shrines to offer public thanks for divine intervention or favors received. The *retablos* collected for this book present a narrative-type manifestation of the plight of twentieth-century Mexicans forced to migrate to the United States in search of jobs. These are religious expressions from the underside of the U.S. Mexican migrant community. The authors have collected these visual religious expressions along with the accompanying prayers for help or thanksgiving, providing the reader with a grassroots entrance into the religious soul of these migrants. Using the *retablos* as the source of their investigation, the authors analyze the social phenomena of the northward migration of Mexican labor.

Elizondo, Virgilio P. *The Future Is Mestizo: Life Where Cultures Meet.* Oak Park, Ill.: Meyer-Stone Books, 1988.

This is one of the first books to ground the Latino/a theological perspective in the *mestizaje* of the people. From the borderlands between the United States and Mexico, a new humanity, a cosmic race, is coming into being. Elizondo attempts to demonstrate from this new space how a commitment to the gospel, one that leads to healing, can be lived out. This healing overcomes the pain of being neither Mexican nor American and celebrates the beginning of something new. Reaching deep into the Mexican American experience of violation, he illustrates how Hispanic theological perspectives are developed. A radical aspect of his message is that these perspectives, born from *mestizaje,* are not limited to Mexican Americans but rather form a paradigm that leads to wholeness and oneness for all humanity.

———. *Galilean Journey: The Mexican-American Promise.* Rev. ed.
Maryknoll, N.Y.: Orbis Books, 2000.

Originally based on the author's doctoral dissertation, this book in-
troduces the concept of *mestizaje,* the distinctive feature of Mexican
American identity, which is defined by the struggle for life, human dig-
nity, and liberation. Elizondo shows how Christ, himself a marginalized
Galilean, also bore the mark of *mestizo.* Latinas/os, like Christ, become
the rejected stone chosen by God to reveal Godself to the entire world.
Hence, Hispanics play a salvific role in the revelation of God to humanity.
The first section deals with the Mexican American experience, specifically
the history and dynamics of *mestizaje,* the cultural birth and maturity of
Mexican Americans, and their faith as a symbol of resistance and survival.
The second section explores the Galilee experience, the struggle toward
fulfillment at Jerusalem, and the call to move beyond all borders. The
final section, from marginalization to new creation, examines the way of
Jesus, the beginning of the new *mestizo* creation, and the paradox of the
Resurrection.

———. *Guadalupe: Mother of the New Creation.* Maryknoll, N.Y.: Orbis
Books, 1997.

Writing in a lyrical style, Elizondo reflects on the story and meaning of the
apparition of the Mother of God to the indigenous peasant Juan Diego.
By interpreting the *Nican mopohura,* the Guadalupe apparition story, Elizondo shows how the bloody conquest of the so-called New World can
be transformed by God into a new creation, specifically the creation of a
new cosmic race. Although the book appears to be a devotional one, the
author deals seriously with the theological themes of *mestizaje,* popular
religion, feminism, and evangelism. Furthermore, rather than keeping the
Guadalupe story as a Mexican icon, or as a Hispanic symbol of spirituality, Elizondo reveals the universal significance of the apparition to the
overall church, a cosmic instance of God's salvific act with relevance in
providing grace to all humanity.

———, ed. *Way of the Cross: Passion of Christ in the Americas.*
Maryknoll, N.Y.: Orbis Books, 1992.

This book consist of short meditations on the stations of the cross, written
by leading Catholic liberation theologians like Gustavo Gutiérrez, Leo-
nardo Boff, Elsa Tamez, and Jon Sobrino. Each meditation focuses on an
aspect of Christ's Passion against the backdrop of the Spanish conquest
of the Americas. While the Americas have been a land of opportunity for
many Europeans, these opportunities existed only because of the sacrifi-

cial death of Amerindians and Africans. This collection takes the reader on a journey by way of the cross to share the suffering, crucifixion, and anticipated hope of Easter for those who have been marginalized in the Americas.

Elizondo, Virgilio P., and Timothy M. Matovina. *Mestizo Worship: A Pastoral Approach to Liturgical Ministry.* Collegeville, Minn.: Liturgical Press, 1998.

The authors provide an analysis of the foundational expressions of faith formulated by the Mexican American community and how they are celebrated within Catholic liturgical life. Close attention is given to the veneration of La Virgen de Guadalupe. The authors study the dynamics between the liturgy and the expressions of faith shaped by the historical struggle of a people. By paying close attention to the symbolic world that underlies the community's devotions and rituals, the authors offer a creative way of incorporating these expressions of faith into the life of the church as an opportunity to encounter Christ in the diverse worship of the parishioners.

———. *San Fernando Cathedral: Soul of the City.* Maryknoll, N.Y.: Orbis Books, 1998.

At first glance, it appears that San Fernando Cathedral, the oldest cathedral in the United States, is the subject of this book. Yet, a closer examination reveals how this sacred space in San Antonio, Texas, manifests the survival of Roman Catholicism over centuries as the focal point for the religiosity of the Mexican American community. This survival is due to the *mestizaje* of the church. While Matovina traces historically the distinct rituals of the cathedral, Elizondo articulates the theological significance the current rituals have for the predominantly Hispanic congregation. Specifically, the *posada* and Good Friday procession through San Antonio's streets are narrated to reveal the Latino/a soul of San Antonio.

Espín, Orlando O. *The Faith of the People: Theological Reflections on Popular Catholicism.* Maryknoll, N.Y.: Orbis Books, 1997.

This collection of essays by Espín provides a critical analysis of popular Catholicism as practiced by the Latino/a masses. Espín insists that the faith of the people, while not theologically sound according to the church, should be, not dismissed, but taken seriously. Furthermore, he shows that while the majority of Latinos/as are Catholics, they practice their faith in a "popular" way that may be at odds with official standards of piety.

Espín also demonstrates how the true "church" is, not the official insti-tution, but the "real" laity composed of average people who participate in a popular expression of their faith, and as such, their way of doing church must be included in Catholic discourse. He goes on to state that the foun-dation of popular religion is the entire community, especially the older women in families. Finally, Espín asserts that because of the authentic reli-gious expression of Hispanics through popular Catholicism, an element of resistance exists in the manifestation of the faith.

Espín, Orlando O., and Miguel H. Díaz, eds. *From the Heart of Our People: Latino/a Explorations in Catholic Systematic Theology.* Maryknoll, N.Y.: Orbis Books, 1999.

The editors assemble a collection of essays that provides a systematic Catholic theology from Latino/a faith and cultural perspectives. When one considers that almost half of all U.S. Catholics are Latinas/os, it becomes puzzling why their voices remain marginalized. Espín and Díaz present the work of leading Catholic theologians and one Protestant on faith from within the Hispanic community, not only to elucidate how Hispanics do theology, but to serve as a challenge to the U.S. Catholic Church to benefit from this discourse. Contributions to the book deal with method-ology, ministry, cosmology, worship, history, grace, sin, ecclesiology, and the Virgin (Our Lady of Charity).

Fernandez, Eduardo. *La Cosecha: Harvesting Contemporary United States Hispanic Theology, 1968–1998.* Collegeville, Minn.: Liturgical Press, 2000.

This book is a history and analysis of the development of Hispanic the-ology, primarily of the Latino/a Catholic context. Fernandez begins by providing general background information regarding the experience of Latinos/as within the culture and church of the United States, focusing primarily on Hispanic Catholicism. He then concentrates on the historical development of the perspectives of Latina/o theologies. Fernandez explores Hispanic theology as contextual by reviewing the theology of seven Catho-lics and one Protestant. He ends the book with a few observations about the development of Latina/o theology in light of future challenges.

García, Ismael. *Dignidad: Ethics through Hispanic Eyes.* Nashville: Abingdon Press, 1997.

A Protestant Christian ethicist, García reflects on the consequences Latinos/as face in being defined as the "Other" of the dominant cul-ture, specifically in the shaping and articulation of their identity. He calls for the *dignidad* (dignity) of a people in the claiming and proclaiming of their own identity. By defending their basic human right to *dignidad*, Latinas/os create a space from which they can form moral behavior and ethical conduct. The sociohistorical experiences of Latinos/as shaped the moral context of Hispanics and so are essential considerations when doing "ethics through Hispanic eyes." García identifies the ordeal of migration, the dilemmas of social integration into the dominant culture, and the struggle to name oneself as a people as some of the important issues for Latinas/os attempting to forge a new identity.

García-Rivera, Alexandro. *The Community of the Beautiful: A Theological Aesthetics.* Collegeville, Minn.: Liturgical Press, 1999.

Through the use of theological aesthetics, this book explores signs and symbols in the popular Catholicism of U.S. Latinos/as. From the struggles of the Latino/a community of faith, beauty is revealed within a violent history of oppression: a beauty that calls for a retrieval of the traditions of the marginalized faith community and a beauty that is fully rooted in the incarnation of God as "the Form." Jesus Christ, as ultimate Form, draws believers toward him, believers whose receptivity to Christ's life is based on beholding the implied difference familiar to the Latino/a construction of history and identity. Investigating the transcendental attributes of God (the true, the good, and the beauty), García-Rivera develops the latter, concluding that the "lifting up of the lowly," which is seen as ugly by the dominant culture, is in fact a different beauty, a community of the beautiful.

———. *St. Martín de Porres: The "Little Stories" and the Semiotics of Culture.* Maryknoll, N.Y.: Orbis Books, 1995.

García-Rivera asserts that much of Latin American history and theology has focused on the "big story," that is, the stories popular to the dominant society, while the "little stories" from the grass roots have been ignored, suppressed, or trivialized. Yet, the power of these "little stories" is evident by the ability of popular religiosity to overcome attempts to silence them. Through a critical analysis of the popular "little" stories about the biracial Peruvian saint Martín de Porres, García-Rivera formulates an understanding of *mestizaje* that informs a world of growing diversity. In a world accustomed to dehumanizing those considered inferior due to race or ethnicity, García-Rivera uses a methodology of semiotics to reread the stories of San Martín in order to reveal the universal "big story" of what it means to be human living under oppression.

Goizueta, Roberto S. *Caminemos con Jesús: Toward a Hispanic/Latino Theology of Accompaniment.* Maryknoll, N.Y.: Orbis Books, 1995.

Goizueta asserts that U.S. Latino/a popular Catholicism is a privileged place for God's revelation to humanity. He articulates a theology grounded in Hispanic experience, from the popular religious celebration of Holy Week to the Virgin of Guadalupe veneration. From these narratives and religious symbols, he constructs an understanding of God, Jesus, Mary, humans, and the interaction among them. The book is designed as a "hermeneutical circle," beginning with experience (chaps. 1–2), moving to analysis of that experience (chaps. 3–6), and concluding with experience informed by the analysis (chap. 7). He introduces a theology grounded in a praxis that makes a preferential option for the faith of the poor understood as a process of "walking with Jesus," or accompaniment.

―――. *Mañana: Christian Theology from a Hispanic Perspective.* Nashville: Abingdon Press, 1990.

This book is a reflection on theology from a Hispanic Protestant perspective, a religious minority among Latinos/as. Besides shattering the myth that all Hispanics are Catholics, González presents his theological views from within the security of his faith, attempting to find a space between the Euroamerican Protestant groups to which he belongs and the Hispanic majority of Catholics to whom he is tied. He calls for a new Reformation, in which the authority of a faith community living out the gospel in relation to the poor has greater authority than learned theological faculties, just as the authority of the Bible supercedes popes and councils. He also encourages Latinas/os to read the Bible in Spanish, meaning not a Spanish translation but from the perspective of U.S. Hispanics. In addition, he elucidates theological concepts such as anthropology, Christology, pneumatology, scriptural inspiration, Trinitarian doctrine, and the doctrine of creation.

―――. *Santa Biblia: The Bible through Hispanic Eyes.* Nashville: Abingdon Press, 1996.

Everyone reads the Bible from his or her social location, that is, through the eyes of his or her culture, as influenced by that culture's history and traditions. Latinas/os are no different. González provides a reading of the Scriptures from the Hispanic perspective, which is influenced by marginality, poverty, *mestizaje*, exile, and solidarity of the community. While he does not attempt to provide the final or ultimate Latino/a perspective, since all Hispanics come to the text from different backgrounds, he tries to provide a particular Latina/o perspective that he hopes will resonate with the majority of Hispanics. González weaves together the biblical interpretations of Hispanic pastors and scholars to provide an exegesis that informs, comforts, and challenges Latinos/as.

————, ed. *We Are a People! Initiatives in Hispanic American Theology.* Minneapolis: Fortress Press, 1992.

This collection of essays from several leading Catholic Latino/a scholars addresses the issues of methodology, Scripture usage, feminism, and major theological concepts from the perspective of Hispanic theologians. They seek to carve out a space between Latin American liberation theology and Euroamerican Catholic theology from which to express a Latina/o voice from within the U.S. underside. These voices, which have been historically ignored, show that even if Hispanics are "a community of communities," from different races, nations, and economic classes, they are still one people.

González, Justo L., ed. *¡Alabadle! Hispanic Christian Worship.* Nashville: Abingdon Press, 1996.

González assembles a series of articles that present a variety of Hispanic worship experiences. The book is designed to debunk the assumption that a typical Latino/a worship style exists by providing illustrations of worship styles practiced in numerous church traditions, such as Assemblies of God, United Methodist, Catholic, American Baptist, Presbyterian, and Disciples of Christ. In spite of these diverse worship traditions, an excitement for the manifestation of God within the worship service serves as a unifying source. This undertaking is among the first to examine worship from an ecumenical perspective, providing insight into different Hispanic worship, music, and liturgy experiences.

————, ed. *Voces: Voices from the Hispanic Church.* Nashville: Abingdon Press, 1996.

This book is a collection of twenty-three essays originally published by *Apuntes,* a journal of Hispanic theology in which Latino/a scholars and laity discuss among themselves, and with the church, issues facing their community. As varied as the Latino/a population, these voices represent different denominations and confession traditions. Some essays deal with specific issues affecting a particular ethnic group; others are relevant to the entire Hispanic community. The book is bilingual, with some essays written in Spanish and others in English. Together, these voices present a challenge to U.S. churches, both Catholic and Protestant, to rethink theology, tradition, and mission.

Guerrero, Andrés G. *A Chicano Theology.* Maryknoll, N.Y.: Orbis Books, 1987.

Guerrero presents the sociohistorical and ecclesiastical situation of Chicanos/as in order to create a liberative response to the systematic oppression this group has endured. In the first part of the book, the author reviews the historical material, starting with the conquest, to illustrate antecedents to Chicana/o oppression. Then he describes the social location and challenges Chicanos/as to face it. In the second part of the book, Guerrero explores oral tradition by interviewing nine Chicana/o leaders. These interviews uncover factors that contribute to Chicano/a oppression, while exploring the themes of *machismo,* racism/classism, education and labor, violence, respect for basic rights, land, fatalistic tendencies, the Catholic Church, theology, exodus symbols, the religious-spiritual symbol of Guadalupe, and the secular-spiritual symbol of the "cosmic race."

Isasi-Díaz, Ada María. *En la Lucha: A Hispanic Women's Liberation Theology.* Minneapolis: Fortress Press, 1993.

*En la lucha* is a Cuban idiom which translates as "in the struggle." Isasi-Díaz conceives of theological ethics within the struggle of a people for survival and liberation and develops a conversation between Latin American liberation theology and the experiences of Latinas living in the United States. While avoiding the abstract, she constructs what she calls *mujerista* (womanist) theology, rooted in the experience of Latinas. By examining the life context of various Latinas' religious practices, Isasi-Díaz describes a feminist perspective designed to empower Latinas who suffer classism from the dominant culture and sexism from both the dominant and Hispanic cultures. While lifting up the experience and theological understandings of Latinas, the book contributes to the overall theological discourse designed to find liberation for all humanity.

———. *Mujerista Theology: A Theology for the Twenty-First Century.* Maryknoll, N.Y.: Orbis Books, 1996.

This book is a collection of essays written by Isasi-Díaz from the perspective of *mujerista* theology. In the first part of the book, which is autobiographical in nature, Isasi-Díaz locates her "self" by elucidating her own life experience in her search for liberation from being the oppressed "Other" in a foreign land, as well as her search for self-identity. She reveals her own space of subjectivity (disproving anyone's claim to objectivity) and conducts her reflection from within the Latina community. In the second part of the book, Isasi-Díaz focuses on the methodology of doing theology through the use of Latinas' grassroots religiosity. She explores and elaborates issues Latinas face in their daily struggles, such as solidarity, justice, anthropology, God's word, liturgy, and rituals.

Isasi-Díaz, Ada María, and Fernando F. Segovia, eds. *Hispanic/Latino Theology: Challenge and Promise*. Minneapolis: Fortress Press, 1996.

Significant in many ways, this is one of the few books that attempt to bring Catholic and Protestant theologians together in a *teología en conjunto* venture. The nineteen essays are arranged under three broad sections: Latino/a theological sources (church history, oral tradition, biblical narrative), social location (the barrio, the diaspora, Latina feminism, social science), and the different trajectories used to articulate a Hispanic theological voice (popular religion, theopoetics, *mujerista* theology, postmodernity). The book attempts to confront the challenge Latinos/as face within the social context of the dominant culture, living not just on the peripheries of power and affluence but as foreigners in an alien land.

Isasi-Díaz, Ada María, and Yolanda Tarango. *Hispanic Women: Prophetic Voice in the Church: Toward a Hispanic Women's Liberation Theology*. Minneapolis: Fortress Press, 1992.

This book is among the earliest articulations of a Hispanic women's liberation theology, a communal process rooted in the stories and struggles of Latinas. These are stories in which sexism interlocks with classism and ethnic prejudice, stories that contribute toward a cultural theology. The presence of classism and ethnic prejudice separates Latina feminism from Euroamerican feminism because the latter is prone to participate in the oppression of its Latina sisters. The core of the liberation theology that Tarango and Isasi-Díaz present is the experience of Latinas and their understanding of those experiences, hence the importance of including their own life journeys in this text.

León, Luis D. *The Religious Impulse in the Life and Work of Cesar Chavez*. Berkeley: University of California Press, forthcoming in 2002.

León focuses his attention on Cesar Chavez, founder of the United Farm Workers (UFW). During his lifetime, Chavez inspired many Chicanas/os to struggle for civil rights. Inasmuch as he was a labor leader, he was also, in effect, a religious leader who preached a gospel of self-sacrifice, nonviolence, and social justice. León uncovers the religious impulse in Chavez's life and work, arguing that (1) Chavez emerged as a mystical prophetic figure in his work with the UFW and that (2) the UFW became not so unlike a religion in itself, with its own distinct symbols, myths, rituals, ethics, and narratives of "redemption" and "condemnation." Chavez was a religious innovator who transcended Christian institutional and "popular" religious forms to address the power structures he confronted. As such, he practiced what León terms "religious poetics," in which the religious and political are inseparable. Certainly, in Chavez's work, the logic, function, and representation of the UFW resemble the operations of a religious movement.

Lucas, Isidro. *The Browning of America: The Hispanic Revolution in the American Church.* Chicago: Fides/Claretian, 1981.

This was among the first books to consider seriously the impact Latinos/as have on churches. Revealing the soul of Hispanics by describing their views on God, faith, country, tradition, and heritage, Lucas moves the discourse away from viewing Hispanics as problems to be solved or objects to be counted. Instead, he exposes the history, struggles, and aspirations of the fastest-growing minority in this nation and the impact that growth will have on churches. Although Lucas writes mainly from a Catholic perspective and a Mexican American point of view, the book, while a bit outdated, serves as a good introduction to the U.S. Latina/o world.

Maldonado, David, ed. *Protestantes/Protestants: Hispanic Christianity within Mainline Traditions.* Nashville: Abingdon Press, 1999.

This collection of essays deals specifically with Hispanic mainline Protestant perspectives and attempts to address what it means to be a Hispanic Protestant within a Hispanic culture that is predominantly Catholic and what it means to be a Hispanic Protestant within a predominantly Euroamerican Protestant denomination. In other words, the book deals with the acquisition of voice and the construction of identity of a twice marginalized group. By exploring sociohistorical antecedents, cultural factors, the theological convictions that inform Protestant mission work, and church growth strategies, these essays consider historical roots and developments, theological, sociological, and contextual dynamics, and the congregational realities of Hispanic Protestantism.

Matovina, Timothy M., and Gerald E. Poyo, eds. *¡Presente! U.S. Latino Catholics from Colonial Origins to the Present.* Maryknoll, N.Y.: Orbis Books, 2000.

The editors of this volume present a history of the U.S. Latino/a Catholic identity by amassing two hundred years of original documents. From the start of the European colonial venture to the struggles for dignity by Hispanics at the close of the twentieth century, the book uses primary sources to reveal the changing nature of Latina/o Catholicism. Bearing witness to the continuous presence of Hispanics in what is now the continental United States and the Catholic Church, this book examines the complex and multiple ways Latinos/as forged their identity within the various experiences of U.S. Catholicism.

Ortiz, Manuel. *The Hispanic Challenge: Opportunities Confronting the Church*. Downers Grove, Ill.: InterVarsity Press, 1993.

Realizing that Latinos/as are the fastest-growing minority group in the United States, Ortiz contemplates the opportunities that can arise from the changing ethnic composition of society and church. First, he explores the unique needs and concerns of U.S. Latinas/os by examining their sociohistorical location, concentrating on the Mexican, Puerto Rican, and Cuban experiences. The second section raises key missiological and ecclesiological issues, specifically those dealing with Catholic-Protestant relationships, racial reconciliation, and justice. In the final section, Ortiz, concerned with the consequences the young face due to barrio life, focuses on leadership and educational training, calling on Hispanic church leaders to develop mentoring programs in order to develop second-generation leadership.

Pazmiño, Roberto W. *Latin American Journey: Insights for Christian Education in North America*. Cleveland: United Church Press, 1994.

Pazmiño, a professor of religious education, journeys to Latin America as a U.S. Latino in search of his "roots." From the barrios of Costa Rica and the Christian base communities of Nicaragua, he uncovers the implications of liberation theology for the discipline of religious and theological education. Relying on the works of the Brazilian educator Paulo Freire, Pazmiño presents a paradigm of Christian education for North America grounded in God's mission to the world as manifested in the Latin American experience. During his journey he discovers that he is a "new" type of Hispanic, one who is Hispanic in North America but not South America. This revelation allows him to introduce U.S. Latina/o culture as a new contributing partner to the emerging multicultural, global partnership in Christian education.

Pedraja, Luis G. *Jesus Is My Uncle: Christology from a Hispanic Perspective*. Nashville: Abingdon Press, 1999.

Pedraja approaches Christology from the social location of Latinos/as, paying close attention to the role played by language and experience. He examines how Hispanics speak about Jesus to show how the christological trajectory of Latinas/os differs from the trajectory of Euroamericans. Jesus is the name of Pedraja's father's brother. Are Hispanics showing disrespect to the holy name of Jesus by using it as a "common" name, or do Hispanics realize that Jesus is a common experience accessible to them? Pedraja also reflects on the Trinitarian aspect of the Deity to provide a clearer comprehension of the Latina/o perspective. Crucial to the Latino/a understanding of Jesus is the phrase "the Verb made flesh" (John 1:14), which portrays Jesus, not as the Word, but as the Verb. God as action moves theological reflections from the abstract to the practical, from doctrine to praxis.

Peterson, Anna, Manuel Vásquez, and Philip Williams. *Christianity, Social Change, and Globalization in the Americas.* New Brunswick, N.J.: Rutgers University Press, forthcoming in 2001.

The book examines how diverse Protestant and Catholic congregations, specifically those with substantial Salvadoran and Peruvian memberships, interpret and respond to globalization. These growing immigrant diasporas do not "melt" into the host cultures but rather maintain multiple ties with their places of origin. The book argues that globalization is felt at the level of everyday and community life, where individuals must draw from their cultural, often religious, resources to negotiate an increasingly baffling and threatening world. Christian churches assist Latinos/as at the margins by helping to build self, community, and space within a still precarious civil society. The authors claim that these churches offer important organizational, pragmatic, and symbolic resources to strengthen both the public sphere and the people's capacity to negotiate the challenges of everyday life. This book concentrates on three main areas: (1) family, youth, and community; (2) democratization, citizenship, and political participation; and (3) transnationalism.

Pineda, Ana María, and Robert Schreiter, eds. *Dialogue Rejoined: Theology and Ministry in the United States Hispanic Reality.* Collegeville, Minn: Liturgical Press, 1995.

This collection of articles undertakes a new dialogue mindful of past evangelistic excess and conscious of the need for new models of evangelism that are unlike the original models brought to the so-called New World by the Spaniards to "save" the heathens. The contributors to this book call for a respectful dialogue with mutual engagement among equals. This book endeavors to establish a conversation between the world of Catholic theological education and the reality of the U.S. Hispanic experience. The first section of the book examines the four major ethnic groups that compose the majority of U.S. Latinos/as (Mexicans, Central Americans, Puerto Ricans, and Cubans), surveying their history and current pastoral challenges. The second section presents the essays of six Catholic theologians (some of whom are not Latinos/as) who investigate the contributions made by Hispanics to the theological dialogue.

Pulido, Albert L. *The Sacred World of the Penitentes.* Washington, D.C.: Smithsonian Institution Press, 2000.

Pulido conducts an exploration of the brotherhood that developed in the isolated frontiers of the early Spanish Empire. Isolated from colonial power, Catholicism flourished in what was to become New Mexico. These Hispano Catholics of the Southwest have been sensationalized as a primitive religion because of their practice of self-flagellation; however, the author focuses on their core religious concepts of doing penance through charity and prayer. He explores how their teachings, which developed apart from institutional Catholicism, provide a creative and practical expression of faith.

Recinos, Harold J. *Hear the Cry! A Latino Pastor Challenges the Church.* Louisville: Westminster/John Knox Press, 1989.

While commending Euroamericans for their sensitivity to the reality of oppression and the need for ministry elsewhere in the world, Recinos challenges them to "hear the cry" of those oppressed within the United States, particularly Latinos/as. Recinos writes about his experience as pastor of the Church of All Nations, which is located in the barrio of the Lower East Side of Manhattan. By interweaving the stories of his congregation with theological reflections and socioeconomic analyses, he fleshes out the Latino/a religious experience. He shows how liberation theology and base communities can concretely function in the United States. His book moves the discussion from a privatized Christianity harmonized with conservative political thinking toward a faith praxis embodied with the gospel where the disenfranchised learn to speak with their own voices.

———. *Jesus Weeps: Global Encounters on Our Doorsteps.* Nashville: Abingdon Press, 1992.

As globalization has heightened Christians' concerns for all humanity, theological schools attempt to equip future leaders for the challenges of worldwide witness and service. While an interest in missions and a need for solidarity with those in the Two-Thirds World have influenced North American Christian global perspectives, Recinos challenges the dominant culture not to overlook the oppressed and poor within the First World, in-

cluding the barrios of the United States. Through a careful analysis of the
biblical text, Recinos shows how the city is central to the process of globalization and mission. Relying on liberationist motifs (Hispanic, as well
as black, Native American, Jewish, and feminist), he emphasizes praxis
over against abstract speculation, forcing the reader to encounter the Two-
Thirds World within First World cities. Mission need not take place in
far-off lands but can be done in the increasingly diverse settings at home.
Recinos guides the church toward a different cultural context within its
own backyard through an approach he calls "pastoral anthropology."

————. *Who Comes in the Name of the Lord? Jesus at the Margins.*
    Nashville: Abingdon Press, 1997.

Recinos argues that God-in-Jesus changed human history. Relying on the
Gospel narratives, he shows how God identified with those who were considered weak and inferior by those with power and privilege. Nazareth,
where the incarnation took place, is the barrio of today. Hence, institutional churches must step out of their privileged status and work among
the marginalized if they want to participate in the work of God in human
history. It is in the barrio where one can find Jesus. If churches choose
not to look there, their future voice will be irrelevant, as the trends of
declining membership continue. The book serves as an invitation to these
mainline churches to discover Christ rather than to create a new culture
and religious synthesis based on conservative ideologies. The future of the
church, if it is to be the church of Christ, will be found among the poor,
the powerless, the despised, and the rejected.

Rivera Pagán, Luis N. *A Violent Evangelism: The Political and Religious
    Conquest of the Americas.* Louisville: Westminster/John Knox Press,
    1992.

Over five hundred years ago, the Iberian culture came into contact with
the Amerindians with devastating results for the latter. Genocide was conducted on a massive scale, justified and supported by the church. Rivera
Pagán examines primary sources to help the reader understand the rea-
soning and motivation behind the conquest of the Americas. Furthermore,
he shows how the biblical text was read, how theology was constructed,
and how philosophy was understood in order to rationalize the decimation of an indigenous people. All Latin Americans and U.S. Latinos/as can
still feel the effects of the Iberian conquest. By examining the past, Rivera
Pagán helps explain the present, elucidating the historical antecedents to
the problems Hispanics are facing.

Rodríguez, Jeanette. *Our Lady of Guadalupe: Faith and Empowerment among Mexican-American Women*. Austin: University of Texas Press, 1994.

This book examines the role played by the most powerful female icon of Mexican culture, Our Lady of Guadalupe, and her relationship to Latinas. Rodríguez communicates the significance of Guadalupe as an active and liberating symbol that confronts the daily struggles of Latinas, a symbol rooted within their own cultural heritage. Guadalupe empowers a people who have been systematically repressed by providing them the dignity and self-belief to subvert the traditional interpretations of this symbol, which call for a womanly model of suffering and servility. Listening to the voices of Latinas creates an understanding about the maternal face of God in Guadalupe. But not only do we discover aspects of the Divine; we also discover something about the believers in Guadalupe.

―――. *Stories We Live/Cuentos Que Vivimos: Hispanic Women's Spirituality*. New York: Paulist Press, 1996.

Rodríguez provides a Latina theological perspective by tapping into the living stories of Latinas, stories told by mothers, grandmothers, aunts, and *comadres*, stories of collective cultural memories. By sharing these stories, Rodríguez hopes to articulate faith and spirituality reflected in the lives and struggles of Latinas. Through these stories, Latinas come in contact with their spirituality and the transformative power of God. Her hope is that stories such as these also enlighten the rest of society, moving it closer toward a more just society.

Rodríguez, José David, and Loida I. Martell-Otero, eds. *Teología en Conjunto: A Collaborative Hispanic Protestant Theology*. Louisville: Westminster/John Knox Press, 1997.

Written from the perspective of Hispanic Protestants, these essays forge an evangelistic methodology that assumes direct involvement by Latinos/as in analyzing their reality, which is tied to a Protestant theological perspective that demands a sociopolitical response to internal and external oppression. These articles show the relationship that has developed between oppressed Hispanics and intellectuals who are aware of the structural crises Latinas/os face in the United States. Throughout the book, the contributors seek healing for their broken existence through the rich diversity found among Latinas/os. These multifarious authors are bound by a holistic collaborative spirit that emerges when they gather to share the Word of God, their stories of suffering, and their pilgrimage in the diaspora. This collection of essays, written from a collective social identity of marginality, shares a commitment to the faith community struggling for justice.

Rodríguez-Díaz, Daniel R., and David Cortés-Fuentes. *Hidden Stories: Unveiling the History of the Latino Church*. Decatur, Ga.: A.E.T.H., 1994.

This volume is a collection of essays presented at the national conference of the Academia para la Historia de la Iglesia Latina (APHILA, Academy for the Study of Latino Church History) in 1993, which was held in Chicago at McCormick Theological Seminary. The wide-ranging essays focus on the need to begin a systematic recovery and documentation of Hispanic church history in the United States, Canada, and Puerto Rico under three broad rubrics: methodological considerations, religion and culture, and Biblical and theological reflections.

Sandoval, Moises. *On the Move: A History of the Hispanic Church in the United States*. Maryknoll, N.Y.: Orbis Books, 1990.

The growth of the Latino/a U.S. population contributes to the prominent role Hispanics play within North American culture, specifically the Catholic Church, where, although they represent nearly the majority of the parishioners, they continue to be marginalized in the church's pastoral work. Sandoval tells the saga of a people struggling to maintain their cultural-religious character from the time the Catholic Church first encountered indigenous people to the present Hispanic experience within the U.S. Catholic Church. His reading is from the underside of church history, uncovering the cruelty and exploitation of the "evangelism" implemented by the conquistadors during the first conquest of the 1500s and by the Euroamericans during the second conquest of the mid-1800s. This work also contains a chapter by Edwin E. Sylvest that summaries the history of Hispanic Protestants in the United States.

Solivan, Samuel. *The Spirit, Pathos, and Liberation: Toward an Hispanic Pentecostal Theology*. Sheffield: Sheffield Academic Press, 1998.

Writing from a Pentecostal perspective, Solivan shows how the oppression and suffering experienced by Latinos/as can be transformed by the Holy Spirit into a life of liberation, hope, joy, and promise. He looks within the Pentecostal community to deal with issues of critical importance to the overall Hispanic theological discussion — specifically, religious experience, suffering, the works of the Spirit, and the importance of language and culture. He integrates into Pentecostal theology some of the biblical and theological contributions of liberation theologians regarding issues relating to the poor and disenfranchised. He introduces "orthopathos" to the discourse, that is, the understanding of theology as a proper relationship between correct belief (orthodoxy) and proper ethics or action (praxis). Orthopathos serves to bridge the dichotomy between orthodoxy and orthopraxis.

Stevens-Arroyo, Anthony M., ed. *Prophets Denied Honor: An Anthology of the Hispano Church of the United States.* Maryknoll, N.Y.: Orbis Books, 1980.

This anthology of essays, poetry, hymns, catechetics, liturgy, political documents, and other writings validates the Latina/o as an important agent within both the Roman Catholic Church and the larger society of the United States. The importance of the Hispanic population in North America is due, not to its growing demographics, but to the ideas and concepts being formulated by *pensadores,* thinkers. The focus, then, is to introduce the reader to emerging U.S. Hispanic voices, which affirms their faith and their identity while simultaneously providing an understanding of the historical development of the Latino/a presence in the church. The collected writings provide sociological, anthropological, and theological background for the new articulation of Catholicism as expressed by U.S. Hispanics.

Stevens-Arroyo, Anthony M., and Gilbert Cadena, eds. *Old Masks, New Faces: Religion and Latino Identities.* New York: Bildner Center for Western Hemisphere Studies, 1995.

As the second of a four-part series focusing on Latino/a religion, these seven essays make connections between the process by which people experience the changing parameters of national identity and the function of religion among Hispanics. Some of the essays deal with contemporary historical events, specifically past studies and research done about Latinas/os, and the impact of Dominicans in New York. Other chapters deal with theoretical themes, as in the case of the study of *pueblo, mujerista* theology, and transformation theory. Two further chapters deal with sociology. One considers demographic data, while the other presents the methodology of "triangulation," by which more accurate data can be obtained.

Stevens-Arroyo, Anthony M., and Ana María Díaz-Stevens, eds. *An Enduring Flame: Studies on Latino Popular Religiosity.* New York: Bildner Center for Western Hemisphere Studies, 1994.

The first of a four-part series, these nine essays deal with the social-scientific study of "popular religiosity." The essayists bring different perspectives for comprehending popular religiosity to create clarity and

insight on how this term, important in the description of Latino/a religiosity, is to be understood. The scholars focus more on the attitudinal than
behavioral, hence the use of the term "religiosity" rather than "religion."
Several articles deal with the process of religious syncretism; others, with
the construction of identity. Still others focus on the resistance and protest
form of popular religiosity, a protest geared toward both the church and
the culture bent on assimilation. Because such expressions of religiosity are
not under the control of the church hierarchy, it becomes a space in which
marginalized Latinas/os find comfort.

———. *Recognizing the Latino Resurgence in U.S. Religion.* Boulder,
    Colo.: Westview Press, 1998.

Through the scriptural story of the encounter between the risen Christ and
his disciples on the road to Emmaus, the authors use the Emmaus paradigm
to challenge the perception of the dominant culture, which views Hispanics
as just another immigrant group awaiting assimilation. For nearly two
centuries, Euroamericans and Latinos/as have walked together with the
dominant culture unaware of the Hispanics' presence. Maintaining that
religion has become a major source of social and symbolic capital in the
creation of Latino/a identity, the authors review the sociohistorical construction of Latina/o identity, showing how a resurgence in Hispanic religious
practice is creating a church-based response to the dominant culture.

Stevens-Arroyo, Anthony M., and Andrés Isidoro Pérez y Mena, eds.
    *Enigmatic Powers: Syncretism with African and Indigenous People's
    Religions among Latinos.* New York: Bildner Center for Western
    Hemisphere Studies, 1995.

The third of a four-part series, this book focuses on indigenous religious expressions of Latinas/os, specifically Santería, spiritism, and South American
and Mesoamerican traditions. For some Hispanics, there is no theological
conflict in attending Sunday morning mass and visiting a *curandera* (healer)
at night. This is the result of the European Christian faith of Spaniards
intermingling with the spiritual cosmology of Africa and Native America.
By employing a social-scientific approach to the phenomenon of syncretism,
this manifestation of religiosity is explored to determine how it meets the
needs of a disenfranchised people seeking to survive.

Villafañe, Eldín. *The Liberating Spirit: Toward an Hispanic American
    Pentecostal Social Ethic.* Grand Rapids: Eerdmans, 1993.

Villafañe focuses on social ethics from the perspective of Latino/a Pentecostals, while simultaneously challenging Pentecostals to develop their

social responsibilities toward justice, breaking the barrier between the profane and sacred. By affirming the cultural heritage of the Hispanic church while coming to terms with the disenfranchised space it occupies, Villafañe calls for the construction of a community ethics as well as a "community of the Spirit" in and for the world, while not being of the world. Villafañe discusses the Latino/a reality, followed by the Hispanic religious dimension. He then moves toward the sociotheological interpretation of the Latina/o urban Pentecostal reality. Finally, he provides a pneumatological paradigm dealing with the Spirit and social spirituality before introducing a Hispanic Pentecostal social ethics.

Villafañe, Eldín, et al. *Seek the Peace of the City: Reflections on Urban Ministries.* Grand Rapids: Eerdmans, 1995.

This book is geared toward the clergy and laity, specifically evangelicals, challenging them and churches to refocus their ministries upon the needs of urban areas. Villafañe provides the reader with a multicultural perspective to theology and ministry. In an age in which churches relocate to the security of the suburbs once the neighborhood begins to "change," Villafañe presents a holistic vision for the city, in which he sees the need for the healing powers of the Holy Spirit. He calls Christians to what he terms "the Jeremiah Paradigm for the City," stemming from a theology of context, mission, and spirituality. Molded on Christ, it is an approach that is critically engaged (presence), seeks wholeness, completeness, and reconciliation (peace), while being undergirded for spiritual warfare (prayer). The last section of the book, through the writings of Douglas Hall, Efraín Agosta, and Bruce Jackson, examines urban theological education from the perspective of seeking the peace of the city.

# Index

201

material religion, 119–20, 124
Matovina, Timothy, 99
Mayans, 31, 146
McDannell, Colleen, 120
Medina, Lara, 113
*mestizaje*
  defined, 13
  Elizondo on, 37, 106
  the future of, 141–45
  Islam and, 134
  Judaism and Islam and, 30
methodology
  anthropology and, 78–79
  the Bible and, 74–76
  epistemology and, 72–74
  the Spanish language and,
    76–77
Mexican American Cultural
  Center, 105, 106
Mexicans
  as aliens, 49–51
  Chicanos/as vs., 152–53
  conquest of, 31–32
  demographics on, 18, 19, 20
  immigration of, 145–46
  income of immigrant, 22
  Our Lady of Guadalupe and, 91,
    92, 93
  the U.S. border and, 44–45
Miami (Dade County), 47–48,
  148–49, 165n.20
Miranda, Jesse, 115
missions, 36
Monserrate, Our Lady of, 150
Moreno, Juan, 91
*mujerista* theology, 110, 111
multiracialism, 55–58. See also
  *mestizaje*

National Council of Churches, 113
Native Americans, 30–33, 36
new ecumenism, the, 113–15,
  138–41
New World Order, the, 156–58
Nicaraguans, 45, 146
North American Free Trade
  Agreement, 156–57

Oboler, Suzanne, 148
Olazabal, Francisco, 100
Olodumare, 128–29
Omi, Michael, 56
option for the poor, the, 79, 156,
  168n.4
organic intellectuals, 153
*orishas*, 33, 34, 129, 130, 131
orthopraxis, 73
Otherness, 26
Our Lady of Guadalupe. *See*
  Guadalupe, La Virgen de
Our Lady of Monserrate, 150
outsiders, 51–53

PADRES, 104
Padres Asociados para Derechos
  Religiosos, Educacionales y
  Sociales, 104
pan-ethnic unity, 147
PARAL, 140
*pastoral de conjunto*, 88–89
paternalism, 108–9
Pedraja, Luis, 77
Penitentes, 168n.6
Pentecostalism
  alternative traditions and, 130
  current increase in Latin America
    of, 35–36, 61

CPSIA information can be obtained
at www.ICGtesting.com
Printed in the USA
LVHW010250050122
707834LV00003B/438

9 781570 754005